America's ★ Best
BRAND-NAME RECIPES

HOMESTYLE COOKING
Made Easy

America's ★ Best

Pictured on the front cover: Mom's Favorite White Cake *(page 326).*

Pictured on the back cover *(clockwise from top left):* Vegetable Lasagna *(page 142),* Chocolate Espresso Cake *(page 336)* and Lemon-Garlic Roasted Chicken *(page 208).*

Nutritional Analysis: The nutritional information included with certain recipes was submitted in part by the participating companies and associations. Every effort has been made to check the accuracy of these numbers. However, because numerous variables account for a wide range of values for certain foods, nutritive analyses in this book should be considered approximate.

The HEALTHY CHOICE® recipes contained in this book have been tested by the manufacturers and have been carefully edited by the publisher. The publisher and the manufacturers cannot be held responsible for any ill effects caused by errors in the recipes, or by spoiled ingredients, unsanitary conditions, incorrect preparation procedures or any other cause.

Microwave Cooking: Microwave ovens vary in wattage. Use the cooking times as guidelines and check for doneness before adding more time.

CONTENTS

SIMPLE
KITCHEN SAVVY

With the fading of summer comes the bounty of the fall harvest, the excitement of a new school year and the anticipation of the coming holiday season. From having the gang over to watch the big game to hosting holiday parties, the fall and winter seasons mean spending time with family and friends. They also mean spending time in the kitchen. Let this wonderful cookbook guide you through fall and winter cooking with recipes for crowd-pleasing appetizers, sandwiches and pizzas, quick soups and casseroles, enticing entrées, spectacular cookies and dazzling desserts. Enjoy the bounty of these seasons, as well as the time you spend in the kitchen, using the hearty recipes and helpful tips found in this fabulous collection.

BEFORE YOU BEGIN

Whether you're preparing an elaborate feast or a simple treat to satisfy a craving, good cooking starts with the basics. Here are some guidelines to keep in mind when you're ready to start.

Look before you leap. Before beginning, read the entire recipe to make sure you have all the necessary ingredients, utensils and supplies.

Follow instructions. Follow the recipe directions and cooking or baking times exactly. Check for doneness using the test given in the recipe.

Measure accurately. Careful measuring of all ingredients is the first step in successful cooking and baking.

Preparation is important. Do any necessary food preparation such as peeling and slicing vegetables, chopping herbs, toasting and chopping nuts, or melting chocolate before proceeding with the recipe.

Use the right size pan. Always use the pan or dish size specified in each recipe. Using a different size pan or dish may cause under or overcooking, or sticking and burnt edges.

MAIN-DISH MAGIC

When planning a meal, it is helpful to select the main course first and then choose side dishes that complement it in flavor and texture. Start by choosing an exciting new recipe from the poultry, meat or seafood chapter and you're on your way to a terrific meal the whole family will love!

Let's Talk Turkey
(and other types of poultry)
Poultry is a great main course choice for everyday as well as for entertaining. It's easy, economical and versatile. With the following tips you'll be cooking poultry like a pro!
• Fresh poultry should be used within two days of purchase or frozen immediately if you do not plan to use it.
• Most poultry can be frozen safely in its original packaging for up to two months. If you are planning to freeze poultry longer, double-wrap it with plastic wrap or foil to keep it airtight.
• Thaw frozen poultry in its original wrapper in the refrigerator. For a whole chicken or turkey, allow 24 hours thawing time for every five pounds. Allow about 5 hours per pound for thawing poultry pieces. Never thaw poultry on the kitchen counter; this promotes bacterial growth.
• Always cook poultry completely before eating or storing. Partially cooking poultry and storing it to finish later promotes bacterial growth.
• If stuffing a whole turkey or chicken, mix stuffing ingredients and stuff the bird immediately before putting it in the oven. Stuff lightly—do not pack. Stuffing cooked in poultry should reach a temperature of 165°F.
• Another easy way to cook stuffing is to place it in a casserole and bake, covered, 45 minutes in a preheated 350°F oven.
• To determine when a whole turkey or chicken is cooked and ready to eat, use a meat thermometer inserted into the meatiest part of the thigh, away from bone or fat. For turkey and chicken, the thigh temperature should be 180°F and breast temperature 170°F. Bone-in chicken pieces are thoroughly cooked when you can insert a fork with ease and the juices run clear, not pink. Boneless chicken pieces are done when the centers are no longer pink.
• Before carving, allow a whole turkey or chicken to stand about 15 minutes. This helps retain more of its flavorful juices and makes it easier to carve.
• Always use a long, sharp carving knife to carve a whole bird and a long-handled meat fork to steady it.

Making the Most of Your Roast (and other cuts of beef, pork, or lamb)

Meat is often the spectacular main course at celebrations throughout the fall and winter seasons. But these days, with more lean cuts available, it is an excellent choice for everyday meals too. Follow these suggestions to get the best flavor and texture from whatever type of meat you're serving.

• Recommended refrigerator storage time for unopened, prepackaged fresh cuts of meat is generally two to three days; for ground meats, one to two days.

• Thaw frozen meat, still wrapped, in the refrigerator about four to seven hours per pound, usually overnight. Once meat is thawed completely, it should be cooked within a day or two and not refrozen.

• To prepare beef, pork, lamb or veal roasts, place meat, fat-side-up, on a rack in a shallow, open roasting pan. Insert a meat thermometer into the thickest part, not resting in fat or on bone. Roasts are usually cooked uncovered in a 325°F oven.

• Standard final temperatures for roast beef, lamb and veal are 140°F for rare, 160°F for medium and 170°F for well done. Pork temperatures should reach 160°F. Fully cooked hams can be warmed to 140°F. Smoked hams that must be cooked before eating should reach 160°F.

• Before carving, allow the roast to stand 10 to 20 minutes. This will make it easier to carve and will help the meat retain more of its flavorful juices.

Go Fish! (and other kinds of seafood)

Because of the great variety of seafood available today, preparing savory seafood recipes is easier than ever! With the recipes in this book and the following guidelines, you can make fish and shellfish a delicious and nutritious addition to your menu.

• Fresh whole fish should have bright, clear, protruding eyes and moist, shiny skin. Gills should be red or pink and the flesh should be firm and elastic. A fresh fish has a fresh, slightly ocean-like, mild smell. Do not buy a fish that has a distinctly fishy, sour smell or one that is slimy to the touch.

• Fresh fish fillets and steaks should have shiny, resilient skin and moist flesh that is free from discoloration. Do not buy fish that has a strong odor.

• All fresh shellfish should have a fresh, mild ocean-like smell. Fresh shrimp should feel firm to the touch. It is recommended that fresh lobsters and crabs are purchased live shortly before cooking.

• Hard-shell clams, mussels and oysters should have tightly closed shells, or should snap tightly closed when tapped. Freshly shucked oysters are usually creamy white, although the color varies with the variety, and should be surrounded by a clear, slightly milky white or light gray liquid. Freshly shucked clams should be plump, moist and shiny.

• Fish cooks quickly, so be careful not to overcook it (this makes the fish tough and destroys the flavor). Fish is done cooking when it turns opaque and flakes easily.

• Clams, mussels and oysters cooked in the shell are done cooking when the shell opens. Remove them as they open. Discard any that do not open.

• Shucked clams, mussels and oysters become opaque when they are cooked.

• When cooked, raw shrimp turn pink and opaque; scallops turn milky white or opaque and firm.

A great meal does more than just taste good. It appeals to other senses too. The aromas, the textures and even how food looks play an important role in our enjoyment. An easy way to enhance even simple foods is to add a garnish. Eye-catching garnishes are simple to make and generally use fruits, vegetables and other ingredients usually on hand.

GREAT IDEAS FOR GARNISHES

Every cook wants the food they make to taste good and look good too. Sometimes all it takes is that special finishing touch to make a dish go from drab to dazzling. Here are some simple tips for dressing up your dinner.

• When choosing a garnish, pick one that enhances and complements the color and texture of the food. For example, crispy and colorful carrot flowers can add much needed excitement to tender grilled meats.

• Remember to consider the size of the garnish too. For example, pair a large garnish with a tray or large platter of food. Garnishes should enhance, not overshadow or hide the food's beauty and flavor.

• If possible, make garnishes ahead of time; wrap in plastic wrap and store in the refrigerator until ready to use. Add garnishes to the food just before serving.

• Choose one of the recipe's ingredients, for example, red onion, and save a few attractive slices as a simple decoration for the top of the dish.

• Garnishes don't have to be elaborate. For example, a sprinkle of chopped fresh herbs or tomatoes can add color to a casserole or side dish. Or, a delicate spray of edible flowers can make an attractive presentation on anything from a savory vegetable dip to a fluffy-frosted birthday cake.

BAKING CAKES & COOKIES

In addition to the guidelines in "Before You Begin" (page 4), the following are a few more tips to make baking easy.

• For best results, use the ingredients called for in the recipe. Butter, margarine and shortening are not always interchangeable.

• When making pastry or pie dough, cut cold butter, margarine or shortening into the flour and salt using a pastry blender or two knives until the mixture forms pea-sized pieces. Then add the liquid, 1 tablespoon at a time, tossing lightly, until the dough is just moist enough to hold together when pressed.

• If pastry or pie dough becomes sticky and difficult to handle, refrigerate it until firm. Then roll out the dough quickly on a lightly floured surface. A tough pie crust is often the result of too much flour worked into the dough or overhandling.

• If two racks are used when baking cakes, arrange the racks so they divide the oven into thirds and then stagger the pans so they are not directly over each other.

• For cakes to rise properly, avoid opening the oven door during the first half of baking. This helps to keep the oven temperature constant.

• For cutout cookies, chill cookie dough before rolling for easier handling. Remove only enough dough from the refrigerator to work with at one time.

• For shaped or drop cookies, dough should be portioned in uniform size and shape on the cookie sheet.

• Space mounds of dough about 2 inches apart on cookie sheets to allow for spreading unless the recipe directs otherwise.

• Allow cookie sheets to cool between batches, as the dough will spread too quickly if placed on hot cookie sheets.

CAKE DECORATING TIPS

Not everybody has the experience to decorate like a pro, but with these simple hints, anyone can decorate a cake with professional-looking results.

• To get a more finished look, trim off the rounded top of the cake. Use a serrated knife long enough to cut across the top in one stroke, such as a bread knife. Cut through the cake horizontally using a gentle sawing motion.

• If making layers, cut the cake horizontally in half or in thirds, using the same technique for trimming the cake as directed above.

• Before frosting the cake, brush off all loose cake crumbs with a soft pastry brush. Then frost the cake with a long, flexible metal spatula for a smoother surface.

• Start with a base coat of frosting first and let it set for a few minutes. This will seal in the crumbs and make it easier to get a smooth finished surface.

• Place the cake on a serving plate before frosting it. To keep the plate clean, simply tuck strips of waxed paper under the edges of the cake, then frost. When you are finished decorating, gently slide the waxed paper out from under the cake. Then add any final decorations around the base of the cake.

SWEET & SIMPLE DECORATIONS

Adding that extra something to desserts or snacks is easier than you think. Choose one of these ideas or try one of your own.

Everybody loves chocolate! Dipping cookies in chocolate adds a festive and flavorful touch. An even easier way to add pizzazz is by drizzling baked goods with melted chocolate.

Colorful glazes: Plain cookies and cakes get a boost of sweetness with powdered sugar glazes. Use the glaze white or color it with food coloring to fit the occasion.

Go nuts! Whole, halved, sliced or chopped nuts can add extra flavor and crunch to anything. Toasted or tinted coconut can add color and flavor to otherwise plain treats.

Sugar, sprinkles and candies: The possibilities are endless—and easy! Simply sprinkle on top and bake. After baking, powdered sugar can be dusted over cooled cakes and cookies.

Prepared toppings: Purchased ice cream toppings such as fudge, caramel or butterscotch are perfect for drizzling over cookies, bars or cakes as an extra-quick decoration.

Melting Chocolate

Chocolate can be used in a variety of ways. Sometimes a recipe may call for chocolate that is already melted. Other times the melted chocolate is used as a garnish. Either way, melting chocolate doesn't have to be tricky. Read through these basic guidelines and follow one of the three easy methods for successful melting every time!

• Make sure all utensils, bowls or saucepans used for melting chocolate are completely dry. Moisture causes chocolate to "seize," which means it becomes stiff and grainy.

• If chocolate seizes, add ½ teaspoon shortening (not butter) for each ounce of chocolate and stir until smooth.

• Watch chocolate carefully. It scorches easily, and once scorched cannot be used.

Double Boiler: This is the safest method because it prevents scorching. Place chocolate in the top of a double boiler or in a heatproof bowl over hot, not boiling, water; stir until smooth. (Make sure that the water remains just below a simmer and is one inch below the bottom of the top pan.) Be careful that no steam or water gets into the chocolate.

Direct Heat: Place chocolate in a heavy saucepan and melt over very low heat, stirring constantly. Remove chocolate from heat as soon as it is melted. Watch the chocolate carefully as it is easily scorched when using this method.

Microwave Oven: Place an unwrapped 1-ounce square or 1 cup of chips in a small microwavable bowl. Microwave on HIGH 1 to 1½ minutes, stirring after 1 minute. Stir chocolate at 30-second intervals until smooth. Be sure to stir microwaved chocolate since it may retain its original shape even when melted.

Drizzling Chocolate

Use a spoon or fork to drizzle melted chocolate over cookies, cakes or other desserts. Or, melt the chocolate in a small resealable plastic freezer bag, cut off a tiny corner of the bag and squeeze out the chocolate in the desired design.

Chocolate Shavings

To add just a little bit more chocolate to your favorite treats, top them off with a sprinkling of shavings. Create shavings by dragging a vegetable peeler across a square of chocolate in short quick strokes.

Toasting Nuts

Toasting nuts brings out their flavor and gives them a wonderful golden color. To toast nuts, spread them in a single layer on a baking sheet. Bake in a 325°F oven 8 to 10 minutes or until golden. Stir nuts occasionally during baking to ensure even toasting. The nuts will darken and become crisper as they cool.

Toasting Coconut

Just as with nuts, toasting brings out the flavor and fragrance of coconut. To toast, spread flaked or shredded coconut in a thin layer on a rimmed baking sheet. Bake in a 325°F oven 7 to 10 minutes. Shake the pan or stir coconut occasionally during baking to ensure even browning and prevent burning.

Tinting Coconut

Tinting coconut is an easy way to add color to any dessert. Dilute a few drops of food coloring with ½ teaspoon milk or water in a small bowl or large plastic food storage bag. Then add 1 to 1⅓ cups flaked or shredded coconut; toss with a fork or seal and shake bag until coconut is evenly tinted. Repeat this process until desired color is reached.

Presenting a magnificent meal before guests or even just family can make sharing that meal so much more enjoyable. Planning and preparing that meal can be a pleasure too. With an abundance of mouthwatering recipes to choose from, it's easy to create an exciting menu for celebrations or any day of the week. Make everyday meals extraordinary and special occasions sensational using the fantastic ideas and tantalizing recipes found in this wonderful cookbook.

ENDLESS

APPETIZERS

Louisiana Crab Dip with Crudités

1 package (8 ounces) cream
   cheese, softened
½ cup sour cream
3 tablespoons horseradish
2 tablespoons chopped fresh
   parsley
1 tablespoon coarse ground
   mustard
2 teaspoons TABASCO® Pepper
   Sauce

1 cup lump crabmeat
1 bunch baby carrots
1 bunch celery, cut into sticks
1 bunch asparagus spears,
   blanched
2 bunches endive
2 red or green bell peppers,
   cored and cut into strips

In medium bowl, blend cream cheese, sour cream, horseradish, parsley, mustard, and TABASCO® Sauce until well mixed. Stir in crabmeat.

On large platter arrange carrots, celery, asparagus, endive and peppers. Serve with crab dip.
Makes about 2 cups dip

Louisiana Crab Dip with Crudités

10

Señor Nacho Dip

4 ounces nonfat cream cheese
½ cup (2 ounces) reduced-fat Cheddar
    cheese
¼ cup mild or medium chunky salsa
2 teaspoons reduced-fat (2%) milk
4 ounces baked tortilla chips or
    assorted fresh vegetable dippers
    Hot peppers for garnish
    Cilantro for garnish

1. Combine cream cheese and Cheddar cheese in small saucepan; stir over low heat until melted. Stir in salsa and milk; heat thoroughly, stirring occasionally.

2. Transfer dip to small serving bowl. Serve with tortilla chips. Garnish with hot peppers and cilantro, if desired.   *Makes 4 servings*

Olé Dip: Substitute reduced fat Monterey Jack cheese or taco cheese for Cheddar cheese.

Spicy Mustard Dip: Omit tortilla chips. Substitute 2 teaspoons spicy brown or honey mustard for salsa. Serve with fresh vegetable dippers or pretzels.

Harvest Sticks with Vegetable Dip

2 packages (3 ounces *each*) cream
    cheese with chives, softened
1 cup sour cream
⅓ cup finely chopped cucumber
2 tablespoons chopped fresh parsley
2 tablespoons dry minced onion *or*
    ¼ cup finely chopped fresh onion
1 garlic clove, minced
¼ teaspoon salt
½ teaspoon curry powder (optional)
6 large carrots, peeled
3 medium zucchini
    Tan raffia

1. Beat cream cheese in small bowl of electric mixer at medium speed until fluffy; blend in sour cream. Stir in cucumber, parsley, onion, garlic and salt. Add curry powder, if desired. Spoon into small serving bowl; cover. Refrigerate at least 1 hour or until serving time.

2. Just before serving, cut carrots lengthwise into thin strips; gather into bundles. Tie raffia around bundles to hold in place. Repeat with zucchini.

3. Place bowl of dip on serving tray; garnish, if desired. Surround with bundles of carrots and zucchini.   *Makes about 2 cups dip*

Señor Nacho Dip

Cucumber Dill Dip

1 package (8 ounces) light cream
    cheese, softened
1 cup HELLMANN'S® or BEST FOODS®
    Real or Light Mayonnaise or Low
    Fat Mayonnaise Dressing
2 medium cucumbers, peeled, seeded
    and chopped
2 tablespoons sliced green onions
1 tablespoon lemon juice
2 teaspoons snipped fresh dill *or*
    ½ teaspoon dried dillweed
½ teaspoon hot pepper sauce

1. In medium bowl beat cream cheese until
smooth. Stir in mayonnaise, cucumbers,
green onions, lemon juice, dill and hot
pepper sauce.

2. Cover; chill to blend flavors.

3. Serve with fresh vegetables, crackers or
chips. Garnish as desired.
Makes about 2½ cups dip

French Onion Dip

1 container (16 ounces) sour cream
½ cup HELLMANN'S® or BEST FOODS®
    Real or Low Fat Mayonnaise
    Dressing
1 package (1.9 ounces) KNORR®
    French Onion Soup and Recipe
    Mix

1. In medium bowl combine sour cream,
mayonnaise and soup mix.

2. Cover; chill to blend flavors.

3. Stir before serving. Accompany with fresh
vegetables or potato chips. Garnish as
desired.   *Makes about 2½ cups dip*

Spinach Dip

1 package (10 ounces) frozen
    chopped spinach, thawed and
    drained
1½ cups sour cream
1 cup HELLMANN'S® or BEST FOODS®
    Real or Low Fat Mayonnaise
    Dressing
1 package (1.4 ounces) KNORR®
    Vegetable Soup and Recipe Mix
1 can (8 ounces) water chestnuts,
    drained and chopped (optional)
3 green onions, chopped

1. In medium bowl combine spinach, sour
cream, mayonnaise, soup mix, water
chestnuts and green onions.

2. Cover; chill to blend flavors.

3. Stir dip before serving. Accompany with
fresh vegetables, crackers or chips. Garnish
as desired.   *Makes about 3 cups dip*

From left to right: French Onion Dip, Cucumber
Dill Dip and Spinach Dip

Sesame Chicken Nuggets

4 tablespoons sesame seeds
1 tablespoon Worcestershire sauce
1 tablespoon water
1 teaspoon granulated sugar
1 teaspoon chili powder
¼ teaspoon garlic powder
1 pound boneless skinless chicken
     breasts, cut into 1-inch pieces
Barbecue Sauce (recipe follows)

Combine sesame seeds, Worcestershire sauce, water, sugar, chili powder and garlic powder in small bowl; mix well. Add chicken and coat evenly. Place chicken on broiling pan. Broil 10 minutes or until lightly browned, turning once. Prepare Barbecue Sauce; serve with chicken nuggets.   *Makes 4 servings*

Barbecue Sauce

1 can (8 ounces) tomato sauce
1 teaspoon granulated sugar
1 teaspoon red wine vinegar
½ teaspoon chili powder
½ teaspoon Worcestershire sauce
¼ teaspoon garlic powder

Combine all ingredients in medium saucepan; simmer 15 minutes, stirring occasionally. Use as a dipping sauce for chicken nuggets.
                    Makes ¾ cups sauce

Note: This recipe can be doubled for an easy dinner dish. Serve any leftover chicken nuggets in pita pocket sandwiches.

Favorite recipe from **The Sugar Association, Inc.**

Crab Canapés

⅔ cup nonfat pasteurized process
     cream cheese product, softened
2 teaspoons lemon juice
1 teaspoon hot pepper sauce
1 package (8 ounces) imitation
     crabmeat or lobster, flaked
⅓ cup chopped red bell pepper
2 green onions with tops, sliced
     (about ¼ cup)
64 cucumber slices (about 2½ medium
     cucumbers cut ⅜ inch thick) or
     melba toast rounds
Chopped parsley for garnish
     (optional)

1. Combine cream cheese, lemon juice and hot pepper sauce in medium bowl; mix well. Stir in crabmeat, bell pepper and green onions; cover. Chill until ready to serve.

2. When ready to serve, spoon 1½ teaspoons crab mixture onto each cucumber slice. Place on serving plate; garnish with parsley, if desired.   *Makes 16 servings*

Note: To allow flavors to blend, chill crab mixture at least 1 hour before spreading onto cucumbers or melba toast rounds.

Crab Canapés

Hot & Spicy Buffalo Chicken Wings

**1 can (15 ounces) DEL MONTE®
   Original Sloppy Joe Sauce**
**¼ cup thick and chunky salsa,
   medium**
**1 tablespoon red wine or cider
   vinegar**
20 chicken wings (about 4 pounds)

1. Preheat oven to 400°F.

2. Combine sloppy joe sauce, salsa and vinegar in small bowl. Remove ¼ cup sauce mixture to serve with cooked chicken wings; cover and refrigerate. Set aside remaining sauce mixture.

3. Arrange wings in single layer in large, shallow baking pan; brush wings with sauce mixture.

4. Bake chicken, uncovered, on middle rack in oven 35 minutes or until chicken is no longer pink in center, turning and brushing with remaining sauce mixture after 15 minutes. Serve with reserved ¼ cup sauce. Garnish, if desired.   *Makes 4 servings*

Prep time: 5 minutes
Cook time: 35 minutes

Hot & Spicy Buffalo Chicken Wings

FRANK'S® Original Buffalo Chicken Wings

**Zesty Blue Cheese Dip
(recipe follows)
2½ pounds chicken wings, split and
    tips discarded
½ cup FRANK'S® Original REDHOT®
    Cayenne Pepper Sauce (or to
    taste)
⅓ cup butter or margarine, melted
Celery sticks**

1. Prepare Zesty Blue Cheese Dip.

2. Deep fry* wings at 400°F 12 minutes or until crisp and no longer pink; drain.

3. Combine RedHot® sauce and butter in large bowl. Add wings to sauce; toss to coat evenly. Serve with Zesty Blue Cheese Dip and celery.   *Makes 24 to 30 wings*

*Or, prepare wings using one of the following cooking methods. Add wings to sauce; toss well to coat completely.

Prep time: 10 minutes
Cook time: 12 minutes

To Bake: Place wings in single layer on rack in foil-lined roasting pan. Bake at 425°F 1 hour or until crisp and no longer pink, turning halfway through baking time.

To Broil: Place wings in single layer on rack in foil-lined roasting pan. Broil 6 inches from heat 15 to 20 minutes or until crisp and no longer pink, turning once.

To Grill: Place wings on oiled grid. Grill, over medium heat, 30 to 40 minutes or until crisp and no longer pink, turning often.

Zesty Blue Cheese Dip

**½ cup blue cheese salad dressing
¼ cup sour cream
2 teaspoons FRANK'S® Original
    REDHOT® Cayenne Pepper Sauce**

Combine all ingredients in medium serving bowl; mix well. Garnish with crumbled blue cheese, if desired.   *Makes ¾ cup dip*

Prep time: 5 minutes

Almond Chicken Cups

1 tablespoon vegetable oil
½ cup chopped red bell pepper
½ cup chopped onion
2 cups chopped cooked chicken
⅔ cup prepared sweet-and-sour sauce
½ cup chopped almonds
2 tablespoons soy sauce
6 flour tortillas (6 to 7 inches)

1. Preheat oven to 400°F. Heat oil in small skillet over medium heat until hot. Add bell pepper and onion. Cook and stir 3 minutes or until crisp-tender.

2. Combine vegetable mixture, chicken, sweet-and-sour sauce, almonds and soy sauce in medium bowl; mix until well blended.

3. Cut each tortilla in half. Place each half in 2¾-inch muffin cup. Fill each with about ¼ cup chicken mixture.

4. Bake 8 to 10 minutes or until tortilla edges are crisp and filling is hot. Remove muffin pan to cooling rack. Let stand 5 minutes before serving.   *Makes 12 chicken cups*

Prep and cook time: 30 minutes

Spicy Chicken Quesadillas

4 boneless skinless chicken breast
    halves
6 to 8 tablespoons vegetable oil,
    divided
½ teaspoon salt
1 large yellow onion, thinly sliced
8 medium-sized flour tortillas
    (6 to 8 inches)
3 cups shredded mild cheddar or
    Monterey Jack cheese (12 ounces)

Flatten chicken breasts and cut into 1×¼-inch strips.

Heat 3 tablespoons oil in heavy skillet. Add chicken and cook, stirring over high heat 3 to 4 minutes or until lightly browned and no longer pink in center. Sprinkle with salt. Remove chicken from skillet with slotted spoon and set aside.

Sauté onion in same skillet until translucent; remove and set aside.

Heat 1 to 2 tablespoons oil in same skillet. Place 1 tortilla in skillet; add ¼ each of chicken, onion and cheese. Place second tortilla on top. Cook quesadilla on both sides until browned and crisp.

Repeat to make 3 more quesadillas.

Cut into wedges and serve with toppings such as salsa, sour cream, or guacamole.
     Makes 8 appetizers

Almond Chicken Cups

Walnut Chicken Pinwheels

2 boneless skinless chicken breasts, halved
12 to 14 spinach leaves
1 package (6.5 ounces) ALOUETTE® Garlic et Herbes Cheese
5 ounces roasted red peppers, sliced or 5 ounces pimiento slices
¾ cup finely chopped California walnuts

Pound chicken to about ¼-inch thickness with flat side of meat mallet or chef's knife. Cover each chicken piece with spinach leaves. Spread each with Alouette®. Top with pepper slices and walnuts. Carefully roll up each breast and secure with wooden toothpicks. Bake at 400°F 20 to 25 minutes until cooked through. Remove from oven; cool. Chill. Remove toothpicks before serving, then slice into ½-inch rounds. Serve cold.   *Makes about 35 appetizers*

Pesto Chicken Bruschetta

2 tablespoons olive oil, divided
1 teaspoon coarsely chopped garlic, divided
8 diagonal slices (¼ inch thick) sourdough bread, divided
½ cup (2 ounces) grated BELGIOIOSO® Asiago Cheese, divided
2 tablespoons prepared pesto
¼ teaspoon black pepper
4 boneless skinless chicken breast halves
12 slices (¼ inch thick) BELGIOIOSO® Fresh Mozzarella Cheese (8 ounces)
2 tomatoes, each cut into 4 slices

In 10-inch skillet, heat 1 tablespoon olive oil and ½ teaspoon garlic. Add 4 slices bread. Cook over medium-high heat, turning once, 5 to 7 minutes or until toasted. Remove from pan. Add remaining 1 tablespoon oil and ½ teaspoon garlic; repeat with remaining bread slices. Sprinkle ¼ cup Asiago cheese on bread. In same skillet, combine pesto and pepper. Add chicken, coating with pesto. Cook over medium-high heat, turning once, 8 to 10 minutes or until chicken is brown and no longer pink in centers. Place 3 slices mozzarella cheese on each bread slice; top with tomato slice. Slice chicken pieces in half horizontally. Place on tomato; sprinkle with remaining ¼ cup Asiago cheese.
Makes 4 servings

Walnut Chicken Pinwheels

Party Chicken Tarts

2 tablespoons butter or margarine
1 cup chopped fresh mushrooms
¼ cup finely chopped celery
¼ cup finely chopped onion
2 tablespoons all-purpose flour
1½ cups chopped cooked chicken
6 tablespoons sour cream
½ teaspoon garlic salt
1 package (10 ounces) flaky
    refrigerator biscuits
    (10 to 12 count)
  Vegetable cooking spray
1 tablespoon butter or margarine,
    melted
  Grated Parmesan cheese

Melt 2 tablespoons butter in large skillet until hot. Add mushrooms, celery and onion; cook and stir 4 to 5 minutes. Sprinkle with flour; stir in chicken and sour cream. Cook until thoroughly heated. Stir in garlic salt; set aside.

Cut each biscuit into quarters; press each piece into miniature muffin tins coated with cooking spray to form tart shell. Brush each piece with melted butter.

Bake at 400°F 6 minutes. Remove from oven. *Reduce oven temperature to 350°F.* Fill each tart with 1 teaspoon chicken mixture; sprinkle with cheese. Bake 14 to 15 minutes. Serve immediately.

Makes 40 to 48 appetizers

Note: For ease in serving at party time, prepare filling ahead and cook tarts 5 minutes. Fill and bake just before serving for best flavor.

Favorite recipe from **National Broiler Council**

Chicken Nachos

22 (about 1 ounce) GUILTLESS
    GOURMET® Baked Tortilla Chips
    (yellow, white or blue corn)
½ cup (4 ounces) cooked and
    shredded boneless chicken breast
¼ cup chopped green onions
¼ cup (1 ounce) grated Cheddar
    cheese
  Sliced green and red chilies
    (optional)

Conventional Directions: Preheat oven to 325°F. Spread tortilla chips on baking sheet. Sprinkle chicken, onions and cheese over chips. Bake about 5 minutes or until cheese starts to bubble. Serve hot. Garnish with chilies, if desired.   *Makes 22 nachos*

Microwave Directions: Spread tortilla chips on flat microwave-safe plate. Sprinkle chicken, onions and cheese over chips. Microwave on HIGH about 30 seconds until cheese starts to bubble. Serve hot. Garnish with chilies, if desired.

Nutrients per Serving:

Calories:	14	Cholesterol:	3 mg
Total Fat:	1 g	Sodium:	23 mg

Party Chicken Tarts

Savory Seafood Spread

2 packages (8 ounces *each*) light
   cream cheese, softened
1 package (8 ounces) imitation crab
   meat, flaked
2 tablespoons minced green onion
1 tablespoon prepared horseradish
1 tablespoon FRANK'S® Original
   REDHOT® Cayenne Pepper Sauce
1 teaspoon FRENCH'S® Worcestershire
   Sauce
½ cup sliced almonds
   Paprika
   Crackers
   Vegetable dippers

1. Preheat oven to 375°F. Beat or process
cream cheese in electric mixer or food
processor until smooth and creamy. Add
crab, green onion, horseradish, RedHot® sauce
and Worcestershire; beat or process until well
blended.

2. Spread cream cheese mixture onto 9-inch
pie plate. Top with almonds and sprinkle
with paprika. Bake 20 minutes or until
mixture is heated through and almonds are
golden. Garnish as desired.

3. Serve with crackers or vegetable dippers.
Makes 3 cups spread

Prep time: 10 minutes
Cook time: 20 minutes

Spectacular Shrimp Spread

½ pound cooked deveined peeled rock
   shrimp
1 can (13 ounces) artichoke hearts,
   drained
1 cup mayonnaise*
½ cup shredded Parmesan cheese
¼ teaspoon ground lemon pepper
⅛ teaspoon salt
   Dash cayenne pepper
   Assorted crackers (optional)

*May substitute ½ cup mayonnaise and ½ cup plain
yogurt for mayonnaise.*

Preheat oven to 400°F. Finely chop shrimp
and artichoke hearts; place in medium bowl.
Add mayonnaise, cheese, lemon pepper, salt
and cayenne pepper; mix well.

Spoon shrimp mixture into 9-inch pie pan or
1-quart shallow baking dish. Bake 10 minutes
or until hot and bubbly. Serve hot with
crackers, if desired.
Makes about 3¾ cups spread

Favorite recipe from **Florida Department of
Agriculture and Consumer Services, Bureau of
Seafood and Aquaculture**

Savory Seafood Spread

Herbed Blue Cheese Spread with Garlic Toasts

1⅓ cups 1% low-fat cottage cheese
1¼ cups (5 ounces) crumbled blue, feta
    or goat cheese
1 large clove garlic
2 teaspoons lemon juice
2 green onions with tops, sliced
    (about ¼ cup)
¼ cup chopped fresh basil or oregano
    or 1 teaspoon dried basil or
    oregano leaves
2 tablespoons toasted slivered
    almonds*
Garlic Toasts (recipe follows)

*To toast almonds, place almonds in shallow baking pan. Bake at 350°F about 10 minutes or until lightly toasted, stirring occasionally. (Watch almonds carefully—they burn easily.)

1. Combine cottage cheese, blue cheese, garlic and lemon juice in food processor; process until smooth. Add green onions, basil and almonds; pulse until well blended but still chunky.

2. Spoon cheese spread into small serving bowl; cover. Refrigerate until ready to serve.

3. When ready to serve, prepare Garlic Toasts. Spread 1 tablespoon cheese spread onto each toast slice. Garnish, if desired.

Makes 16 servings

Garlic Toasts

32 French bread slices, ½ inch thick
    Nonstick cooking spray
¼ teaspoon garlic powder
⅛ teaspoon salt

Place bread slices on nonstick baking sheet. Lightly coat both sides of bread slices with nonstick cooking spray. Combine garlic powder and salt in small bowl; sprinkle evenly onto bread slices. Broil, 6 to 8 inches from heat, 30 to 45 seconds on each side or until bread slices are lightly toasted.

Makes 32 pieces

Chunky Hawaiian Spread

1 package (3 ounces) light cream
    cheese, softened
½ cup fat free or light sour cream
1 can (8 ounces) DOLE® Crushed
    Pineapple, well-drained
¼ cup mango chutney*
    Low fat crackers

*If there are large pieces of fruit in chutney, cut into small pieces.

• Beat cream cheese, sour cream, pineapple and chutney in bowl until blended. Cover and chill 1 hour or overnight. Serve with crackers. Refrigerate any leftover spread in airtight container for up to one week.

Makes 2½ cups spread

Herbed Blue Cheese Spread with Garlic Toasts

Nutty Broccoli Spread

1 box (10 ounces) BIRDS EYE® frozen Chopped Broccoli
4 ounces cream cheese
¼ cup grated Parmesan cheese
1 teaspoon dried basil
¼ cup walnuts
1 loaf frozen garlic bread

• Cook broccoli according to package directions; drain well.

• Preheat oven to 400°F. Place broccoli, cream cheese, Parmesan cheese and basil in food processor or blender; process until ingredients are mixed. (Do not overmix.) Add walnuts; process 3 to 5 seconds.

• Split garlic bread lengthwise. Spread broccoli mixture evenly over bread.

• Bake 10 to 15 minutes or until bread is toasted and broccoli mixture is heated through.

• Cut bread into bite-size pieces; serve hot.

Makes about 2 cups spread

Prep time: 10 minutes
Cook time: 10 to 15 minutes

Wisconsin Edam and Beer Spread

1 ball (2 pounds) Wisconsin Edam Cheese*
¾ cup butter, cubed and softened
2 tablespoons snipped fresh chives
2 teaspoons Dijon mustard
½ cup amber or dark beer, at room temperature
Cocktail rye or pumpernickel bread slices

*Wisconsin Gouda can be substituted for Edam. Since Gouda is not available in ball form, this spread may be served in your favorite serving bowl.

Cut one fifth from top of cheese to create flat surface. With butter curler or melon baller, remove cheese from center of ball leaving ½-inch-thick shell. Shred enough of cheese removed from ball and top to measure 4 cups. Reserve remaining cheese.

Place shredded cheese, butter, chives and mustard in large bowl; mix with spoon until blended. Stir in beer until blended. Spoon spread into hollowed cheese ball; reserve remaining spread for refills. Chill until serving time. Serve with cocktail bread.

Makes 4 cups spread

Favorite recipe from **Wisconsin Milk Marketing Board**

Nutty Broccoli Spread

SNAPPY SOUPS
& SANDWICHES

Beefy Broccoli & Cheese Soup

2 cups chicken broth
1 package (10 ounces) frozen
   chopped broccoli, thawed
¼ cup chopped onion
¼ pound ground beef
1 cup milk
2 tablespoons all-purpose
   flour

4 ounces (1 cup) shredded
   sharp Cheddar cheese
1½ teaspoons chopped fresh
   oregano *or* ½ teaspoon
   dried oregano
Salt and freshly ground
   black pepper
Hot pepper sauce

Bring broth to a boil in medium saucepan. Add broccoli and onion; cook 5 minutes or until broccoli is tender.

Meanwhile, brown ground beef in small skillet; drain. Gradually add milk to flour, mixing until well blended. Add milk mixture and ground beef to broth mixture; cook, stirring constantly, until mixture is thickened and bubbly.

Add cheese and oregano; stir until cheese is melted. Season with salt, pepper and hot pepper sauce to taste. *Makes 4 to 5 servings*

Beefy Broccoli & Cheese Soup

32

Vegetable Soup

2 tablespoons FILIPPO BERIO® Olive
    Oil
2 medium potatoes, peeled and
    quartered
2 medium onions, sliced
3 cups beef broth
8 ounces fresh green beans, trimmed
    and cut into 1-inch pieces
3 carrots, peeled and chopped
8 ounces fresh spinach, washed,
    drained, stems removed and
    chopped
1 green bell pepper, diced
2 tablespoons chopped fresh parsley
1 tablespoon chopped fresh basil *or*
    1 teaspoon dried basil leaves
1 clove garlic, finely minced
½ teaspoon ground cumin
    Salt and freshly ground black
    pepper

In Dutch oven, heat olive oil over medium-high heat until hot. Add potatoes and onions; cook and stir 5 minutes. Add beef broth, green beans and carrots. Bring mixture to a boil. Cover; reduce heat to low and simmer 10 minutes, stirring occasionally. Add spinach, bell pepper, parsley, basil, garlic and cumin. Cover; simmer an additional 15 to 20 minutes or until potatoes are tender. Season to taste with salt and black pepper. Serve hot.   *Makes 6 to 8 servings*

Fresh Tomato Pasta Soup

1 tablespoon olive oil
½ cup chopped onion
1 clove garlic, minced
3 pounds fresh tomatoes, coarsely
    chopped
3 cups ⅓-less-salt chicken broth
1 tablespoon minced fresh basil
1 tablespoon minced fresh marjoram
1 tablespoon minced fresh oregano
1 teaspoon fennel seed
½ teaspoon black pepper
¾ cup uncooked rosamarina or other
    small pasta
½ cup (2 ounces) shredded part-skim
    mozzarella cheese
Marjoram sprigs for garnish

1. Heat oil in large saucepan over medium heat. Add onion and garlic; cook and stir until onion is tender. Add tomatoes, broth, basil, marjoram, oregano, fennel seed and pepper.

2. Bring to a boil; reduce heat. Cover; simmer 25 minutes. Remove from heat; cool slightly.

3. Purée tomato mixture in food processor or blender in batches. Return to saucepan; bring to a boil. Add pasta; cook 7 to 9 minutes or until tender. Transfer to serving bowls. Sprinkle with mozzarella. Garnish with marjoram sprigs, if desired.
          Makes 8 (¾-cup) servings

Vegetable Soup

Roasted Winter Vegetable Soup

1 small or ½ medium acorn squash, halved
2 medium tomatoes
1 medium onion, unpeeled
1 green bell pepper, halved
1 red bell pepper, halved
2 small red potatoes
3 cloves garlic, unpeeled
1½ cups tomato juice
½ cup water
4 teaspoons vegetable oil
1 tablespoon red wine vinegar
¼ teaspoon black pepper
¾ cup chopped fresh cilantro
4 tablespoons nonfat sour cream

1. Preheat oven to 400°F. Spray baking sheet with nonstick cooking spray. Place acorn squash, tomatoes, onion, bell peppers, potatoes and garlic on baking sheet. Bake 40 minutes, removing garlic and tomatoes after 10 minutes. Let stand 15 minutes or until cool enough to handle.

2. Peel vegetables and garlic; discard skins. Coarsely chop vegetables. Combine half of chopped vegetables, tomato juice, water, oil and vinegar in food processor or blender; process until smooth.

3. Combine puréed vegetables, remaining chopped vegetables and black pepper in large saucepan. Bring to a simmer over medium-high heat. Simmer 5 minutes or until heated through, stirring constantly. Top servings evenly with cilantro and sour cream.

Makes 4 servings

Grandma's Chicken Soup

8 broiler-fryer chicken thighs, skinned, fat trimmed
2 carrots, cut into ¼-inch slices
2 ribs celery, cut in ¼-inch slices
2 medium turnips, pared, cubed
1 large onion, chopped
8 cups water
½ teaspoons salt
¼ teaspoon black pepper
¼ teaspoon poultry seasoning
⅛ teaspoon dried thyme leaves
1 cup wide egg noodles, uncooked

In large saucepan or Dutch oven, layer chicken, carrots, celery, turnips and onion. Add water, salt, pepper, poultry seasoning and thyme. Cook, covered, over medium heat until liquid boils. Reduce heat and simmer about 45 minutes or until chicken and vegetables are fork tender. Remove chicken; cool. Separate meat from bones; discard bones. Cut chicken into bite-size pieces. Heat soup mixture to boiling; stir in noodles. Cook, uncovered, about 5 to 7 minutes or until noodles are done. Stir in chicken.

Makes 8 servings

Favorite recipe from **Delmarva Poultry Industry, Inc.**

Chicken Rotini Soup

½ **pound boneless skinless chicken breasts, cut into ½-inch pieces**
1 **cup water**
2 **tablespoons butter or margarine**
4 **ounces fresh mushrooms, sliced**
½ **medium onion, chopped**
4 **cups canned chicken broth**
1 **teaspoon Worcestershire sauce**
¼ **teaspoon dried tarragon leaves, crushed**
¾ **cup uncooked rotini**
1 **small zucchini**
   Fresh basil for garnish

Combine chicken and water in medium saucepan. Bring to a boil over high heat. Reduce heat to medium-low; simmer 2 minutes. Drain water and rinse chicken.

Melt butter in 5-quart Dutch oven or large saucepan over medium heat. Add mushrooms and onion. Cook and stir until onion is tender. Stir in chicken, chicken broth, Worcestershire sauce and tarragon. Bring to a boil over high heat. Stir in pasta. Reduce heat to medium-low; simmer, uncovered, 5 minutes.

Cut zucchini into ⅛-inch slices; halve any large slices. Add to soup; simmer, uncovered, about 5 minutes, or until pasta is tender. Ladle into bowls. Garnish, if desired.

Makes 4 servings

Chicken Rotini Soup

Cream of Chicken and Wild Rice Soup

½ cup uncooked wild rice
 5 cups canned chicken broth, divided
¼ cup butter
 1 large carrot, sliced
 1 medium onion, chopped
 2 ribs celery, chopped
¼ pound fresh mushrooms, sliced
 2 tablespoons all-purpose flour
¼ teaspoon salt
¼ teaspoon white pepper
 1½ cups chopped cooked chicken
¼ cup dry sherry

1. Rinse rice under cold water; drain.

2. Combine 2½ cups chicken broth and rice in 2-quart saucepan. Bring to a boil over medium-high heat. Reduce heat to low; simmer, covered, 1 hour or until rice is tender. Drain; set aside.

3. Melt butter in 3-quart saucepan over medium heat. Add carrot; cook and stir 3 minutes. Add onion, celery and mushrooms; cook and stir 3 to 4 minutes until vegetables are tender.

4. Remove from heat. Whisk in flour, salt and pepper until smooth.

5. Gradually stir in remaining 2½ cups chicken broth. Bring to a boil over medium heat; cook and stir 1 minute or until thickened.

6. Stir in chicken and sherry. Reduce heat to low; simmer, uncovered, 3 minutes or until heated through.

7. Spoon ¼ cup rice into each serving bowl. Ladle soup over rice.

Makes 4 to 6 servings

Tortellini Soup

1 tablespoon FLEISCHMANN'S®
    Original Spread (70% Corn Oil)
2 cloves garlic, minced
2 (14¼-ounce) cans COLLEGE INN®
    Chicken or Beef Broth
1 (8-ounce) package fresh or frozen
    cheese-filled tortellini, thawed
1 (14½-ounce) can stewed tomatoes,
    cut up, undrained
1 (10-ounce) package fresh or frozen
    spinach, thawed
Grated Parmesan cheese

In large saucepan, melt margarine over medium-high heat. Add garlic; cook and stir 2 to 3 minutes or until lightly browned. Add broth and tortellini; bring to a boil. Reduce heat to low; simmer 10 minutes, stirring occasionally. Add tomatoes and spinach; simmer an additional 5 minutes. Top individual servings with Parmesan cheese.

Makes 6 servings

Cream of Chicken and Wild Rice Soup

Ravioli Soup

8 ounces sweet Italian sausage, casing removed
1 clove garlic, crushed
2 (13¾-ounce) cans lower sodium chicken broth
2 cups water
1 (9-ounce) package frozen miniature cheese-filled ravioli
1 (15-ounce) can garbanzo beans, drained
1 (14½-ounce) can stewed tomatoes
⅓ cup GREY POUPON® Dijon Mustard
½ teaspoon dried oregano leaves
¼ teaspoon coarsely ground black pepper
1 cup torn fresh spinach leaves
Grated Parmesan cheese

In 4-quart heavy pot, over medium heat, brown sausage and cook garlic until tender, stirring to break up sausage, about 5 minutes. Pour off excess fat; remove sausage mixture from pot and set aside.

In same pot, over medium-high heat, heat chicken broth and water to a boil. Add ravioli; cook for 4 to 5 minutes or until tender. Stir in beans, stewed tomatoes, sausage mixture, mustard, oregano and pepper; heat through. Stir in spinach and cook until wilted, about 1 minute. Serve topped with Parmesan cheese.

Makes 8 servings

Grilled Corn Soup

4 ears Grilled Corn-on-the-Cob (recipe follows)
5 green onions
4 cups chicken broth, divided
Salt and black pepper

Cut kernels from cobs to make 2 to 2½ cups. Slice green onions, separating the white part from the green. Place corn, white part of onions and 2 cups chicken broth in blender or food processor; process until mixture is slightly lumpy. Place corn mixture in large saucepan; add remaining chicken broth. Simmer gently 15 minutes. Stir in sliced green onion tops; season to taste with salt and pepper. *Makes 4 to 6 servings*

Grilled Corn-on-the-Cob
Turn back corn husks; do not remove. Remove silks with stiff brush; rinse corn under cold running water. Smooth husks back into position. Grill ears, on a covered grill, over medium-hot **KINGSFORD®** briquets, about 25 minutes or until tender, turning corn often. Remove husks and serve.

Ravioli Soup

Split Pea Soup

1 package (16 ounces) dried green or
yellow split peas
1 pound smoked pork hocks *or*
4 ounces smoked sausage link,
sliced and quartered *or* 1 meaty
ham bone
7 cups water
1 medium onion, chopped
2 medium carrots, chopped
¾ teaspoon salt
½ teaspoon dried basil leaves
¼ teaspoon dried oregano leaves
¼ teaspoon black pepper
Ham and carrot strips for garnish

Rinse peas under cold water. Place peas, pork
hocks and water in 5-quart Dutch oven.

Add onion, carrots, salt, basil, oregano and
pepper to Dutch oven. Bring to a boil over
high heat. Reduce heat to medium-low;
simmer, uncovered, 1 hour 15 minutes or
until peas are tender, stirring occasionally.
Stir frequently near end of cooking to keep
soup from scorching.

Remove pork hocks; cool. Cut meat into
bite-size pieces.

Carefully ladle 3 cups hot soup into food
processor or blender; cover and process until
mixture is smooth.

Return puréed soup and meat to Dutch oven.
(If soup is too thick, add a little water until
desired consistency is reached.) Heat
through. Ladle into bowls. Garnish, if
desired.   *Makes 6 servings*

Creamy Asparagus Potato Soup

1 can (14½ ounces) DEL MONTE®
FreshCut™ Brand Whole New
Potatoes, drained
1 can (12 ounces) DEL MONTE®
FreshCut™ Asparagus Spears,
drained
½ teaspoon dried thyme, crushed
⅛ teaspoon garlic powder
1 can (14 ounces) chicken broth
1 cup milk or half & half

1. Place potatoes, asparagus, thyme and garlic
powder in food processor or blender
(in batches, if needed); process until smooth.

2. Pour into medium saucepan; add broth.
Bring to a boil. Stir in milk; heat through.
(Do not boil.) Season with salt and pepper to
taste, if desired. Serve hot or cold. Thin with
additional milk or water, if desired.
                    Makes 4 servings

Prep time: 5 minutes
Cook time: 5 minutes

Split Pea Soup

Beef Soup with Noodles

2 tablespoons soy sauce
1 teaspoon minced fresh ginger
¼ teaspoon crushed red pepper
1 boneless beef top sirloin steak, cut
    1 inch thick (about ¾ pound)
1 tablespoon peanut or vegetable oil
2 cups sliced fresh mushrooms
2 cans (about 14 ounces *each*) beef
    broth
1 cup (3 ounces) fresh snow peas, cut
    diagonally into 1-inch pieces
1½ cups hot cooked fine egg noodles
    (2 ounces uncooked)
1 green onion, cut diagonally into
    thin slices
1 teaspoon dark sesame oil (optional)
    Red bell pepper strips for garnish
    (optional)

1. Combine soy sauce, ginger and crushed red pepper in small bowl. Spread mixture evenly over both sides of steak. Marinate at room temperature 15 minutes.

2. Heat deep skillet over medium-high heat. Add peanut oil; heat until hot. Drain steak; reserve soy sauce mixture (there will only be a small amount of mixture). Add steak to skillet; cook 4 to 5 minutes per side.* Let stand on cutting board 10 minutes.

3. Add mushrooms to skillet; stir-fry 2 minutes. Add broth, snow peas and reserved soy sauce mixture; bring to a boil, scraping up browned meat bits. Reduce heat to medium-low. Stir in noodles.

4. Cut steak across the grain into ⅛-inch slices; cut each slice into 1-inch pieces. Stir into soup; heat through. Stir in green onion and sesame oil. Ladle into soup bowls. Garnish with bell pepper strips, if desired.
Makes 4 servings (about 6 cups)

Cooking time is for medium-rare doneness. Adjust time for desired doneness.

Minestrone Soup

2 (14¼-ounce) cans COLLEGE INN®
    Beef or Chicken Broth
1 (16-ounce) can mixed vegetables,
    undrained
1 (16-ounce) can stewed tomatoes,
    undrained and coarsely chopped
1 (10½-ounce) can red kidney beans,
    drained
¼ cup uncooked shell macaroni
1 teaspoon garlic powder
1 teaspoon dried basil leaves

In large saucepan, over medium-high heat, heat all ingredients to a boil. Reduce heat; simmer 20 minutes or until macaroni is cooked.
Makes 6 servings

Beef Soup with Noodles

Bistro Turkey Sandwiches

¼ cup reduced-calorie mayonnaise
2 tablespoons finely chopped fresh basil
2 tablespoons chopped drained sun-dried tomatoes in oil
2 tablespoons finely chopped pitted kalamata olives
⅛ teaspoon red pepper flakes
1 loaf focaccia bread, quartered and split *or* 8 slices sourdough bread
1 jar (7 ounces) roasted red bell peppers, rinsed and drained
4 romaine or red leaf lettuce leaves
2 packages (4 ounces each) HEBREW NATIONAL® Sliced Oven Roasted or Smoked Turkey Breast

Combine mayonnaise, basil, sun-dried tomatoes, olives and red pepper flakes in small bowl; mix well. Spread evenly over cut sides of bread. Remove excess liquid from roasted peppers with paper towels. Layer roasted peppers, lettuce and turkey breast between bread slices. *Makes 4 servings*

Spinach and Beef Pita Sandwiches

1 pound ground beef
1 package (10 ounces) frozen chopped spinach, thawed and drained of as much moisture as possible
1 bunch green onions, chopped
1 can (2¼ ounces) sliced black olives, drained
2 teaspoons LAWRY'S® Lemon Pepper, divided
1 large tomato, diced
1 cup plain nonfat yogurt or dairy sour cream
½ cup reduced-calorie mayonnaise
6 (6-inch) pita breads, warmed
Lettuce leaves
1 cup (4 ounces) crumbled feta cheese

In large skillet, brown ground beef until crumbly; drain fat. Add spinach, green onions, olives and 1 teaspoon Lemon Pepper to beef; cook 2 minutes. Stir in tomato. In small bowl, combine yogurt, mayonnaise and remaining 1 teaspoon Lemon Pepper. Split open pita breads. Line insides with lettuce. Stir cheese into beef mixture and divide among pita pockets. Serve with yogurt sauce. *Makes 6 servings*

Serving Suggestion: Pass the remaining yogurt sauce separately.

Hint: Use scissors to cut open pita breads.

Bistro Turkey Sandwich

Eggplant & Pepper Cheese Sandwiches

1 (8-ounce) eggplant, cut into
   18 slices
   Salt and black pepper, to taste
⅓ cup GREY POUPON® COUNTRY
   DIJON® Mustard
¼ cup olive oil
2 tablespoons REGINA® Red Wine
   Vinegar
1 clove garlic, crushed
¾ teaspoon dried oregano leaves
6 (4-inch) pieces French bread, cut in
   half
1 (7-ounce) jar roasted red peppers,
   cut into strips
1½ cups shredded mozzarella cheese
   (6 ounces)

Place eggplant slices on greased baking sheet, overlapping slightly. Sprinkle lightly with salt and pepper. Bake at 400°F for 10 to 12 minutes or until tender.

Blend mustard, oil, vinegar, garlic and oregano. Brush eggplant slices with ¼ cup mustard mixture; broil eggplant for 1 minute.

Brush cut sides of French bread with remaining mustard mixture. Layer 3 slices eggplant, a few red pepper strips and ¼ cup cheese on each bread bottom. Place on broiler pan with roll tops, cut-sides up; broil until cheese melts. Close sandwiches with bread tops and serve immediately; garnish as desired.
Makes 6 sandwiches

Mediterranean Chicken Salad Sandwiches

4 boneless skinless chicken breast
   halves
½ cup water
1 teaspoon dried basil leaves
¼ teaspoon salt
¼ teaspoon black pepper
1 cup chopped cucumber
½ cup mayonnaise
¼ cup chopped roasted red pepper
¼ cup pitted sliced ripe olives
¼ cup yogurt
¼ teaspoon garlic powder
6 Kaiser rolls, split
   Additional mayonnaise
   Lettuce leaves

Place chicken, water, basil, salt and black pepper in medium saucepan; bring to a boil. Reduce heat; simmer, covered, 10 to 12 minutes or until chicken is no longer pink in center. Remove chicken from saucepan; cool. Cut into ½-inch pieces.

Combine chicken, cucumber, mayonnaise, red pepper, olives, yogurt and garlic powder in medium bowl; toss to coat well.

Spread rolls with additional mayonnaise. Top with lettuce and chicken salad mixture.
Makes 6 servings

Eggplant & Pepper Cheese Sandwiches

Mighty Hero Sandwich

1 (16-ounce) round loaf sourdough
    bread
¼ cup balsamic vinegar
1 tablespoon olive oil
2 cloves garlic, minced
1 teaspoon dried oregano leaves
1 teaspoon dried parsley flakes
¼ teaspoon black pepper
1 cup sliced fresh mushrooms
6 (¼-inch-thick) tomato slices
2 (¼-inch-thick) red onion slices,
    separated into rings
2 cups shredded zucchini
1 cup (4 ounces) HEALTHY CHOICE®
    Fat Free Mozzarella Shreds
4 ounces HEALTHY CHOICE® Deli
    Thin Sliced Bologna
4 ounces HEALTHY CHOICE® Deli
    Thin Oven Roasted Turkey Breast

Slice bread in half horizontally. Remove soft bread from inside each half, leaving ½-inch-thick shells; set shells aside. Reserve soft inside bread for another use.

Combine vinegar and next 5 ingredients in a shallow dish; add mushrooms, tomato and onion. Let stand 15 minutes.

Drain vegetables, reserving marinade. Brush marinade inside bread shells. Layer half each of zucchini, mushroom mixture and cheese in bottom half of loaf; top with bologna. Repeat layers; top with turkey and remaining half of loaf. Wrap in plastic wrap; chill. To serve, unwrap loaf and cut into wedges.

Makes 8 servings

Nutrients per Serving:

Calories:	192	Cholesterol:	16 mg
Total Fat:	4 g	Sodium:	591 mg

French Dip Sandwiches

½ cup A.1.® Original or A.1.® Bold &
    Spicy Steak Sauce, divided
1 tablespoon GREY POUPON® Dijon
    Mustard
4 steak rolls, split horizontally
8 ounces sliced cooked roast beef
1 (13¾-ounce) can beef broth

In small bowl, blend ¼ cup steak sauce and mustard; spread mixture evenly on cut sides of roll tops. Arrange 2 ounces beef on each roll bottom; replace roll tops over beef. Slice sandwiches in half crosswise if desired. In small saucepan, heat broth and remaining ¼ cup steak sauce, stirring occasionally. Serve as a dipping sauce with sandwiches. Garnish as desired. *Makes 4 servings*

French Dip Sandwich

Meatless Muffaletta Sandwich

1 (12-inch) loaf French- or Italian-style bread, unsliced
½ cup LAWRY'S® Classic Red Wine Vinaigrette with Cabernet Sauvignon Dressing
½ cup mayonnaise
2 teaspoons capers
1 ripe avocado, peeled, pitted and sliced
½ cup sliced green Spanish olives
1 can (2¼ ounces) sliced pitted black olives, drained
4 ounces sliced Swiss cheese
Fresh basil leaves
4 Roma tomatoes, sliced, *or* 4 ounces roasted red pepper slices
3 thin slices red onion, separated into rings

Slice bread horizontally. Hollow out each half, leaving ¾-inch shell. (Tear removed bread into crumbs; freeze for another use.) Set bread shells aside. In food processor or blender, combine Classic Red Wine Vinaigrette with Cabernet Sauvignon Dressing, mayonnaise and capers; process until well blended. Spread vinaigrette mixture evenly onto insides of shells. Into bottom bread shell, evenly layer remaining ingredients. Cover with top half of bread; press bread halves together firmly. Wrap tightly in plastic wrap; refrigerate 30 minutes.

Makes 4 servings

Meatless Muffaletta Sandwich

Serving Suggestion: Unwrap loaf; slice into four 3-inch portions. Flavors are best when sandwich is served at room temperature. For crispier crust, place uncut loaf in 225°F. oven. Bake 15 to 20 minutes. Remove from oven. Cut and fill loaf as directed.

Hint: If desired, rinse olives in cold water to reduce saltiness.

Combine yogurt, celery, spinach, green onions, lemon juice, dill and mustard in large bowl. Stir in chicken, apple and walnuts. Season with salt and pepper, if desired. Spoon ½ cup salad and 1 lettuce leaf into each pita bread half.   *Makes 4 sandwiches*

Favorite recipe from **Walnut Marketing Board**

Walnut Chicken Salad Sandwich

⅔ **cup nonfat plain yogurt**
½ **cup finely chopped celery**
½ **cup finely chopped fresh spinach**
     ***or* 3 tablespoons drained thawed**
     chopped frozen spinach
¼ **cup chopped green onions**
1 **tablespoon lemon juice**
1 **tablespoon chopped fresh dill or**
     tarragon *or* ½ teaspoon dried
     dillweed or tarragon leaves
1 **teaspoon ground mustard**
3 **cups diced cooked chicken breasts**
1 **apple, cored and diced**
½ **cup (2 ounces) chopped California**
     walnuts
  Salt and black pepper (optional)
4 **iceberg lettuce leaves or other crisp**
     lettuce leaves
4 **pita breads, halved**

Veggie Club Sandwiches

¼ **cup reduced-fat mayonnaise**
1 **clove garlic, minced**
⅛ **teaspoon dried marjoram leaves**
⅛ **teaspoon dried tarragon leaves**
8 **slices whole-grain bread**
8 **washed leaf lettuce leaves**
1 **large tomato, thinly sliced**
1 **small cucumber, thinly sliced**
4 **slices reduced-fat Cheddar cheese**
1 **medium red onion, thinly sliced**
     and separated into rings
½ **cup alfalfa sprouts**

1. To prepare mayonnaise spread, combine mayonnaise, garlic, marjoram and tarragon in small bowl. Refrigerate until ready to use.

2. To assemble sandwiches, spread each of 4 bread slices with 1 tablespoon mayonnaise spread. Divide lettuce, tomato, cucumber, cheese, onion and sprouts evenly among bread slices. Top with remaining bread. Cut sandwiches into halves and serve immediately.   *Makes 4 sandwiches*

Tuna Monte Cristo Sandwiches

**4 thin slices (2 ounces) Cheddar
   cheese**
**4 slices sourdough or challah (egg)
   bread**
½ pound deli tuna salad
¼ cup milk
1 egg, beaten
2 tablespoons butter or margarine

1. Place 1 slice cheese on each bread slice. Spread tuna salad evenly over two slices of cheese-topped bread. Top with remaining bread.

2. Combine milk and egg in shallow bowl. Dip sandwiches in egg mixture, turning to coat well.

3. Melt butter in large nonstick skillet over medium heat. Add sandwiches; cook 4 to 5 minutes per side or until bread is golden brown and cheese is melted.

Makes 2 servings

Prep and cook time: 20 minutes

Tuna Monte Cristo Sandwich

Egg Salad Sandwiches

1 cup EGG BEATERS® Healthy Real Egg Substitute, hard-cooked and chopped
¼ cup chopped celery
¼ cup chopped onion
2 tablespoons fat-free mayonnaise
12 slices whole wheat bread
6 lettuce leaves
1 large tomato, cut into 6 thin slices

In small bowl, combine hard-cooked Egg Beaters®, celery, onion and mayonnaise. On each of 6 bread slices, place lettuce leaf and tomato slice; top each with about ¼ cup egg salad and remaining bread slice.

Makes 6 servings

Prep time: 20 minutes

Hummus Pita Sandwiches

1 to 2 cloves garlic, peeled
1 can (15 ounces) garbanzo beans, drained, reserve liquid
¼ cup loosely packed parsley sprigs
3 tablespoons fresh lemon juice
1 tablespoon olive oil
¼ teaspoon ground black pepper
2 tablespoons sesame seeds, toasted
4 pita breads
2 tomatoes, thinly sliced
1 cucumber, sliced
1 cup alfalfa sprouts, rinsed and drained
2 tablespoons crumbled feta cheese

1. Place garlic in food processor; process until minced. Add garbanzo beans, parsley, lemon juice, olive oil and pepper. Process until almost smooth, scraping sides of bowl once. If mixture is very thick, add 1 to 2 tablespoons reserved garbanzo bean liquid. Pour hummus into medium bowl. Stir in sesame seeds.

2. Cut pita breads in half. Spread about 3 tablespoons hummus in each pita bread half. Divide tomatoes, cucumber slices and alfalfa sprouts evenly among pita breads. Sprinkle with feta cheese. *Makes 4 servings*

Grilled Steak and Pepper Sandwiches

1 (1-pound) beef top round steak
¾ cup A.1.® Steak Sauce
2 bell peppers (1 red and 1 green), sliced
4 large hard rolls, split and grilled
4 ounces thinly sliced mozzarella cheese

Place steak in nonmetal dish; coat with ¼ cup steak sauce. Cover; chill 1 hour, turning occasionally.

In medium skillet, over medium heat, cook and stir peppers in remaining steak sauce until tender-crisp, about 10 minutes; keep warm.

Remove steak from marinade. Grill over medium heat for 6 minutes on each side or until done. Thinly slice steak; arrange on roll bottoms. Top each with warm pepper sauce, cheese slice and roll top; serve immediately.

Makes 4 servings

Grilled Chicken Breast and Peperonata Sandwiches

1 tablespoon olive oil or vegetable oil
1 medium red bell pepper, sliced into strips
1 medium green bell pepper, sliced into strips
¾ cup onion slices (about 1 medium)
2 cloves garlic, minced
¼ teaspoon salt
¼ teaspoon black pepper
4 boneless skinless chicken breast halves (about 1 pound)
4 small French rolls, split and toasted

1. Heat oil in large nonstick skillet over medium heat until hot. Add bell peppers, onion and garlic; cook and stir 5 minutes. Reduce heat to low; cook and stir about 20 minutes or until vegetables are soft. Sprinkle with salt and black pepper.

2. Grill chicken, on covered grill over medium-hot coals, 10 minutes on each side or until chicken is no longer pink in center. Or, broil chicken, 6 inches from heat source, 7 to 8 minutes on each side or until chicken is no longer pink in center.

3. Place chicken on rolls. Divide bell pepper mixture evenly; spoon over chicken.

Makes 4 servings

Spicy Barbecue Beef Sandwich

1 cup A.1.® Steak Sauce
⅔ cup chili sauce
½ cup water
3 tablespoons GREY POUPON® Dijon Mustard
1 (2-pound) beef top round steak
2 tablespoons vegetable oil
2 large onions, sliced
8 sandwich rolls, split and toasted

In small bowl, combine steak sauce, chili sauce, water and mustard; set aside.

In large heavy saucepan, over medium-high heat, brown steak in oil. Add onions, stirring until lightly browned. Stir in sauce mixture; heat to a boil. Cover; reduce heat and simmer 1½ hours or until steak is tender. Remove steak; cut into julienne strips. Return steak to pan; cook and stir until hot. Spoon steak mixture onto roll bottoms; replace tops. Serve immediately. *Makes 8 servings*

Grilled Chicken Breast and Peperonata Sandwich

SENSATIONAL

SALADS

Roasted Red Pepper, Corn & Garbanzo Bean Salad

2 cans (15 ounces each) garbanzo beans
1 jar (11.5 ounces) GUILTLESS GOURMET® Roasted Red Pepper Salsa
1 cup frozen corn, thawed, drained

½ cup GUILTLESS GOURMET® Green Tomatillo Salsa
2 green onions, thinly sliced
8 lettuce leaves

Rinse and drain beans well; place in 2-quart casserole dish. Add roasted red pepper salsa, corn, tomatillo salsa and onions; stir to combine. Cover and refrigerate 1 hour or up to 24 hours.

To serve, line serving platter with lettuce. Spoon bean mixture over top. Garnish with tomato wedges and sprouts, if desired. *Makes 8 servings*

Roasted Red Pepper, Corn & Garbanzo Bean Salad

58

Chicken and Couscous Salad

1 can (14½ ounces) low-sodium chicken broth, defatted
½ teaspoon ground cinnamon
¼ teaspoon curry powder
¼ teaspoon ground nutmeg
1 cup uncooked couscous
1½ pounds boneless skinless chicken breasts, cooked
2 cups fresh pineapple chunks
2 cups cubed seeded cucumber
2 cups cubed red bell pepper
2 cups cubed yellow bell pepper
1 cup sliced celery
½ cup sliced green onions with tops
3 tablespoons water
3 tablespoons apple cider vinegar
2 tablespoons vegetable oil
1 tablespoon fresh mint *or*
    1 teaspoon dried mint leaves
    Lettuce leaves

1. In nonstick Dutch oven or large nonstick saucepan, heat chicken broth, cinnamon, curry powder and nutmeg to a boil. Stir in couscous; remove pan from heat and let stand, covered, 5 minutes. Fluff couscous with fork; cool to room temperature.

2. Cut chicken into ½-inch pieces. Add chicken, pineapple, cucumber, bell peppers, celery and green onions to couscous; toss to combine.

3. In small jar with tight-fitting lid, combine water, vinegar, oil and mint; shake well. Pour over couscous mixture; toss to coat. Serve immediately in lettuce-lined bowl. Garnish as desired. *Makes 6 servings*

Chinese Chicken Salad

3 cups cooked rice, cooled
1½ cups cooked chicken breast cubes (about 1 whole breast)
1 cup sliced celery
1 can (8 ounces) sliced water chestnuts, drained
½ cup sliced fresh mushrooms
¼ cup sliced green onions
¼ cup chopped red bell pepper
¼ cup sliced black olives
2 tablespoons vegetable oil
2 tablespoons lemon juice
1 tablespoon soy sauce
½ teaspoon ground ginger
¼ to ½ teaspoon ground white pepper
    Lettuce leaves

Combine rice, chicken, celery, water chestnuts, mushrooms, green onions, bell pepper, and olives in large bowl. Place oil, lemon juice, soy sauce, ginger, and white pepper in small jar with lid; shake well. Pour over rice mixture. Toss lightly. Serve on lettuce leaves. *Makes 4 servings*

Nutrients per Serving:

Calories:	350	Cholesterol:	41 mg
Total Fat:	10 g	Sodium:	644 mg

Favorite recipe from **USA Rice Federation**

Chicken and Couscous Salad

Creole Red Beans and Rice Salad

1 cup dried red beans, rinsed and
  drained
½ teaspoon salt, divided
6 sun-dried tomatoes (not packed in
  oil), chopped
1 cup water
½ cup basmati or Texmati rice
  Creole Dressing (recipe follows)
6 green onions, sliced
1 medium yellow squash, cut into
  ½-inch cubes
¾ cup finely diced red bell pepper
¾ cup finely diced celery
  Lettuce leaves
  Cherry tomatoes for garnish

1. Place beans in large saucepan; cover with
2 inches water. Bring to a boil over high heat.
Cover and remove from heat. Let stand
1 hour. Return to a boil over high heat.
Reduce heat to low. Simmer, covered, 30
minutes; stir in ¼ teaspoon salt. Cook 15 to
30 minutes more or until tender, adding
tomatoes during last 5 minutes.

2. Bring 1 cup water to a boil in medium
saucepan. Add rice and remaining ¼
teaspoon salt. Reduce heat to low. Cover and
simmer 25 to 30 minutes or until liquid is
absorbed and rice is tender. Cool.

3. Meanwhile, prepare Creole Dressing. Set
aside.

4. Drain bean mixture in colander. Rinse
under cold water; drain. Place beans in large
bowl.

5. Add rice, green onions, squash, bell pepper
and celery to beans.

6. Pour Creole Dressing over bean mixture;
toss to blend. Serve on lettuce leaves.
Garnish, if desired.   *Makes 4 servings*

Creole Dressing

¼ cup olive oil
2 tablespoons tomato juice
2 tablespoons Creole or other whole-
  grain mustard
4 teaspoons red wine vinegar
1 teaspoon Worcestershire sauce
2 cloves garlic, minced
½ teaspoon dried thyme leaves
¼ teaspoon cayenne pepper

Combine all ingredients in small bowl; whisk
until blended.   *Makes 1 cup dressing*

Dilled Carrot Salad

¼ teaspoon dill weed
1 can (8¼ ounces) DEL MONTE®
  FreshCut™ Brand Sliced Carrots,
  drained
5 cups torn romaine lettuce
  Dijon dressing

1. In large bowl, sprinkle dill over carrots.

2. Add lettuce; toss with dressing.
          Makes 4 servings

Prep time: 5 minutes

Creole Red Beans and Rice Salad

Fruity Brown Rice Salad with Raspberry Vinaigrette

2 cups cooked brown rice
2 cups small broccoli flowerets, blanched and chilled
2 cups fresh or canned pineapple chunks
1 can (11 ounces) mandarin oranges, drained
½ cup slivered red bell pepper
½ cup chopped red onion
    Raspberry Vinaigrette Dressing (recipe follows)
1 can (12 ounces) STARKIST® Solid White Tuna, drained and chunked
6 to 8 Bibb lettuce cups

In large bowl, mix together rice, broccoli, pineapple, oranges, bell pepper and onion. Add Raspberry Vinaigrette Dressing; toss. Refrigerate several hours before serving. Just before serving, add tuna; toss gently. Serve in lettuce cups. *Makes 6 to 8 servings*

Raspberry Vinaigrette Dressing

¼ cup raspberry vinegar or apple cider vinegar
2 tablespoons orange or lemon juice
1 tablespoon brown sugar
1 teaspoon seasoned salt
½ teaspoon crushed red pepper
1 medium clove garlic, finely minced or pressed
½ cup olive oil

In small bowl, whisk together vinegar, orange juice, brown sugar, seasoned salt, crushed red pepper and garlic. Slowly add oil, whisking continuously until well blended.
Makes about 1 cup dressing

Prep time: 15 minutes

Honey Dijon Fruit Salad

½ cup prepared HIDDEN VALLEY® Honey Dijon Ranch Creamy Dressing
½ cup low-fat pineapple-flavored yogurt
¼ cup finely chopped fresh pineapple or drained canned crushed pineapple
1 teaspoon grated lemon peel
1 teaspoon lemon juice
4 cups assorted fresh fruit (grapes, berries, sliced apples, pears or bananas)
    Lettuce leaves

Combine dressing, yogurt, pineapple, lemon peel and lemon juice in medium bowl. Arrange fruit on lettuce-lined serving plate or 4 individual plates. Serve dressing with salad.
Makes 4 servings

Fruity Brown Rice Salad with Raspberry Vinaigrette

Sparkling Berry Salad

2 cups cranberry juice
2 packages (4-serving size) or
    1 package (8-serving size) JELL-O®
    Brand Sugar Free Gelatin, any red
    flavor
1½ cups cold club soda
    ¼ cup crème de cassis liqueur
        (optional)
    1 teaspoon lemon juice
    1 cup raspberries
    1 cup blueberries
    ½ cup sliced strawberries
    ½ cup whole strawberries, cut into
        fans
    Mint leaves (optional)

Bring cranberry juice to a boil in medium saucepan. Completely dissolve gelatin in boiling cranberry juice. Stir in club soda, liqueur and lemon juice. Chill until slightly thickened.

Reserve a few raspberries and blueberries for garnish, if desired. Stir remaining raspberries, blueberries and the sliced strawberries into gelatin mixture. Spoon into 6-cup mold that has been lightly sprayed with nonstick cooking spray. Chill until firm, about 4 hours. Unmold. Surround with reserved berries, strawberry fans and mint leaves, if desired.

Makes 8 servings

Nutrients per Serving:

Calories:	100	Cholesterol:	0 mg
Total Fat:	0 g	Sodium:	70 mg

Sunset Yogurt Salad

2 packages (4-serving size) or
    1 package (8-serving size) JELL-O®
    Brand Orange or Lemon Flavor
    Sugar Free Gelatin
2 cups boiling water
1 container (8 ounces) plain low-fat
    yogurt
¼ cup cold water
1 can (8 ounces) crushed pineapple
    in unsweetened juice, undrained
1 cup shredded carrots

Completely dissolve gelatin in boiling water. Measure 1 cup gelatin into medium mixing bowl; chill until slightly thickened. Stir in yogurt. Pour into medium serving bowl. Chill until set but not firm.

Add cold water to remaining gelatin. Stir in pineapple with juice and carrots. Chill until slightly thickened. Spoon over gelatin-yogurt mixture in bowl. Chill until firm, about 4 hours. Garnish with carrot curl, celery leaf and pineapple slice, if desired.

Makes 5 cups (10 servings)

Nutrients per Serving (½ cup):

Calories:	40	Cholesterol:	0 mg
Total Fat:	0 g	Sodium:	65 mg

Sparkling Berry Salad

Gingered Pear Salad

1 can (8½ ounces) pear halves in juice, undrained
1 package (4-serving size) JELL-O® Brand Lemon Flavor Sugar Free Gelatin
¾ cup boiling water
2 teaspoons lemon juice
Ice cubes
1 cup (8 ounces) 2% low-fat cottage cheese
⅛ teaspoon salt
⅛ teaspoon ground ginger

Drain pears, reserving juice; set juice aside. Finely chop pears; set aside.

Dissolve gelatin in boiling water; add lemon juice. Add enough ice cubes to reserved pear juice to measure 1 cup. Add to gelatin; stir until slightly thickened. Remove any unmelted ice; pour gelatin into blender container. Add cottage cheese, salt and ginger; cover. Blend until smooth. Stir in pears. Pour into 3 individual plastic containers or serving dishes. Chill until firm, about 2 hours.

Makes 3 cups (3 entrée servings)

Nutrients per Serving:

Calories:	120	Cholesterol:	5 mg
Total Fat:	2 g	Sodium:	480 mg

Mandarin Chicken Salad

1 can (15½ ounces) DEL MONTE® *FreshCut*™ Brand Pineapple Chunks in Heavy Syrup, undrained
3 tablespoons vegetable oil
3 tablespoons cider vinegar
1 tablespoon soy sauce
4 cups shredded cabbage or iceberg lettuce
1 can (14½ ounces) DEL MONTE® *FreshCut*™ Diced Tomatoes, drained
2 cups cubed cooked chicken
⅓ cup packed cilantro, chopped, *or* ½ cup sliced green onions

1. Drain pineapple, reserving ¼ cup syrup. In small bowl, combine reserved syrup, oil, vinegar and soy sauce; stir briskly with fork.

2. Toss cabbage with pineapple, tomatoes, chicken and cilantro in large bowl. Add dressing as desired; gently toss.

3. Sprinkle with toasted slivered almonds or toasted sesame seeds, if desired.

Makes 4 servings

Prep time: 15 minutes

Tip: For an extra crunchy salad, top with crumbled dry noodles from an Oriental noodle soup mix.

Mandarin Chicken Salad

Grilled Chicken Caesar Salad

1 pound boneless skinless chicken breast halves
½ cup extra-virgin olive oil
3 tablespoons fresh lemon juice
2 cloves garlic, minced
2 teaspoons anchovy paste
½ teaspoon salt
½ teaspoon black pepper
6 cups torn romaine lettuce leaves
4 plum tomatoes, quartered
¼ cup grated Parmesan cheese
1 cup purchased garlic croutons
  Anchovy fillets (optional)
  Additional black pepper (optional)

1. Place chicken in large resealable plastic food storage bag. Combine oil, lemon juice, garlic, anchovy paste, salt and ½ teaspoon pepper in small bowl. Reserve ⅓ cup of marinade; cover and refrigerate until serving. Pour remaining marinade over chicken in bag. Seal bag tightly, turning to coat. Marinate in refrigerator at least 1 hour or up to 4 hours, turning occasionally.

2. Combine lettuce, tomatoes and cheese in large bowl. Cover; refrigerate until serving.

3. Prepare grill for direct cooking.

4. Drain chicken; reserve marinade from bag. Place chicken on grid. Grill chicken, on covered grill, over medium coals 10 to 12 minutes or until chicken is no longer pink in center, brushing with reserved marinade from bag after 5 minutes and turning halfway through grilling time. Discard remaining marinade from bag. Cool chicken slightly.

5. Slice warm chicken crosswise into ½-inch-wide strips; add chicken and croutons to lettuce mixture in bowl. Drizzle with ⅓ cup reserved marinade; toss to coat well. Top with anchovy fillets and serve with additional pepper, if desired. *Makes 4 servings*

Cobb Salad

1 package (10 ounces) torn mixed salad greens *or* 8 cups packed torn romaine lettuce
6 ounces deli chicken, turkey or smoked turkey breast, cut ¼ inch thick
1 large tomato, seeded and chopped
⅓ cup real bacon bits or crumbled crisp-cooked bacon
1 large ripe avocado, peeled, seeded and diced
⅓ cup prepared blue cheese or Caesar salad dressing

1. Arrange lettuce in salad bowl.

2. Dice chicken; arrange in a row down center of lettuce.

3. Arrange tomato, bacon and avocado attractively in rows on either side of chicken. Cover; refrigerate until serving time (up to 2 hours).

4. Just before serving, add dressing; toss salad and arrange on chilled serving plates. Serve with freshly ground black pepper, if desired.
Makes 4 main-dish or 8 side-dish servings

Grilled Chicken Caesar Salad

Zesty Taco Salad

2 tablespoons vegetable oil
1 clove garlic, finely chopped
¾ pound ground turkey
1¾ teaspoons chili powder
¼ teaspoon ground cumin
3 cups washed, torn lettuce leaves
1 can (14½ ounces) Mexican-style
   diced tomatoes, drained
1 cup rinsed, drained canned
   garbanzo beans (chick-peas)
⅔ cup chopped peeled cucumber
⅓ cup frozen corn, thawed
¼ cup chopped red onion
1 to 2 jalapeño peppers, seeded,
   finely chopped* (optional)
1 tablespoon red wine vinegar
12 nonfat tortilla chips
   Fresh greens (optional)

Jalapeño peppers can sting and irritate the skin; wear rubber gloves when handling peppers and do not touch eyes. Wash hands after handling.

1. Combine oil and garlic in small bowl; let stand 1 hour at room temperature.

2. Combine turkey, chili powder and cumin in large nonstick skillet. Cook over medium heat 5 minutes or until turkey is no longer pink, stirring to crumble.

3. Combine turkey, lettuce, tomatoes, beans, cucumber, corn, onion and jalapeño pepper, if desired, in large bowl. Remove garlic from oil; discard garlic. Combine oil and vinegar in small bowl. Drizzle over salad; toss to coat. Serve on tortilla chips and fresh greens, if desired. Serve with additional tortilla chips and garnish with cilantro, if desired.

Makes 4 servings

Zesty Taco Salad

Layered Mexican Salad

⅔ cup dried black turtle beans *or*
    1 can (15 ounces) black turtle
    beans, rinsed and drained
    Salsa Cruda (recipe follows)
1 small head romaine lettuce, washed
    and cored
1 cup frozen corn, thawed and
    drained
1 large cucumber, peeled
1 can (2¼ ounces) sliced ripe olives,
    drained
1 large lemon
¾ cup nonfat mayonnaise
3 tablespoons plain nonfat yogurt
2 to 3 cloves garlic, minced
½ cup (2 ounces) shredded low-fat
    Cheddar cheese
1 green onion, thinly sliced

Rinse and sort beans. Place in medium saucepan with 4 cups water. Bring to a boil over high heat. Reduce heat to medium-low; simmer 5 minutes. Remove from heat; cover and let stand 1 to 2 hours. Drain. Return beans to pan with 4 cups fresh water. Bring to a boil. Reduce heat to medium-low; cover and simmer 1½ to 2 hours or until tender. Drain; rinse and drain again.

Prepare Salsa Cruda. Layer romaine leaves and slice crosswise into ½-inch strips. Place half of lettuce in large serving bowl. Layer Salsa Cruda, beans and corn over lettuce.

Halve cucumber lengthwise; scoop out and discard seeds. Slice thinly. Place cucumber on top of corn; sprinkle with olives. Top with remaining lettuce.

Grate lemon peel; blend with mayonnaise, yogurt and garlic. Juice lemon; stir 3 to 4 tablespoons juice into mayonnaise dressing. Spread dressing evenly on top of salad. Sprinkle with cheese and green onion. Cover salad and refrigerate 2 hours or up to 1 day.
Makes 12 servings

Salsa Cruda

1 cup chopped seeded tomato
2 tablespoons minced onion
2 tablespoons minced fresh cilantro
    (optional)
2 tablespoons lime juice
½ jalapeño pepper, seeded and
    minced*
1 clove garlic, minced

Jalapeño peppers can sting and irritate the skin; wear rubber gloves when handling peppers and do not touch eyes. Wash hands after handling.

Combine all ingredients in small bowl. Refrigerate 1 hour before serving.
Makes 4 servings

Grilled Steak Caesar Salad

½ cup A.1.® Original or A.1.® Bold &
    Spicy Steak Sauce
3 tablespoons lemon juice
1 teaspoon minced anchovy fillets
1 teaspoon minced garlic
½ cup olive oil
1 (1-pound) beef top round steak,
    about 1 inch thick
4 (1-inch-thick) slices French bread
4 cups torn romaine lettuce leaves
2 ounces shaved Parmesan cheese

In small bowl, blend steak sauce, lemon juice, anchovies and garlic; slowly whisk in oil until well blended. Place steak in nonmetal dish; coat with ⅓ cup steak sauce mixture. Cover; refrigerate 1 hour, turning occasionally. Reserve remaining steak sauce mixture for dressing.

Remove steak from marinade; discard marinade. Grill steak over medium-high heat 6 minutes on each side or to desired doneness. Lightly brush cut sides of bread with some reserved dressing. Grill bread 2 to 3 minutes on each side or until golden.

In small saucepan, heat remaining reserved dressing until warm. Arrange lettuce on serving platter. Thinly slice steak; arrange on lettuce. Drizzle with warm dressing; top with cheese. Serve immediately with grilled bread.

Makes 4 servings

Honey-Dijon Salad with Shrimp

8 cups torn romaine lettuce leaves
1 pound large shrimp, cleaned and
    cooked
3 cups sliced mushrooms
2 cups sliced carrots
½ cup EGG BEATERS® Healthy Real Egg
    Substitute
¼ cup corn oil
¼ cup white wine vinegar
¼ cup GREY POUPON® Dijon Mustard
¼ cup honey
2 cups plain croutons (optional)
Carrot curls, for garnish

In large bowl, combine lettuce, shrimp, mushrooms and sliced carrots; set aside.

In small bowl, whisk together Egg Beaters®, oil, vinegar, mustard and honey until well blended. To serve, pour dressing over salad, tossing until well coated. Top with croutons, if desired. Garnish with carrot curls.

Makes 8 servings

Prep time: 25 minutes

Nutrients per Serving:

Calories:	252	Cholesterol:	111 mg
Total Fat:	9 g	Sodium:	538 mg

Grilled Steak Caesar Salad

Seafood Salad

1 pound calamari salad*
2 tablespoons FRANK'S® Original
    REDHOT® Cayenne Pepper Sauce
2 tablespoons orange juice
1 tablespoon olive oil
⅛ teaspoon sugar
½ pound raw bay scallops
1 red or yellow bell pepper, seeded
    and cut into thin strips
¼ cup chopped fresh basil *or*
    2 teaspoons dried basil leaves
1 tablespoon grated orange peel
    Lettuce leaves (optional)

*Calamari salad can be found in the seafood section
of most supermarkets or seafood markets.*

1. Drain calamari salad; reserve dressing.
Combine reserved dressing, RedHot® sauce,
orange juice, oil and sugar in medium skillet.
Add scallops and bell pepper. Bring to a boil
over medium-high heat. Reduce heat to low.
Cook, covered, 3 to 5 minutes or until
scallops are opaque and bell pepper is crisp-
tender. Cool slightly.

2. Combine calamari salad, scallop mixture,
basil and orange peel in large bowl; toss to
coat evenly. Cover; refrigerate 1 hour, stirring
occasionally. Serve on lettuce-lined plates, if
desired.

Makes 6 servings (about 5 cups)

Prep time: 30 minutes
Cook time: 5 minutes
Chill time: 1 hour

Gingered Pork Tenderloin Salad

3 pounds pork tenderloin, thinly
    sliced
¼ cup teriyaki sauce
3 tablespoons grated fresh ginger
3 tablespoons chopped cilantro
1 tablespoon cracked black pepper
1 tablespoon olive oil
12 artichoke hearts, quartered
2 tablespoons butter
    Tangy Vinaigrette Dressing
    (recipe follows)
6 red potatoes, boiled, peeled and
    sliced
2 red onions, peeled and thinly sliced
    Lettuce leaves

Marinate pork slices in teriyaki sauce, ginger,
cilantro and pepper for 1 hour. Drain pork
from marinade and stir-fry quickly in hot oil;
set aside. Sauté artichokes in butter until
lightly browned. Prepare Tangy Vinaigrette
Dressing. Toss pork, potatoes, artichokes and
onions with dressing. Refrigerate. Arrange
salad on lettuce-lined plates. Serve with
remaining dressing.   *Makes 12 servings*

Tangy Vinaigrette Dressing

1 cup olive oil
¾ cup rice vinegar
¼ cup chopped parsley
¼ cup chopped chives
2 tablespoons chopped gherkins
3 chopped anchovies
1 tablespoon capers
2 cloves garlic, minced
2 teaspoons curry powder
    Salt and black pepper to taste

Combine all ingredients in small jar with tight-fitting lid. Shake well.

Makes about 2 cups dressing

Prep time: 20 minutes

Favorite recipe from **National Pork Producers Council**

Szechuan Pork Salad

½ pound boneless lean pork
4 tablespoons KIKKOMAN® Teriyaki Sauce, divided
⅛ to ¼ teaspoon crushed red pepper
1 cup water
2 tablespoons cornstarch
1 tablespoon distilled white vinegar
2 tablespoons vegetable oil, divided
1 onion, chunked and separated
12 radishes, thinly sliced
2 medium zucchini, cut into julienne strips
Salt
4 cups shredded lettuce

Cut pork across grain into thin slices, then into narrow strips. Combine pork, 1 tablespoon teriyaki sauce and red pepper in small bowl; set aside. Combine water, cornstarch, remaining 3 tablespoons teriyaki sauce and vinegar; set aside. Heat 1 tablespoon oil in hot wok or large skillet over high heat. Add pork and stir-fry 2 minutes; remove. Heat remaining 1 tablespoon oil in same pan. Add onion; stir-fry 2 minutes. Add radishes and zucchini; lightly sprinkle with salt and stir-fry 1 minute longer. Stir in pork

and teriyaki sauce mixture. Cook and stir until mixture boils and thickens. Spoon over bed of lettuce on serving platter; serve immediately. *Makes 2 to 3 servings*

Chicken Pasta Salad

½ cup vegetable oil
½ cup GREY POUPON® Dijon Mustard
½ cup lemon juice
2 cloves garlic, minced
4 cups bow-tie pasta, cooked and drained
2 cups cubed cooked chicken
1½ cups halved cherry tomatoes
1½ cups cooked asparagus, cut into 1½-inch pieces
1 small yellow bell pepper, cut into strips
Lettuce leaves

In small bowl, whisk oil, mustard, lemon juice and garlic; set aside.

In large bowl, mix pasta, chicken, tomatoes, asparagus and bell pepper; add ¾ cup mustard mixture, tossing to coat well. Chill salad and reserved dressing at least 2 hours. Just before serving, stir reserved dressing into salad; arrange on lettuce-lined serving platter.

Makes 6 servings

Caribbean Pasta Salad with Tropical Island Dressing

1 can black beans, drained and rinsed
½ cup thawed frozen orange juice
   concentrate
½ teaspoon ground allspice
6 ounces mafalda pasta
1 teaspoon vegetable oil
4 cups washed and torn romaine
   lettuce leaves
1½ cups fresh pineapple chunks
1 mango, peeled and sliced
1 cup shredded cabbage
⅓ cup chopped onion
⅓ cup chopped red bell pepper
8 ounces pina colada-flavored yogurt
½ cup orange juice
1 tablespoon finely chopped orange
   peel
1 teaspoon grated fresh ginger
2 oranges, sectioned

1. Combine beans, orange juice concentrate and allspice in medium bowl. Cover and refrigerate 1 hour; drain and discard liquid from beans.

2. Cook pasta according to package directions. Drain. Rinse under cold water until cool; drain again. Return to pan; toss with oil.

3. To assemble salad, divide lettuce, pasta, pineapple, beans, mango, cabbage, onion and bell pepper among 6 plates.

4. To prepare dressing, combine yogurt, orange juice, orange peel and ginger in small bowl. Arrange orange sections on salads. Serve with dressing.   *Makes 6 servings*

Tuna Louie Salad

   Bibb lettuce
1 can (12 ounces) STARKIST® Solid
   White Tuna, drained and chunked
2 avocados, peeled, sliced
2 to 4 hard-cooked eggs, sliced
4 plum tomatoes, sliced
16 ounces canned grapefruit sections,
   drained and juice reserved
⅓ cup whipping cream, whipped
½ cup Thousand Island dressing
   Lime wedges

On four serving plates, arrange lettuce, tuna, avocados, eggs, tomatoes and grapefruit. In small bowl, fold whipped cream into Thousand Island dressing. For thinner dressing, add 1 to 2 tablespoons reserved grapefruit juice. Spoon dressing over salads or serve separately. Garnish with lime wedges.   *Makes 4 servings*

Prep time: 8 minutes

Caribbean Pasta Salad with Tropical Island Dressing

Chicken, Tortellini and Roasted Vegetable Salad

3 cups whole medium mushrooms
2 cups cubed zucchini
2 cups cubed eggplant
¾ cup red onion wedges (about 1 medium)
Nonstick olive oil cooking spray
1½ packages (9-ounce size) reduced-fat cheese tortellini
6 cups bite-size pieces leaf lettuce and arugula
1 pound boneless skinless chicken breasts, cooked and cut into 1½-inch pieces
Sun-Dried Tomato and Basil Vinaigrette (recipe follows)

1. Heat oven to 425°F. Place mushrooms, zucchini, eggplant and onion in 15×10-inch jelly-roll pan. Spray generously with cooking spray; toss to coat. Bake 20 to 25 minutes or until vegetables are browned. Cool to room temperature.

2. Cook tortellini according to package directions; drain. Cool to room temperature.

3. Combine roasted vegetables, tortellini, lettuce and chicken in large bowl. Drizzle with Sun-Dried Tomato and Basil Vinaigrette; toss to coat. Serve immediately.

Makes 8 servings

Sun-Dried Tomato and Basil Vinaigrette

4 sun-dried tomato halves, not packed in oil
Hot water
½ cup defatted low-sodium chicken broth
2 tablespoons finely chopped fresh basil *or* 2 teaspoons dried basil leaves
2 tablespoons water
2 tablespoons olive oil
2 tablespoons lemon juice
1 clove garlic, minced
¼ teaspoon salt
¼ teaspoon black pepper

1. Place sun-dried tomatoes in small bowl. Pour hot water over tomatoes to cover. Let stand 10 to 15 minutes or until tomatoes are soft. Drain well; chop tomatoes.

2. In small jar with tight-fitting lid, combine tomatoes and remaining ingredients; shake well. Refrigerate until ready to use; shake before using.

Makes about 1 cup dressing

Chicken, Tortellini and Roasted Vegetable Salad

BOUNTIFUL

BRUNCHES

Blintzes with Raspberry Sauce

Raspberry Sauce (recipe follows)	3 tablespoons EGG BEATERS® Healthy Real Egg Substitute
1 (16-ounce) container low-fat cottage cheese (1% milkfat)	½ teaspoon sugar 10 prepared Crêpes (page 84)

Prepare Raspberry Sauce. Set aside. In small bowl, combine cottage cheese, Egg Beaters® and sugar; spread about 2 tablespoonfuls mixture down center of each crêpe. Fold crêpes into thirds; fold top and bottom of each crêpe to meet in center, forming blintzes. In lightly greased nonstick skillet, over medium heat, place blintzes seam-side down; cook 4 minutes or until golden brown. Turn over; cook 4 more minutes or until golden brown. Top with Raspberry Sauce and garnish as desired. *Makes 10 servings*

Raspberry Sauce
In blender or food processor, purée 1 (16-ounce) package thawed frozen raspberries; strain. Stir in 2 tablespoons sugar. *(continued on page 84)*

Blintzes with Raspberry Sauce

(Blintzes with Raspberry Sauce,
continued from page 82)

Crêpes

1 cup all-purpose flour
1 cup skim milk
½ cup EGG BEATERS® Healthy Real Egg
    Substitute
1 tablespoon FLEISCHMANN'S®
    Original Spread (70% Corn Oil),
    melted

In medium bowl, blend flour, milk, Egg Beaters® and margarine; let stand 30 minutes.

Heat lightly greased 8-inch nonstick skillet or crêpe pan over medium-high heat. Pour in scant ¼ cup batter, tilting pan to cover bottom. Cook 1 to 2 minutes; turn crêpe over and cook 30 seconds to 1 minute more. Place on waxed paper. Stir batter and repeat process to make a total of 10 crêpes.

Makes 10 servings

Nutrients per Serving:

| Calories: | 161 | Cholesterol: | 2 mg |
| Total Fat: | 2 g | Sodium: | 231 mg |

Huevos Rancheros

1 cup GUILTLESS GOURMET® Salsa
2 eggs
2 corn tortillas (6 inches each)
2 tablespoons low-fat sour cream
1 tablespoon chopped fresh cilantro

Bring salsa to a boil in small nonstick skillet over medium heat. Gently break eggs into salsa, being careful not to break yolks. Reduce heat to medium-low; cover and simmer 5 minutes or to desired firmness.

Meanwhile to soften tortillas, wrap in damp paper towel. Microwave on HIGH (100% power) 20 seconds. Or, to soften tortillas in oven, preheat oven to 300°F. Wrap tortillas in foil. Bake 10 minutes. To serve, arrange 1 tortilla on serving plate; top with 1 egg and half of the salsa. Dollop with 1 tablespoon sour cream and sprinkle with ½ tablespoon cilantro. Repeat with remaining ingredients.

Makes 2 servings

Brunch Eggs Olé

Fresh Salsa (page 85)
8 eggs
½ cup all-purpose flour
1 teaspoon baking powder
¾ teaspoon salt
2 cups (8 ounces) shredded Monterey
    Jack cheese with jalapeño
    peppers
1½ cups (12 ounces) small curd cottage
    cheese
1 cup (4 ounces) shredded sharp
    Cheddar cheese
1 jalapeño pepper, seeded and
    chopped*
½ teaspoon hot pepper sauce

Jalapeño peppers can sting and irritate the skin; wear rubber gloves when handling peppers and do not touch eyes. Wash hands after handling.

1. Prepare Fresh Salsa. Preheat oven to 350°F. Grease 9-inch square baking pan.

2. Beat eggs in large bowl at high speed with electric mixer 4 to 5 minutes or until slightly thickened and lemon colored.

3. Combine flour, baking powder and salt in small bowl. Stir flour mixture into eggs until blended.

4. Combine Monterey Jack cheese, cottage cheese, Cheddar cheese, jalapeño pepper and hot pepper sauce in medium bowl; mix well. Fold into egg mixture until well blended. Pour into prepared pan.

5. Bake 45 to 50 minutes or until golden brown and firm in center. Let stand 10 minutes before cutting into squares to serve. Serve with Fresh Salsa. Garnish as desired.

Makes 8 servings

Fresh Salsa

3 medium plum tomatoes, seeded and chopped
2 tablespoons chopped onion
1 small jalapeño pepper, stemmed, seeded and minced
1 tablespoon chopped fresh cilantro
1 tablespoon lime juice
¼ teaspoon salt
⅛ teaspoon black pepper

Combine tomatoes, onion, jalapeño pepper, cilantro, lime juice, salt and black pepper in small bowl. Refrigerate until ready to serve.

Makes 1 cup salsa

Brunch Eggs Olé

Sausage Vegetable Frittata

5 eggs
¼ cup milk
2 tablespoons grated Parmesan
   cheese
½ teaspoon dried oregano leaves
½ teaspoon black pepper
1 (10-ounce) package BOB EVANS®
   Skinless Link Sausage
2 tablespoons butter or margarine
1 small zucchini, sliced (about 1 cup)
½ cup shredded carrots
⅓ cup sliced green onions with tops
¾ cup (6 ounces) shredded Swiss
   cheese
   Carrot curls (optional)

Whisk eggs in medium bowl; stir in milk, Parmesan cheese, oregano and pepper. Set aside. Cook sausage in large skillet over medium heat until browned, turning occasionally. Drain off any drippings. Remove sausage from skillet and cut into ½-inch lengths. Melt butter in same skillet. Add zucchini, shredded carrots and green onions; cook and stir over medium heat until tender. Top with sausage, then Swiss cheese. Pour egg mixture over vegetable mixture. Stir gently to combine. Cook, without stirring, over low heat 8 to 10 minutes or until center is almost set. Remove from heat. Let stand 5 minutes before cutting into wedges; serve hot. Garnish with carrot curls, if desired. Refrigerate leftovers.

Makes 4 to 6 servings

Brunch Quesadillas with Fruit Salsa

1 pint fresh strawberries, hulled and
   diced
1 fresh ripe Anjou pear, cored and
   diced
1 tablespoon chopped fresh cilantro
1 tablespoon honey
1 cup (4 ounces) SARGENTO®
   Preferred Light Fancy Supreme
   Shredded Mozzarella Cheese
4 flour tortillas (8 inches in diameter)
2 teaspoons light margarine, melted
2 tablespoons light sour cream

To make Fruit Salsa, combine strawberries, pear, cilantro and honey in medium bowl; set aside.

Sprinkle 2 tablespoons cheese on one half of each tortilla. Top with ⅓ cup Fruit Salsa (drain and discard any liquid from fruit) and another 2 tablespoons cheese. Fold tortillas in half. Brush top of each folded tortilla with some of the melted margarine.

Grill folded tortillas, greased sides down, in dry preheated skillet until light golden brown and crisp, about 2 minutes. Brush tops with remaining melted margarine; turn and brown other sides. Remove to serving plate or platter. Cut each tortilla in half. Serve with remaining Fruit Salsa. Garnish with sour cream. Serve immediately.

Makes 4 servings

Nutrients per Serving:

Calories:	278	Cholesterol:	14 mg
Total Fat:	9 g	Sodium:	264 mg

Sausage Vegetable Frittata

Eggs Benedict

Mock Hollandaise Sauce
    (recipe follows)
4 eggs, divided
2 English muffins, halved
    Fresh spinach leaves, washed and
        drained
8 ounces sliced lean Canadian bacon
4 (¼-inch-thick) tomato slices
    Paprika

1. Prepare Mock Hollandaise Sauce. Set aside.

2. Bring 6 cups water to a boil in large saucepan over high heat. Reduce heat to low. Carefully break 1 egg into small dish and slide egg into water. Repeat with remaining 3 eggs. Simmer, uncovered, about 5 minutes or until yolks are just set.

3. Meanwhile, toast muffin halves; place on serving plates. Top each muffin half with spinach leaves, 2 ounces Canadian bacon, 1 tomato slice and 1 egg. Spoon Mock Hollandaise Sauce over eggs; sprinkle with paprika. Serve with fresh fruit, if desired.

Makes 4 servings

Mock Hollandaise Sauce

4 ounces fat-free cream cheese
3 tablespoons plain nonfat yogurt
1 tablespoon lemon juice
1 teaspoon Dijon mustard

Process all ingredients in food processor or blender until smooth. Heat in small saucepan over medium-high heat until hot.

Makes about ¾ cup sauce

Banana Pancakes

1 cup all-purpose flour
1 tablespoon sugar
1 teaspoon baking powder
½ teaspoon baking soda
½ teaspoon salt
1 container (6 ounces) banana
    custard-style yogurt
½ cup skim milk
1 egg, beaten
2 tablespoons vegetable oil
1 cup cooked rice
1 cup puréed or finely diced banana
    Vegetable cooking spray

Combine flour, sugar, baking powder, baking soda and salt in large bowl. Add yogurt, milk, egg and oil; stir until smooth. Stir in rice and banana. Pour ¼ cup batter onto hot griddle coated with cooking spray. Cook over medium heat until bubbles form on top and underside is lightly browned. Turn to brown other side.

Makes 6 servings

Tip: For Cinnamon-Banana Pancakes, add ¼ teaspoon ground cinnamon to dry ingredients.

Nutrients per Serving:

Calories:	246	Cholesterol:	42 mg
Total Fat:	6 g	Sodium:	482 mg

Favorite recipe from **USA Rice Federation**

Eggs Benedict

Breakfast in a Loaf

Scrambled Eggs (recipe follows)
1 round loaf bread (8- to 9-inch
    diameter)
4 ounces sliced ham
½ red bell pepper, thinly sliced into
    rings
½ cup (2 ounces) shredded Monterey
    Jack cheese
½ cup (2 ounces) shredded Cheddar
    cheese
½ cup sliced pitted ripe olives
1 medium tomato, thinly sliced
8 ounces mushrooms, sliced and
    cooked

1. Prepare Scrambled Eggs. Remove from heat; cover to keep warm.

2. Preheat oven to 350°F. Cut 2-inch slice from top of loaf; set aside for lid. Remove soft interior of loaf, leaving a 1-inch-thick wall and bottom.

3. Place ham on bottom of loaf. Top with bell pepper rings; sprinkle with half of cheeses. Layer Scrambled Eggs, olives and tomato over cheeses. Top with remaining cheeses and mushrooms.

4. Place lid on loaf. Wrap in foil. Place on baking sheet. Bake about 30 minutes or until heated through. Cut into 8 wedges.

Makes 8 servings

Scrambled Eggs

1 tablespoon butter or margarine
6 eggs, lightly beaten
½ teaspoon salt
¼ teaspoon ground black pepper

1. Melt butter in 10-inch skillet over medium heat.

2. Season eggs with salt and pepper. Add eggs to skillet; cook, stirring gently and lifting to allow uncooked eggs to flow under cooked portion. (Do not overcook; eggs should be soft with no liquid remaining.)

Makes 4 servings

Breakfast Hash

1 pound BOB EVANS® Special
    Seasonings or Sage Roll Sausage
2 cups chopped potatoes
¼ cup chopped red and/or green bell
    peppers
2 tablespoons chopped onion
6 eggs
2 tablespoons milk

Crumble sausage into large skillet. Add potatoes, bell peppers and onion. Cook over low heat until sausage is browned and potatoes are fork-tender, stirring occasionally. Drain off any drippings. Whisk eggs and milk in small bowl until blended. Add to sausage mixture; scramble until eggs are set but not dry. Serve hot. Refrigerate leftovers.

Makes 6 to 8 servings

Serving Suggestion: Serve with fresh fruit.

Breakfast in a Loaf

Silver Dollar Pancakes with Mixed Berry Topping

1¼ cups all-purpose flour
2 tablespoons sugar
2 teaspoons baking soda
1½ cups buttermilk
½ cup EGG BEATERS® Healthy Real Egg
   Substitute
3 tablespoons margarine, melted,
   divided
Mixed Berry Topping (page 93)

In large bowl, combine flour, sugar and baking soda. Stir in buttermilk, Egg Beaters® and 2 tablespoons margarine just until blended.

Brush large nonstick griddle or skillet with some of remaining margarine; heat over medium-high heat. Using 1 heaping tablespoon batter for each pancake, spoon batter onto griddle. Cook until bubbly; turn and cook until lightly browned. Repeat with remaining batter using remaining margarine as needed to make 28 pancakes. Serve hot with Mixed Berry Topping.

Makes 28 (2-inch) pancakes

Silver Dollar Pancakes with Mixed Berry Topping

Mixed Berry Topping

In medium saucepan, over medium-low heat, combine 1 (12-ounce) package thawed frozen mixed berries,* ¼ cup honey and ½ teaspoon grated gingerroot (or ⅛ teaspoon ground ginger). Cook and stir just until hot and well blended. Serve over pancakes.

Three cups mixed fresh berries may be substituted.

Prep time: 20 minutes
Cook time: 20 minutes

Nutrients per Serving:

Calories:	228	Cholesterol:	2 mg
Total Fat:	6 g	Sodium:	491 mg

Golden Apple French Toast

1 Washington Golden Delicious apple, cored and sliced
½ cup apple juice
1 egg, beaten
¼ teaspoon vanilla extract
2 slices bread
1 teaspoon cornstarch
⅛ teaspoon salt
⅛ teaspoon ground cardamom
1 tablespoon cold water

1. Combine apple slices and apple juice in small pan; heat to a simmer. Cook apple slices until tender but still retain their shape, about 8 minutes. Remove from heat and set aside while preparing French toast.

2. To make French toast, in wide, shallow bowl, combine egg and vanilla. Dip bread slices in egg mixture to coat both sides. In nonstick skillet, cook bread slices until lightly browned on both sides. Remove French toast to serving plates; with slotted spoon, remove apple slices from pan and arrange on top of French toast. To make syrup, combine cornstarch, salt, cardamom, and water; stir into reserved apple juice. Bring mixture to a boil, stirring constantly; cook until thickened and clear. Spoon syrup over apple slices and French toast. Serve immediately.

Makes 2 servings

Favorite recipe from **Washington Apple Commission**

Nectarine Whirl

1 Chilean nectarine or peach, cut into chunks
½ cup 1% milk
½ cup orange juice
1 tablespoon honey
¼ teaspoon almond extract
2 ice cubes, cracked

Place all ingredients in blender. Blend at high speed 15 seconds or until smooth. Serve immediately.   *Makes 1 serving*

Favorite recipe from **Chilean Winter Fruit Association**

Bloody Mary's RedHot® Style

1 quart tomato juice
½ cup vodka
2 tablespoons FRANK'S® Original
    REDHOT® Cayenne Pepper Sauce
2 tablespoons FRENCH'S®
    Worcestershire Sauce
2 tablespoons prepared horseradish
1 tablespoon lemon juice
1 teaspoon celery salt

Combine all ingredients in large pitcher;
refrigerate. Serve over ice.

Makes 4 servings

Prep time: 5 minutes
Chill time: 30 minutes

Dole® Juice Spritzer

½ cup DOLE® Country Raspberry Juice
    or other DOLE® Juice
½ cup mineral or sparkling water

• Pour juice and mineral water over ice cubes
in large glass. Garnish with lime wedge and
citrus curl, if desired.   *Makes 1 serving*

Prep time: 5 minutes

Nutrients per Serving:

Calories:	70	Cholesterol:	0 mg
Total Fat:	0 g	Sodium:	3 mg

Bloody Mary's RedHot® Style

Strawberry-Banana Yogurt Energy Drink

**1 box (10 ounces) BIRDS EYE® frozen
 Strawberries, partially thawed
2 medium bananas
¾ cup plain yogurt**

• Place all ingredients in blender or food processor; blend until smooth.

Makes 2½ cups

Prep time: 5 minutes

Hot Cocoa Au Lait

**2 tablespoons HERSHEY'S European
 Style Cocoa or HERSHEY'S Cocoa
¼ cup hot water
1½ cups skim milk
 Granulated sugar substitute to equal
 8 teaspoons sugar
¼ teaspoon vanilla extract**

In small saucepan, place cocoa; gradually stir in water. Cook over medium heat, stirring constantly, until mixture boils. Boil and stir until smooth and hot, about 1 minute. Immediately stir in milk; continue cooking and stirring until mixture is hot. *Do not boil.* Remove from heat; stir in sugar substitute and vanilla. Serve immediately.

Makes 3 servings

Nutrients per Serving:

Calories:	70	Cholesterol:	<5 mg
Total Fat:	1 g	Sodium:	65 mg

Touchdown Cheese Scones

**2 cups all-purpose flour
2½ teaspoons baking powder
½ teaspoon baking soda
¼ teaspoon salt
2 tablespoons cold butter or
 margarine, cut in pieces
1 cup shredded mild Cheddar cheese
⅔ cup buttermilk
2 large eggs, divided
¼ teaspoon TABASCO® Pepper Sauce**

Preheat oven to 350°F. In large bowl, sift together flour, baking powder, baking soda and salt. Cut in butter until mixture resembles cornmeal. Stir in cheese. In small bowl blend together buttermilk, 1 egg and TABASCO® Sauce. Make a well in center of dry ingredients; add buttermilk mixture. Stir quickly and lightly with fork to form sticky dough. Turn dough out on lightly floured board. Knead gently 10 times. Divide dough in half; pat each half into circle about ½ inch thick. Cut each circle into 4 wedges. Combine remaining egg and 1 tablespoon water. Brush each wedge with egg mixture. Arrange on greased baking sheet. Bake 13 to 15 minutes or until golden.

Makes 8 scones

Nutrients per Serving:

Calories:	225	Cholesterol:	92 mg
Total Fat:	9 g	Sodium:	385 mg

Oatmeal Apple Cranberry Scones

2 cups all-purpose flour
1 cup uncooked rolled oats
⅓ cup sugar
2 teaspoons baking powder
½ teaspoon salt
½ teaspoon baking soda
½ teaspoon ground cinnamon
¾ cup MOTT'S® Natural Apple Sauce, divided
2 tablespoons margarine
½ cup coarsely chopped cranberries
½ cup peeled, chopped apple
¼ cup skim milk
¼ cup plus 2 tablespoons honey, divided

1. Preheat oven to 425°F. Spray baking sheet with nonstick cooking spray.

2. In large bowl, combine flour, oats, sugar, baking powder, salt, baking soda and cinnamon. Add ½ cup apple sauce and margarine; cut in with pastry blender or fork until mixture resembles coarse crumbs. Stir in cranberries and apple.

3. In small bowl, combine milk and ¼ cup honey. Add milk mixture to flour mixture; stir together until dough forms a ball.

4. Turn out dough onto well-floured surface; knead 10 to 12 times. Pat dough into 8-inch circle. Place on prepared baking sheet. Use tip of knife to score dough into 12 wedges.

5. In another small bowl, combine remaining ¼ cup apple sauce and 2 tablespoons honey. Brush mixture over top of dough.

6. Bake 12 to 15 minutes or until lightly browned. Immediately remove from baking sheet; cool on wire rack 10 minutes. Serve warm or cool completely. Cut into 12 wedges. *Makes 12 servings*

Nutrients per Serving:

Calories:	170	Cholesterol:	0 mg
Total Fat:	2 g	Sodium:	200 mg

Harvest Apple Oatmeal

1 cup water
1 cup apple juice
1 medium apple, cored and chopped
1 cup uncooked old-fashioned rolled oats
¼ cup raisins
⅛ teaspoon salt
⅛ teaspoon ground cinnamon

Combine water, apple juice and apple in 2-quart microwavable bowl. Microwave on HIGH (100% power) 3 minutes, stirring halfway through cooking time. Add oats, raisins, salt and cinnamon; stir until well blended. Microwave on MEDIUM (50% power) 4 to 5 minutes or until thick; stir before serving. Garnish with apple slices, if desired. *Makes 2 servings*

Conventional Directions: Bring water, apple juice and apple to a boil in medium saucepan over medium-high heat. Stir in oats, raisins, salt and cinnamon until well blended. Cook, uncovered, over medium heat 5 to 6 minutes or until thick, stirring occasionally.

Oatmeal Apple Cranberry Scones

Triple Berry Breakfast Parfaits

2 cups vanilla sugar-free nonfat yogurt
¼ teaspoon ground cinnamon
1 cup sliced strawberries
½ cup blueberries
½ cup raspberries
1 cup low-fat granola without raisins
Mint leaves for garnish

1. Combine yogurt and cinnamon in small bowl. Combine strawberries, blueberries and raspberries in medium bowl.

2. For each parfait, layer ¼ cup fruit mixture, 2 tablespoons granola and ¼ cup yogurt mixture in parfait glass. Repeat layers. Garnish with mint leaves, if desired.

Makes 4 servings

Fruit-N-Grain Breakfast Salad

3 cups water
¼ teaspoon salt
¾ cup quick-cooking brown rice
¾ cup bulgur
1 Washington Granny Smith apple
1 Washington Red Delicious apple
1 orange
1 cup raisins
8 ounces low-fat vanilla yogurt

Bring water and salt to a boil in large saucepan over high heat. Add rice and bulgur; reduce heat to low. Cover and cook 10 minutes. Remove from heat and set aside

Triple Berry Breakfast Parfait

for 2 minutes. Spread hot grains on baking sheet to cool. (Grains can be cooked ahead of time and stored in refrigerator up to one week.) Just before serving, prepare fruit. Core and chop apples. Peel orange and cut into sections. Add chopped apple, orange sections and raisins to cooled grain mixture. Add yogurt and stir to coat grains and fruit.

Makes 6 servings

Nutrients per Serving:

Calories:	187	Cholesterol:	1 mg
Total Fat:	1 g	Sodium:	117 mg

Favorite recipe from **Washington Apple Commission**

Scotch Eggs

BISCUITS
>   2 cups sifted all-purpose flour
>   1 tablespoon baking powder
>   1 teaspoon salt
>   ⅓ **CRISCO**® **Stick or ⅓ cup CRISCO**®
>   **all-vegetable shortening**
>   ¾ **cup milk**

TOPPING
>   1 pound pork sausage
>   ¼ **Butter Flavor* CRISCO**® **Stick or**
>   ¼ **cup Butter Flavor* CRISCO**
>   **all-vegetable shortening**
>   6 tablespoons all-purpose flour
>   2½ cups milk
>   1 cup shredded Cheddar cheese
>   ½ teaspoon salt
>   ¼ teaspoon black pepper
>   12 hard cooked eggs, peeled and diced

*Butter Flavor Crisco is artificially flavored.

1. For biscuits, heat oven to 425°F. Combine flour, baking powder and salt in medium bowl. Cut in shortening using pastry blender (or 2 knives) until coarse crumbs form. Add milk. Stir with fork until blended.

2. Transfer dough to lightly floured surface. Knead gently 8 to 10 times. Roll dough ½ inch thick. Cut with floured 2-inch round cutter. Place on ungreased baking sheet.

3. Bake at 425°F for 12 to 15 minutes, or until brown. *Do not overbake.*

4. For topping, heat skillet on medium-high heat. Add sausage, breaking it up into small pieces with fork. Cook until brown. Drain.

5. Melt shortening in 2-quart saucepan on low heat. Stir in flour. Cook and stir on low heat 2 minutes. Add milk slowly, whisking constantly. Increase heat to medium. Bring to a boil, stirring constantly. Stir in cheese, salt and pepper. Add eggs and sausage. Serve immediately over halved biscuits.

Makes 6 servings

Note: Substitute chopped ham for sausage, if desired.

Easy Morning Strata

1 pound BOB EVANS® Original Recipe
    Roll Sausage
8 eggs
10 slices bread, cut into cubes
    (about 10 cups)
3 cups milk
2 cups (8 ounces) shredded Cheddar
    cheese
2 cups (8 ounces) sliced fresh
    mushrooms
1 (10-ounce) package frozen cut
    asparagus, thawed and drained
2 tablespoons all-purpose flour
2 tablespoons butter or margarine,
    melted
1 tablespoon dry mustard
2 teaspoons dried basil leaves
1 teaspoon salt

Crumble sausage into large skillet. Cook over medium heat until browned, stirring occasionally. Drain off any drippings. Whisk eggs in large bowl. Add sausage and remaining ingredients; mix well. Spoon into greased 13×9-inch baking dish. Cover; refrigerate 8 hours or overnight. Preheat oven to 350°F. Bake 60 to 70 minutes or until knife inserted near center comes out clean. Let stand 5 minutes before cutting into squares; serve hot. Refrigerate leftovers.

Makes 10 to 12 servings

Serving Suggestion: Serve with slices of fresh plums.

Egg & Sausage Casserole

½ pound pork sausage
3 tablespoons margarine or butter,
    divided
2 tablespoons all-purpose flour
¼ teaspoon salt
¼ teaspoon black pepper
1¼ cups milk
2 cups frozen hash brown potatoes
4 eggs, hard-boiled and sliced
½ cup cornflake crumbs
¼ cup sliced green onions

Preheat oven to 350°F. Spray 2-quart oval baking dish with nonstick cooking spray.

Crumble sausage into large skillet; brown over medium-high heat until no longer pink, stirring to separate meat. Drain sausage on paper towels. Discard fat and wipe skillet with paper towel.

Melt 2 tablespoons margarine in same skillet over medium heat. Stir in flour, salt and pepper until smooth. Gradually stir in milk; cook and stir until thickened. Add sausage, potatoes and eggs; stir to combine. Pour into prepared dish.

Melt remaining 1 tablespoon margarine. Combine cornflake crumbs and melted margarine in small bowl; sprinkle evenly over casserole.

Bake, uncovered, 30 minutes or until hot and bubbly. Sprinkle with green onions.

Makes 6 servings

Easy Morning Strata

Blueberry Muffins

1 cup fresh or thawed, frozen
    blueberries
1¾ cups plus 1 tablespoon all-purpose
    flour, divided
2 teaspoons baking powder
1 teaspoon grated lemon peel
½ teaspoon salt
½ cup MOTT'S® Apple Sauce
½ cup sugar
1 whole egg
1 egg white
2 tablespoons vegetable oil
¼ cup skim milk

1. Preheat oven to 375°F. Line 12 (2½-inch) muffin cups with paper liners or spray with nonstick cooking spray.

2. In small bowl, toss blueberries with 1 tablespoon flour.

3. In large bowl, combine remaining 1¾ cups flour, baking powder, lemon peel and salt.

4. In another small bowl, combine apple sauce, sugar, whole egg, egg white and oil.

5. Stir apple sauce mixture into flour mixture alternately with milk. Mix just until moistened. Fold in blueberry mixture. Spoon evenly into prepared muffin cups.

6. Bake 20 minutes or until toothpick inserted in centers comes out clean. Immediately remove from pan; cool on wire rack 10 minutes. Serve warm or cool completely.   *Makes 12 servings*

Blueberry Muffins

Double Oat Muffins

2 cups QUAKER® Oat Bran hot cereal, uncooked
⅓ cup firmly packed brown sugar
¼ cup all-purpose flour
2 teaspoons baking powder
¼ teaspoon salt (optional)
¼ teaspoon ground nutmeg (optional)
1 cup skim milk
2 egg whites, lightly beaten
3 tablespoons vegetable oil
1½ teaspoons vanilla
¼ cup QUAKER® Oats (quick or old fashioned, uncooked)
1 tablespoon firmly packed brown sugar

Heat oven to 400°F. Line 12 medium muffin cups with paper baking cups or grease lightly. Combine oat bran cereal, ⅓ cup brown sugar, flour, baking powder, salt and nutmeg. Add combined milk, egg whites, oil and vanilla, mixing just until moistened. Fill muffin cups almost full. Combine oats and 1 tablespoon brown sugar; sprinkle evenly over muffin tops. Bake 18 to 22 minutes or until golden brown. Remove to wire rack. Cool completely.   *Makes 12 muffins*

Microwave Directions: Line 6 microwavable muffin cups with double paper baking cups. Combine oat bran cereal, ⅓ cup brown sugar, flour, baking powder, salt and nutmeg. Add combined milk, egg whites, oil and vanilla, mixing just until moistened. Fill muffin cups almost full. Combine oats and 1 tablespoon brown sugar; sprinkle evenly over muffin tops. Microwave at HIGH (100% power) 2½ to 3 minutes or until wooden toothpick inserted in centers come out clean. Remove from pan; cool 5 minutes before serving. Line muffin cups with additional double paper baking cups. Repeat procedure with remaining batter.

Tips: To freeze muffins, wrap securely in foil or place in freezer bag. Seal, label and freeze. To reheat frozen muffins, unwrap muffins. Microwave at HIGH (100% power) about 30 seconds per muffin.

Nutrients per Serving *(1 muffin):*

Calories:	140	Cholesterol:	0 mg
Total Fat:	5 g	Sodium:	90 mg

Peach Gingerbread Muffins

2 cups all-purpose flour
2 teaspoons baking powder
1 teaspoon ground ginger
½ teaspoon salt
½ teaspoon ground cinnamon
¼ teaspoon ground cloves
½ cup sugar
½ cup MOTT'S® Chunky Apple Sauce
¼ cup MOTT'S® Apple Juice
¼ cup GRANDMA'S® Molasses
1 egg
2 tablespoons vegetable oil
1 (16-ounce) can peaches in juice, drained and chopped

1. Preheat oven to 400°F. Line 12 (2½-inch) muffin cups with paper liners or spray with nonstick cooking spray.

2. In large bowl, combine flour, baking powder, ginger, salt and spices.

3. In small bowl, combine sugar, apple sauce, apple juice, molasses, egg and oil.

4. Stir apple sauce mixture into flour mixture just until moistened. Fold in peaches. Spoon evenly into prepared muffin cups.

5. Bake 20 minutes or until toothpick inserted in centers comes out clean. Immediately remove from pan; cool on wire rack 10 minutes. Serve warm or cool.

Makes 12 servings

Nutrients per Serving:

Calories:	190	Cholesterol:	20 mg
Total Fat:	3 g	Sodium:	150 mg

Orange Streusel Coffeecake

Cocoa Streusel (recipe follows)
¾ cup (1½ sticks) butter or margarine, softened
1 cup sugar
3 eggs
1 teaspoon vanilla extract
½ cup dairy sour cream
3 cups all-purpose flour
2 teaspoons baking powder
1 teaspoon baking soda
1 cup orange juice
2 teaspoons grated orange peel
½ cup orange marmalade

Prepare Cocoa Streusel. Heat oven to 350°F. Grease 12-cup fluted tube pan. In large bowl, beat butter and sugar until well blended. Add eggs and vanilla; beat well. Add sour cream; beat until blended. Stir together flour, baking powder and baking soda; add alternately with orange juice to butter mixture, beating until well blended. Stir in orange peel. Spread marmalade in bottom of prepared pan; sprinkle half of streusel over marmalade. Pour half of batter into pan, spreading evenly. Sprinkle remaining streusel over batter; spread remaining batter over streusel. Bake about 1 hour or until toothpick inserted in center of cake comes out clean. Loosen cake from side of pan with spatula; invert onto serving plate. *Makes 12 servings*

Cocoa Streusel

Stir together ⅔ cup packed light brown sugar, ½ cup chopped walnuts, ¼ cup HERSHEY'S Cocoa and ½ cup MOUNDS® Sweetened Coconut Flakes, if desired.

Orange Streusel Coffeecake

Spring Break Blueberry Coffeecake

TOPPING
- ½ cup flaked coconut
- ¼ cup firmly packed brown sugar
- 2 tablespoons butter or margarine, softened
- 1 tablespoon all-purpose flour

CAKE
- 1 package DUNCAN HINES® Blueberry Muffin Mix
- 1 can (8 ounces) crushed pineapple with juice, undrained
- 1 egg
- ¼ cup water

1. Preheat oven to 350°F. Grease 9-inch square pan.

2. For topping, combine coconut, brown sugar, butter and flour in small bowl. Mix with fork until well blended. Set aside.

3. Rinse blueberries from Mix with cold water and drain.

4. For cake, place muffin mix in medium bowl. Break up any lumps. Add pineapple with juice, egg and water. Stir until moistened, about 50 strokes. Fold in blueberries. Spread in pan. Sprinkle topping over batter. Bake at 350°F for 30 to 35 minutes or until toothpick inserted in center comes out clean. Serve warm or cool completely. *Makes 9 servings*

Tip: To keep blueberries from discoloring batter, drain on paper towels after rinsing.

Cinnamon-Raisin Rolls

- 1 package (16 ounces) hot roll mix, plus ingredients to prepare mix
- ⅓ cup raisins
- 4 tablespoons margarine, softened, divided
- ¼ cup granulated sugar
- 2 teaspoons ground cinnamon
- ½ teaspoon ground nutmeg
- 1½ cups powdered sugar
- 1 to 2 tablespoons skim milk, divided
- ½ teaspoon vanilla

Preheat oven to 375°F. Spray 13×9-inch baking pan with nonstick cooking spray. Prepare hot roll mix according to package directions; mix in raisins. Knead dough on lightly floured surface until smooth and elastic, about 5 minutes. Cover dough with plastic wrap; let stand 5 minutes.

Roll out dough on floured surface to 16×10-inch rectangle. Spread dough with 2 tablespoons margarine. Combine granulated sugar, cinnamon and nutmeg; sprinkle evenly over dough. Roll up dough starting at long end. Pinch to seal. Gently stretch sealed dough until about 18 inches long. Cut dough into 1-inch pieces; place, cut side up, in prepared pan. Cover pan loosely with towel. Let stand 20 to 30 minutes or until doubled in size.

Bake 20 to 25 minutes or until golden. Cool in pan on wire rack 2 to 3 minutes. Remove from pan; cool on wire rack.

Combine powdered sugar, remaining margarine, 1 tablespoon milk and vanilla in medium bowl. Spread glaze over warm rolls. *Makes 1½ dozen rolls*

Cinnamon-Raisin Rolls

Apple Sauce Cinnamon Rolls

ROLLS

    4 cups all-purpose flour, divided
    1 package active dry yeast
    1 cup MOTT'S® Natural Apple Sauce, divided
    ½ cup skim milk
    ⅓ cup plus 2 tablespoons granulated sugar, divided
    2 tablespoons margarine
    ½ teaspoon salt
    1 egg, beaten lightly
    2 teaspoons ground cinnamon

ICING

    1 cup sifted powdered sugar
    1 tablespoon skim milk
    ½ teaspoon vanilla extract

1. To prepare Rolls, in large bowl, combine 1½ cups flour and yeast. In small saucepan, combine ¾ cup apple sauce, ½ cup milk, 2 tablespoons granulated sugar, margarine and salt. Cook over medium heat, stirring frequently, until mixture reaches 120°F to 130°F and margarine is almost melted (milk will appear curdled). Add to flour mixture along with egg. Beat with electric mixer on low speed 30 seconds, scraping bowl frequently. Beat on high speed 3 minutes. Stir in 2¼ cups flour until soft dough forms.

2. Turn out dough onto lightly floured surface; flatten slightly. Knead 3 to 5 minutes or until smooth and elastic, adding remaining ¼ cup flour to prevent sticking if necessary. Shape dough into ball; place in large bowl sprayed with nonstick cooking spray. Turn dough over so that top is greased. Cover with towel; let rise in warm place about 1 hour or until doubled in bulk.

3. Spray two 8- or 9-inch round baking pans with nonstick cooking spray.

4. Punch down dough; turn out onto lightly floured surface. Cover with towel; let rest 10 minutes. Roll out dough into 12-inch square. Spread remaining ¼ cup apple sauce over dough, to within ½ inch of edges. In small bowl, combine remaining ⅓ cup granulated sugar and cinnamon; sprinkle over apple sauce. Roll up dough jelly-roll style. Moisten edge with water; pinch to seal seam. Cut roll into 12 (1-inch) slices with sharp floured knife. Arrange 6 rolls ½ inch apart in each prepared pan. Cover with towel; let rise in warm place about 30 minutes or until nearly doubled in bulk.

5. Preheat oven to 375°F. Bake 20 to 25 minutes or until lightly browned. Cool on wire rack 5 minutes. Invert each pan onto serving plate.

6. To prepare Icing, in small bowl, combine powdered sugar, 1 tablespoon milk and vanilla until smooth. Drizzle over tops of rolls. Serve warm. *Makes 12 servings*

Nutrients per Serving:

Calories:	260	Cholesterol:	25 mg
Total Fat:	3 g	Sodium:	100 mg

Apple Sauce Cinnamon Rolls

Cozy

CASSEROLES

Layered Mexican Casserole

8 ounces ground beef
1 (12-ounce) can corn, drained
1 (12-ounce) jar chunky salsa
1 (2¼-ounce) can sliced pitted
   ripe olives, drained
1 cup cottage cheese

1 (8-ounce) carton sour cream
5 cups tortilla chips, divided
2 cups (8 ounces) shredded
   Wisconsin Cheddar
   cheese, divided
½ cup chopped tomato

Brown ground beef in large skillet; drain. Add corn and salsa; cook until thoroughly heated. Reserve 2 tablespoons olives; stir remaining olives into beef mixture. Combine cottage cheese and sour cream in medium bowl. In 2-quart casserole, layer 2 cups chips, half of meat mixture, ¾ cup Cheddar cheese and half of cottage cheese mixture. Repeat layers; cover. Bake in preheated 350°F oven 35 minutes. Line edge of casserole with remaining chips; top with tomato, reserved olives and remaining Cheddar cheese. Bake 10 minutes or until cheese is melted. *Makes 4 to 6 servings*

Favorite recipe from **Wisconsin Milk Marketing Board**

Layered Mexican Casserole

Beef Stroganoff Casserole

1 pound lean ground beef
¼ teaspoon salt
⅛ teaspoon black pepper
1 teaspoon vegetable oil
8 ounces sliced mushrooms
1 large onion, chopped
3 cloves garlic, minced
¼ cup dry white wine
1 can (10¾ ounces) condensed cream
   of mushroom soup, undiluted
½ cup sour cream
1 tablespoon Dijon mustard
4 cups cooked egg noodles
   Chopped fresh parsley (optional)

Preheat oven to 350°F. Spray 13×9-inch baking dish with nonstick cooking spray.

Place beef in large skillet; season with salt and pepper. Brown beef over medium-high heat until no longer pink, stirring to separate. Drain fat from skillet; set beef aside.

Heat oil in same skillet over medium-high heat until hot. Add mushrooms, onion and garlic; cook and stir 2 minutes or until onion is tender. Add wine. Reduce heat to medium-low and simmer 3 minutes. Remove from heat; stir in soup, sour cream and mustard until well combined. Return beef to skillet.

Place noodles in prepared dish. Pour beef mixture over noodles; stir until noodles are well coated.

Bake, uncovered, 30 minutes or until heated through. Sprinkle with parsley, if desired.
Makes 6 servings

Classic Hamburger Casserole

1 pound ground beef
1 package (9 ounces) frozen cut green
   beans, thawed and drained
1 can (10¾ ounces) condensed
   tomato soup
¼ cup water
½ teaspoon seasoned salt
⅛ teaspoon black pepper
2 cups hot mashed potatoes
1⅓ cups (2.8-ounce can) FRENCH'S®
   French Fried Onions, divided
½ cup (2 ounces) shredded Cheddar
   cheese

Preheat oven to 350°F. Brown ground beef in medium skillet; drain. Stir in green beans, soup, water and seasonings; pour into 1½-quart casserole. Combine mashed potatoes and ⅔ cup French Fried Onions in medium bowl. Spoon potato mixture in mounds around edge of casserole. Bake, uncovered, at 350°F 25 minutes or until heated through. Top potatoes with cheese and remaining ⅔ cup onions; bake, uncovered, 5 minutes or until onions are golden brown. *Makes 4 to 6 servings*

Beef Stroganoff Casserole

Patchwork Casserole

2 pounds ground beef
2 cups chopped green bell pepper
1 cup chopped onion
2 pounds frozen Southern-style
    hash-brown potatoes, thawed
2 cans (8 ounces *each*) tomato sauce
1 cup water
1 can (6 ounces) tomato paste
1 teaspoon salt
½ teaspoon dried basil, crumbled
¼ teaspoon ground black pepper
1 pound pasteurized process
    American cheese, thinly sliced,
    divided

Preheat oven to 350°F.

Cook and stir beef in large skillet over medium heat until crumbled and brown, about 10 minutes; drain off fat.

Add bell pepper and onion; cook and stir until tender, about 4 minutes. Stir in potatoes, tomato sauce, water, tomato paste, salt, basil and black pepper.

Spoon half of mixture into 13×9×2-inch baking pan or 3-quart baking dish; top with half of cheese. Spoon remaining meat mixture evenly on top of cheese. Cover pan with foil; bake 45 minutes.

Cut remaining cheese into decorative shapes; place on top of casserole. Let stand loosely covered until cheese melts, about 5 minutes.

Makes 8 to 10 servings

Crazy Lasagna Casserole

1½ pounds ground beef
1 teaspoon LAWRY'S® Seasoned Salt
1 package (1.5 ounces) LAWRY'S®
    Original-Style Spaghetti Sauce
    Spices & Seasonings
1 can (8 ounces) tomato sauce
1 can (6 ounces) tomato paste
1½ cups water
1 package (10 ounces) medium-size
    shell macaroni, cooked and
    drained
1 carton (16 ounces) small curd
    cottage cheese
1½ cups (6 ounces) grated cheddar
    cheese

In large skillet, brown ground beef until crumbly; drain fat. Add Seasoned Salt, Original-Style Spaghetti Sauce Spices & Seasonings, tomato sauce, tomato paste and water; mix well. Bring to a boil over medium-high heat; reduce heat to low and cook, uncovered, 10 minutes, stirring occasionally. In shallow 2-quart casserole, layer half each of macaroni, cottage cheese and meat sauce. Sprinkle ½ cup cheddar cheese over meat sauce. Repeat layers, ending with meat sauce. Top with remaining 1 cup cheddar cheese. Bake, uncovered, in 350°F oven 30 to 40 minutes or until bubbly and cheese is melted.

Makes 8 servings

Serving Suggestion: Serve with garlic bread.

Patchwork Casserole

Chili Wagon Wheel Casserole

8 ounces uncooked wagon wheel or
  other pasta
1 pound lean ground sirloin or
  ground turkey breast
¾ cup chopped green bell pepper
¾ cup chopped onion
1 can (14½ ounces) no-salt-added
  stewed tomatoes
1 can (8 ounces) no-salt-added tomato
  sauce
½ teaspoon ground black pepper
¼ teaspoon ground allspice
½ cup (2 ounces) shredded reduced-
  fat Cheddar cheese

1. Preheat oven to 350°F. Cook pasta
according to package directions. Drain and
rinse; set aside.

2. Spray large nonstick skillet with nonstick
cooking spray. Add ground sirloin, bell
pepper and onion; cook 5 minutes or until
meat is no longer pink, stirring frequently.
(Drain mixture if using ground sirloin.)

3. Stir in tomatoes, tomato sauce, black
pepper and allspice; cook 2 minutes. Stir in
pasta. Spoon mixture into 2½-quart casserole.
Sprinkle with cheese.

4. Bake 20 to 25 minutes or until heated
through. *Makes 6 servings*

Chili Meatloaf & Potato Casserole

MEATLOAF
1½ pounds lean ground beef
  ¾ cup finely chopped onion
  ⅓ cup saltine cracker crumbs
  1 egg, slightly beaten
  3 tablespoons milk
  1 tablespoon chili powder
  ¾ teaspoon salt

POTATO TOPPING
  3 cups prepared mashed potatoes
  1 can (11 ounces) corn with red and
    green bell peppers, drained
  ¼ cup thinly sliced green onions
  ½ to 1 cup shredded taco seasoned
    cheese

1. Preheat oven to 375°F. In large bowl,
combine meatloaf ingredients, mixing lightly
but thoroughly; gently press into bottom of 9-
inch square baking pan. Bake 20 to 25
minutes or until no longer pink and juices
run clear. Carefully pour off drippings.

2. Meanwhile in medium bowl, combine all
topping ingredients *except* cheese. Spread
over meatloaf to edges of pan; sprinkle with
cheese. Broil 3 to 4 inches from heat 3 to
5 minutes or until top is lightly browned.
Makes 6 servings

Favorite recipe from **National Cattlemen's
Beef Association**

Chili Wagon Wheel Casserole

Mexican Chicken Casserole

8 ounces elbow or mini-shell
    macaroni
2 teaspoons olive oil
1 large carrot, shredded
1 medium green bell pepper, finely
    chopped
1 tablespoon minced garlic
¾ pound chicken tenders, cut in
    ¾-inch pieces
2 teaspoons ground cumin
1½ teaspoons dried oregano leaves
½ teaspoon salt
¼ to ½ teaspoon crushed red pepper
2 cups (8 ounces) shredded Monterey
    Jack cheese, divided
1 jar (6 ounces) tomato salsa, divided

1. Cook pasta according to package
directions. Meanwhile, heat oil in large
nonstick skillet over medium heat. Add
carrot, bell pepper and garlic; cook and stir
3 minutes or until vegetables soften. Add
chicken; increase heat to medium-high. Cook
and stir 3 to 4 minutes or until chicken
pieces are cooked through. Add cumin,
oregano, salt and crushed red pepper; cook
and stir 1 minute. Remove from heat and set
aside.

Mexican Chicken Casserole

2. Drain and rinse pasta; place in large bowl. Add chicken mixture, 1 cup cheese and 1 cup salsa; stir well to blend. Pour into lightly greased 13×9-inch microwave-safe baking dish. Top with remaining 1 cup salsa and 1 cup cheese; cover with plastic wrap. Microwave on HIGH 4 to 6 minutes, turning dish halfway through cooking time to heat casserole evenly. Remove plastic wrap and serve immediately.   *Makes 4 to 6 servings*

Down-Home Corn and Chicken Casserole

2 chickens (2 to 3 pounds *each*), each cut into 10 pieces
3 tablespoons CHEF PAUL PRUDHOMME'S Poultry Magic®, divided
⅓ cup vegetable oil
8 cups fresh corn, cut off cob (about twelve 8-inch ears), divided
3½ cups finely chopped onions
1½ cups finely chopped green bell peppers
1 pound tomatoes, peeled and chopped
3½ cups chicken stock or water
2 cups uncooked converted rice

Remove excess fat from chicken pieces; season chicken with 2 tablespoons Poultry Magic® and place in plastic bag. Seal and refrigerate overnight.

Heat oil in 8-quart roasting pan over high heat about 6 minutes. Add 10 largest pieces of chicken, skin-side-down, and brown about 5 minutes on each side. Remove chicken and reheat oil about 1 minute or until oil stops sizzling. Brown remaining chicken 5 minutes on each side. Remove and keep warm.

Add half of corn to hot oil. Scrape bottom of pan well to get up all browned chicken bits and stir to mix well. Cook corn without stirring, about 6 minutes. Add 1½ teaspoons Poultry Magic® and stir to combine. Cook, without stirring, about 7 minutes. Stir in onions, bell peppers and remaining 1½ teaspoons Poultry Magic®. Cover with tight-fitting lid and cook about 5 minutes. Add remaining 4 cups corn and tomatoes. Stir to mix well; cover and cook 10 minutes. Transfer corn mixture to another pan and keep warm.

Preheat oven to 400°F. Add chicken stock and rice to roasting pan. Bring to a boil stirring occasionally. Layer chicken pieces on top of rice and cover chicken layer with corn mixture. Cover and bake 25 minutes.

Remove casserole from oven. Let stand 10 minutes, covered. Serve.

Makes 8 servings

Chicken Asparagus Casserole

2 teaspoons vegetable oil
1 cup seeded and chopped green and/or red bell peppers
1 medium onion, chopped
2 cloves garlic, minced
1 can (10¾ ounces) condensed cream of asparagus soup
2 eggs
1 container (8 ounces) ricotta cheese
2 cups (8 ounces) shredded Cheddar cheese, divided
1½ cups chopped cooked chicken
1 package (10 ounces) frozen chopped asparagus, thawed and drained*
8 ounces noodles, cooked
Ground black pepper (optional)

*Or, substitute ½ pound cooked fresh asparagus cut into ½-inch pieces.

1. Preheat oven to 350°F. Grease 13×9-inch casserole; set aside.

2. Heat oil in small skillet over medium heat. Add bell peppers, onion and garlic; cook and stir until crisp-tender.

3. Mix soup, eggs, ricotta cheese and 1 cup Cheddar cheese in large bowl until well blended. Add onion mixture, chicken, asparagus and noodles; mix well. Season with black pepper, if desired. Spread mixture evenly in prepared casserole. Top with remaining 1 cup Cheddar cheese.

4. Bake 30 minutes or until center is set and cheese is bubbly. Let stand 5 minutes before serving. Garnish as desired.

Makes 12 servings

Chicken and Zucchini Casserole

3 cups STOVE TOP® Chicken Flavor or Cornbread Stuffing Mix in the Canister
1¼ cups hot water
3 tablespoons margarine or butter, divided
¾ pound boneless skinless chicken breasts, cubed
2 medium zucchini, cut into ½-inch pieces
1½ cups (6 ounces) shredded cheddar cheese
1 can (8 ounces) water chestnuts, drained, halved (optional)
½ teaspoon dried basil leaves
¼ teaspoon black pepper

MIX stuffing mix, water and 2 tablespoons margarine in large bowl just until margarine is melted and stuffing mix is moistened.

PLACE chicken, zucchini and remaining 1 tablespoon margarine in 3-quart microwavable casserole. Cover loosely with wax paper.

MICROWAVE on HIGH 4 minutes, stirring halfway through cooking time. Stir in prepared stuffing, cheese, water chestnuts, basil and pepper until well mixed. Cover.

MICROWAVE 10 minutes, stirring halfway through cooking time. Let stand 5 minutes.

Makes 6 servings

Prep time: 10 minutes
Cook time: 20 minutes

Chicken Asparagus Casserole

Chicken-Mac Casserole

1½ cups elbow macaroni, cooked in unsalted water and drained
6 slices bacon, fried crisp and crumbled
2 cups (10 ounces) cubed cooked chicken
1⅓ cups (2.8-ounce can) FRENCH'S® French Fried Onions, divided
1 can (10¾ ounces) condensed cream of mushroom soup
1 package (10 ounces) frozen chopped spinach, thawed and well drained
1½ cups (6 ounces) shredded Cheddar cheese, divided
1 cup sour cream
⅛ teaspoon garlic powder

Preheat oven to 375°F. Return hot macaroni to saucepan; stir in bacon, chicken and ⅔ *cup* French Fried Onions. Combine soup, spinach, *1 cup* Cheddar cheese, sour cream and garlic powder in medium bowl. Spoon half of macaroni mixture into greased 12×8-inch baking dish; cover with half of spinach mixture. Repeat layers. Bake, covered, at 375°F 30 minutes or until heated through. Top with remaining ½ *cup* cheese and ⅔ *cup* onions. Bake, uncovered, 3 minutes or until onions are golden brown.

Makes 6 to 8 servings

Turkey Meatball & Olive Casserole

2 cups uncooked rotini
½ pound ground turkey
¼ cup dry bread crumbs
1 egg, slightly beaten
2 teaspoons dried minced onion
2 teaspoons white wine Worcestershire sauce
½ teaspoon salt
½ teaspoon dried Italian seasoning
⅛ teaspoon black pepper
1 tablespoon vegetable oil
1 can (10¾ ounces) condensed cream of celery soup
½ cup low-fat plain yogurt
¾ cup pimiento-stuffed green olives, sliced
3 tablespoons Italian-style bread crumbs
1 tablespoon margarine or butter, melted
Paprika (optional)

Preheat oven to 350°F. Spray 2-quart round casserole with nonstick cooking spray.

Cook pasta according to package directions until al dente. Drain and set aside.

Meanwhile, combine turkey, bread crumbs, egg, onion, Worcestershire, salt, Italian seasoning and pepper in medium bowl. Shape mixture into ½-inch meatballs.

Heat oil in medium skillet over high heat until hot. Add meatballs in single layer; cook until lightly browned on all sides and still pink in centers, turning frequently. *Do not overcook.* Remove from skillet; drain on paper towels.

Mix soup and yogurt in large bowl. Add pasta, meatballs and olives; stir gently to combine. Transfer to prepared dish.

Combine bread crumbs and margarine in small bowl; sprinkle evenly over casserole. Sprinkle lightly with paprika, if desired.

Bake, covered, 30 minutes. Uncover and bake 12 minutes or until meatballs are no longer pink in centers and casserole is hot and bubbly. *Makes 6 to 8 servings*

Turkey Meatball & Olive Casserole

Polish Reuben Casserole

2 cans (10¾ ounces *each*) condensed
    cream of mushroom soup
1⅓ cups milk
  ½ cup chopped onion
  1 tablespoon prepared mustard
  2 cans (16 ounces *each*) sauerkraut,
    rinsed and drained
  1 package (8 ounces) uncooked
    medium noodles
1½ pounds Polish sausage, cut into
    ½-inch pieces
  2 cups (8 ounces) shredded Swiss
    cheese
  ¾ cup whole wheat bread crumbs
  2 tablespoons butter, melted

Preheat oven to 350°F. Grease 13×9-inch
baking pan. Combine soup, milk, onion and
mustard in medium bowl; blend well. Spread
sauerkraut into prepared pan. Top with
uncooked noodles. Spoon soup mixture
evenly over noodles; cover with sausage. Top
with cheese. Combine bread crumbs and
butter in small bowl; sprinkle over cheese.
Cover pan tightly with foil. Bake 1 hour or
until noodles are tender. Garnish as desired.

Makes 8 to 10 servings

Sausage & Noodle Casserole

1 pound BOB EVANS® Original Recipe
    Roll Sausage
1 cup chopped onion
¼ cup chopped green bell pepper
1 (10-ounce) package frozen peas
1 (10¾-ounce) can condensed cream
    of chicken soup
1 (8-ounce) package egg noodles,
    cooked according to package
    directions and drained
  Salt and black pepper to taste
1 (2.8-ounce) can French fried
    onions, crushed

Preheat oven to 350°F. Crumble sausage into
large skillet. Add onion and bell pepper.
Cook over medium heat until meat is
browned and vegetables are tender, stirring
occasionally. Drain off any drippings. Cook
peas according to package directions. Drain,
reserving liquid in 2-cup glass measuring
cup; set aside. Add enough water to pea
liquid to obtain 1⅓ cups liquid. Combine
liquid and soup in large bowl; stir in sausage
mixture, noodles, reserved peas, salt and black
pepper. Mix well. Spoon mixture into
greased 2½-quart baking dish. Sprinkle with
onions. Bake 30 minutes or until bubbly.
Serve hot. Refrigerate leftovers.

Makes 6 servings

Polish Reuben Casserole

Spinach-Cheese Pasta Casserole

8 ounces uncooked pasta shells
2 eggs
1 package (10 ounces) frozen
   chopped spinach, thawed and
   squeezed dry
1 cup ricotta cheese
1 jar (26 ounces) marinara sauce
1 teaspoon salt
1 cup (4 ounces) shredded mozzarella
   cheese
¼ cup grated Parmesan cheese

Preheat oven to 350°F. Spray 1½-quart round casserole with nonstick cooking spray.

Cook pasta according to package directions until al dente. Drain.

Meanwhile, whisk eggs in large bowl until blended. Add spinach and ricotta to eggs; stir until combined. Stir in pasta, marinara sauce and salt until pasta is well coated. Pour into prepared dish. Sprinkle mozzarella and Parmesan evenly over casserole.

Bake, covered, 30 minutes. Uncover and bake 15 minutes or until hot and bubbly.

Makes 6 to 8 servings

Spinach-Cheese Pasta Casserole

Spaghetti & Egg Casserole

12 ounces uncooked spaghetti
 3 tablespoons FILIPPO BERIO® Olive Oil
¾ cup sliced onion
 4 eggs, beaten
 3 tablespoons grated Parmesan cheese
   Additional grated Parmesan cheese (optional)
   Additional beaten egg (optional)

Preheat oven to 350°F. Cook pasta according to package directions until al dente (tender but still firm). Drain. Meanwhile, in medium skillet, heat olive oil over medium heat until hot. Add onion; cook and stir 5 minutes or until softened. Remove with slotted spoon to large bowl. When oil is cool, grease 9-inch square baking pan with a portion of oil from skillet.

Add 4 beaten eggs and 3 tablespoons Parmesan cheese to onion; mix well. Add pasta; toss until lightly coated. Pour into prepared pan. Bake 10 to 20 minutes or until egg is firm.

Sprinkle with additional Parmesan cheese or brush with additional beaten egg, if desired. Broil, 4 to 5 inches from heat, until golden brown.   *Makes 6 servings*

Pasta Primavera Casserole

8 ounces uncooked rotini pasta
1 jar (12 ounces) chicken gravy
½ cup milk
1⅓ cups (2.8-ounce can) FRENCH'S® French Fried Onions, divided
1 small zucchini, thinly sliced
1 tomato, chopped
1 cup frozen peas, thawed and drained
1 cup (4 ounces) shredded mozzarella cheese
½ cup grated Parmesan cheese
2 tablespoons minced fresh basil *or* 1 teaspoon dried basil leaves

Preheat oven to 350°F. Grease 2-quart oblong baking dish. Cook pasta according to package directions using shortest cooking time. Drain. Return pasta to saucepan.

Add gravy, milk, ⅔ *cup* French Fried Onions, and remaining ingredients to pasta; toss lightly. Spoon into prepared baking dish.

Bake, uncovered, 35 minutes or until heated through, stirring halfway through cooking time. Top with remaining ⅔ *cup* onions. Bake, uncovered, 5 minutes or until onions are golden brown.   *Makes 6 servings*

Prep time: 15 minutes
Cook time: 40 minutes

Savory Lentil Casserole

1¼ cups uncooked dried brown or
    green lentils, rinsed and drained
2 tablespoons olive oil
1 large onion, chopped
3 cloves garlic, minced
8 ounces fresh shiitake or button
    mushrooms, sliced
2 tablespoons all-purpose flour
1½ cups canned beef broth
4 ounces Canadian bacon, minced
1 tablespoon Worcestershire sauce
1 tablespoon balsamic vinegar
½ teaspoon salt
½ teaspoon black pepper
½ cup grated Parmesan cheese
2 to 3 plum tomatoes, seeded and
    chopped
    Thyme and Italian parsley for
    garnish

1. Preheat oven to 400°F. Place lentils in medium saucepan; cover with 1 inch water. Bring to a boil over high heat. Reduce heat to low. Simmer, covered, 20 to 25 minutes until lentils are barely tender; drain.

2. Meanwhile, heat oil in large skillet over medium heat. Add onion and garlic; cook and stir 10 minutes. Add mushrooms; cook and stir 10 minutes or until liquid is evaporated and mushrooms are tender. Sprinkle flour over mushroom mixture; stir well. Cook and stir 1 minute. Stir in broth, bacon, Worcestershire sauce, vinegar, salt and pepper. Cook and stir until mixture is thick and bubbly.

3. Grease 1½-quart casserole. Stir lentils into mushroom mixture. Spread evenly into prepared casserole. Sprinkle with cheese. Bake 20 minutes.

4. Sprinkle tomatoes over casserole just before serving. Garnish with thyme and Italian parsley, if desired.

Makes 4 servings

Swissed Ham and Noodles Casserole

2 tablespoons butter
½ cup chopped onion
½ cup chopped green bell pepper
1 can (10½ ounces) condensed cream
    of mushroom soup, undiluted
1 cup dairy sour cream
1 package (8 ounces) medium
    noodles, cooked and drained
2 cups (8 ounces) shredded
    Wisconsin Swiss cheese
2 cups cubed cooked ham
    (about ¾ pound)

In 1-quart saucepan, melt butter; sauté onion and bell pepper. Remove from heat; stir in soup and sour cream. In buttered 2-quart casserole, layer one-third of the noodles, one-third of the Swiss cheese, one-third of the ham and half of the soup mixture. Repeat layers, ending with final one-third layer of ham. Bake in preheated 350°F oven 30 to 45 minutes or until heated through.

Makes 6 to 8 servings

Favorite recipe from **Wisconsin Milk Marketing Board**

Savory Lentil Casserole

Pronto

PASTA

Shrimp & Asparagus Fettuccine

12 ounces uncooked fettuccine
1 box (10 ounces) BIRDS EYE®
  frozen Asparagus Cuts*
1 tablespoon vegetable oil
1 package (16 ounces) frozen,
  uncooked cocktail-size
  shrimp

1 jar (12 ounces) prepared
  alfredo sauce
1 jar (4 ounces) sliced
  pimiento, drained

*Or, substitute 1½ cups Birds Eye® frozen Green Peas or Birds Eye® frozen Broccoli Cuts.

Cook pasta according to package directions, adding asparagus to water
8 minutes before pasta is done. Drain; keep warm. Meanwhile, heat oil in large
skillet over medium-high heat. Add shrimp; cover and cook 3 minutes or until
shrimp turn pink. Drain excess liquid, leaving shrimp and about 2 tablespoons
liquid in skillet. Reduce heat to low. Stir in alfredo sauce and pimiento. Cover;
cook 5 minutes. Do not boil. Toss fettuccine and asparagus with shrimp
mixture.   *Makes about 4 servings*

Shrimp & Asparagus Fettuccine

Angel Hair Pasta with Seafood Sauce

2 teaspoons olive oil
½ cup chopped onion
2 cloves garlic, minced
3 pounds fresh plum tomatoes, seeded and chopped
¼ cup chopped fresh basil
2 tablespoons chopped fresh oregano
1 teaspoon crushed red pepper
½ teaspoon sugar
2 bay leaves
½ pound firm whitefish, such as sea bass, monkfish or grouper, cut into ¾-inch pieces
½ pound fresh bay scallops or shucked oysters
8 ounces uncooked angel hair pasta
2 tablespoons chopped fresh parsley

1. Heat oil in large nonstick skillet over medium heat; add onion and garlic. Cook and stir 3 minutes or until onion is tender. Reduce heat to low; add tomatoes, basil, oregano, crushed red pepper, sugar and bay leaves. Cook, uncovered, 15 minutes, stirring occasionally.

2. Add whitefish and scallops. Cook, uncovered, 3 to 4 minutes or until fish flakes easily when tested with fork and scallops are opaque. Remove bay leaves; discard. Set seafood sauce aside.

3. Cook pasta according to package directions, omitting salt. Drain well.

4. Combine pasta with seafood sauce in large serving bowl. Mix well. Sprinkle with parsley. Serve immediately.

Makes 6 servings

Pasta, Chicken & Broccoli Pesto Toss

4 ounces (about 2 cups) uncooked vegetable spiral pasta
2 cups cubed, cooked chicken or turkey breast meat
2 cups small broccoli florets, cooked crisp-tender, cooled
1½ cups (6 ounces) SARGENTO® Light Fancy Shredded Mozzarella Cheese
⅔ cup lightly packed fresh basil leaves
2 cloves garlic
1 cup mayonnaise
1 tablespoon lemon juice
½ teaspoon salt
½ cup (1½ ounces) SARGENTO® Fancy Shredded Parmesan Cheese
½ cup pine nuts or coarsely chopped walnuts, toasted

Cook pasta according to package directions until tender; drain and cool. Combine pasta, chicken, broccoli and mozzarella cheese in large bowl. Process basil and garlic in covered blender or food processor until finely chopped. Add mayonnaise, lemon juice and salt. Process to combine thoroughly. Stir in Parmesan cheese. Add to pasta mixture; toss to coat well. Stir in pine nuts. Serve immediately or cover and refrigerate. For maximum flavor, remove from refrigerator and toss gently 30 minutes before serving.

Makes 8 servings

Angle Hair Pasta with Seafood Sauce

Pasta Primavera with Roasted Garlic Sauce

3 large heads garlic
2 tablespoons FLEISCHMANN'S®
    Original Spread (70% Corn Oil),
    melted
3 tablespoons GREY POUPON®
    COUNTRY DIJON® Mustard
3 tablespoons lemon juice
¼ teaspoon coarsely ground black
    pepper
1 cup sliced fresh mushrooms
½ cup julienned zucchini
½ cup julienned carrot
½ cup COLLEGE INN® Lower Sodium
    Chicken Broth or water
1 cup chopped tomato
1 tablespoon chopped fresh basil
    leaves *or* 1 teaspoon dried basil
    leaves
8 ounces angel hair pasta, cooked and
    drained

Brush each head of garlic lightly with
1 teaspoon melted spread; wrap each head
separately in foil. Place in small baking pan;
bake at 400°F for 45 minutes or until tender.
Cool 10 minutes. Separate cloves; squeeze
cloves to extract pulp (discard skins).

In blender or food processor, purée garlic
pulp, mustard, lemon juice and pepper; set
aside.

In skillet over medium-high heat, sauté
mushrooms, zucchini and carrot in remaining
spread until tender-crisp, about 3 minutes;
add garlic mixture, broth or water, tomato
and basil. Reduce heat to low; cook and stir
until sauce is heated through. Toss with hot
cooked pasta. Serve immediately.

Makes 4 servings

Lemon Pepper Pasta with Piccatta Style Vegetables

1 (12-ounce) package PASTA LABELLA®
    Lemon Pepper Pasta
2 tablespoons butter
1 tablespoon extra virgin olive oil
1 cup julienned red onions
1 cup julienned carrots
2 teaspoons minced garlic
1 cup white wine
1½ tablespoons capers
1 cup julienned snow peas
    Salt and black pepper to taste
2 tablespoons chopped parsley
⅓ cup grated Parmesan cheese

Cook pasta according to package directions.
In large skillet, heat butter and olive oil. Add
onions, carrots and garlic and sauté for 4
minutes. Add wine and capers and simmer
for 2 minutes. Mix in hot Lemon Pepper
Pasta and snow peas; toss and blend well.
Season with salt and pepper and sprinkle
with parsley. Top with Parmesan cheese and
serve. *Makes 3 servings*

Macaroni and Cheese Dijon

1¼ cups milk
12 ounces pasteurized process
    Cheddar cheese spread, cubed
½ cup GREY POUPON® Dijon Mustard
⅓ cup sliced green onions
6 slices bacon, cooked and crumbled
⅛ teaspoon ground red pepper
12 ounces tri-color rotelle or spiral-
    shaped pasta, cooked
1 (2.8-ounce) can French fried onion
    rings

In medium saucepan over low heat, heat milk, cheese and mustard until cheese melts and mixture is smooth. Stir in green onions, bacon and red pepper; remove from heat.

In large bowl, combine hot pasta and cheese mixture, tossing until well coated; spoon into greased 2-quart casserole. Cover; bake at 350°F for 15 to 20 minutes. Uncover and stir; top with onion rings. Bake, uncovered, for 5 minutes more. Let stand 10 minutes before serving. Garnish as desired.

Makes 6 servings

Macaroni and Cheese Dijon

Pad Thai (Thai Fried Noodles)

7¼ cups water, divided
12 ounces dried thin rice stick
    noodles*
4 tablespoons vegetable oil, divided
3 tablespoons brown sugar
¼ cup soy sauce
2 tablespoons lime juice
1 tablespoon anchovy paste
2 eggs, lightly beaten
12 ounces medium shrimp, peeled and
    deveined
2 cloves garlic, minced
1 tablespoon paprika
¼ to ½ teaspoon crushed red pepper
1 cup canned bean sprouts, rinsed,
    drained and divided
½ cup coarsely chopped unsalted dry
    roasted peanuts
4 green onions with tops, cut into
    1-inch pieces
½ of 1 lime, cut lengthwise into
    4 wedges, for garnish

If rice stick noodles are unavailable, use fine egg noodles, thin spaghetti, vermicelli or angel hair pasta.

Bring 6 cups water to a boil in wok over high heat. Add noodles; cook 2 minutes or until tender but still firm, stirring frequently. Drain; rinse. Place noodles in large bowl. Add 1 tablespoon oil and toss lightly to coat; set aside.

Combine remaining 1¼ cups water, brown sugar, soy sauce, lime juice and anchovy paste in small bowl; set aside.

Heat wok over medium heat 2 minutes or until hot. Drizzle 1 tablespoon oil into wok and heat 30 seconds. Add eggs; stir-fry 1 minute or just until set on bottom. Turn eggs over; stir to scramble. Remove to medium bowl. Increase heat to high.

Drizzle 1 tablespoon oil into wok and heat 30 seconds. Add shrimp and garlic; stir-fry 2 minutes or until shrimp begin to turn pink and opaque. Remove shrimp to bowl with eggs. Reduce heat to medium.

Drizzle remaining 1 tablespoon oil into wok and heat 15 seconds. Stir in paprika and red pepper to taste. Add noodles and anchovy mixture; cook and stir about 5 minutes or until noodles are softened. Stir in ¾ cup bean sprouts. Add peanuts and green onions; toss and cook about 1 minute or until green onions are tender. Add eggs and shrimp; stir-fry until heated through. Transfer to serving plate; top with remaining bean sprouts. Garnish with lime wedges.

Makes 4 servings

Pad Thai

Savory Lo Mein

2 tablespoons olive or vegetable oil
1 medium clove garlic, finely
    chopped*
1 small head bok choy, cut into
    2-inch pieces (about 5 cups)**
1 envelope LIPTON® Recipe Secrets®
    Onion Soup Mix
1 cup water
2 tablespoons sherry (optional)
1 teaspoon soy sauce
¼ teaspoon ground ginger (optional)
8 ounces linguine or spaghetti,
    cooked and drained

*If using LIPTON® Recipe Secrets® Savory Herb with
Garlic Soup Mix, omit garlic.*

**Substitution: Use 5 cups coarsely shredded green
cabbage. Decrease 10 minute cook time to 3
minutes.*

In 12-inch skillet, heat oil over medium heat
and cook garlic and bok choy, stirring
frequently, 10 minutes or until crisp-tender.
Stir in onion soup mix blended with water,
sherry, soy sauce and ginger. Bring to a boil
over high heat. Reduce heat to low and
simmer uncovered, stirring occasionally,
5 minutes. Toss with hot linguine. Sprinkle, if
desired, with toasted sesame seeds.

Makes about 4 servings

Tip: This dish is also terrific made with
LIPTON® Recipe Secrets® Onion-Mushroom,
Savory Herb with Garlic, Golden Herb with
Lemon or Golden Onion Soup Mix.

Penne with Arrabiatta Sauce

½ pound uncooked penne or other
    tube-shaped pasta
2 tablespoons olive oil or oil from
    sun-dried tomatoes
8 cloves garlic
1 can (28 ounces) crushed tomatoes
    in purée
¼ cup chopped sun-dried tomatoes
    packed in oil
8 kalamata olives, pitted and
    chopped*
3 tablespoons FRANK'S® Original
    REDHOT® Cayenne Pepper Sauce
6 fresh basil leaves *or* 1½ teaspoons
    dried basil leaves
1 tablespoon capers

*To pit olives, place olives on cutting board. Press
with side of knife until olives split. Remove pits.*

1. Cook pasta according to package
directions; drain.

2. Heat oil in large nonstick skillet over
medium heat. Add garlic; cook until golden,
stirring frequently. Add remaining
ingredients. Bring to a boil. Simmer, partially
covered, 10 minutes. Stir occasionally.

3. Toss pasta with half of the sauce mixture.
Spoon into serving bowl. Pour remaining
sauce mixture over pasta. Garnish with fresh
basil or parsley, if desired.

Makes 4 servings (3 cups sauce)

Prep time: 15 minutes
Cook time: 20 minutes

Penne with Arrabiatta Sauce

Ricotta-Stuffed Chicken with Sun-Dried Tomato Linguine

1 broiler-fryer chicken (3 pounds)
1 cup reduced-fat ricotta cheese
1 cup chopped fresh spinach leaves
4 cloves garlic, minced
2 teaspoons dried basil leaves
2 teaspoons minced fresh parsley
1 teaspoon dried oregano leaves
¼ teaspoon salt
   Nonstick olive oil cooking spray
   Paprika
   Sun-Dried Tomato Linguine
   (recipe follows)

1. Preheat oven to 375°F. Split chicken in half with sharp knife or poultry shears, cutting through breastbone. Place chicken, skin-side-up, on counter and press with palm of hand to crack bone so that chicken will lie flat.

2. Loosen skin over top of chicken using fingers and sharp paring knife; do not loosen skin over wings and drumsticks.

3. Combine ricotta cheese, spinach, garlic, basil, parsley, oregano and salt in small bowl. Spread mixture under skin of chicken.

4. Place chicken in roasting pan. Spray top of chicken lightly with cooking spray; sprinkle with paprika. Bake about 1 hour 15 minutes or until chicken is no longer pink in center and juices run clear. Prepare Sun-Dried Tomato Linguine; serve with chicken. Garnish as desired.   *Makes 6 servings*

Sun-Dried Tomato Linguine

6 sun-dried tomato halves, not packed in oil
   Nonstick olive oil cooking spray
1 cup sliced mushrooms
3 cloves garlic, minced
1 tablespoon minced fresh parsley
¾ teaspoon dried rosemary
1 can (15 ounces) low-sodium chicken broth
2 tablespoons cornstarch
¼ cup cold water
1 package (9 ounces) linguine, cooked in salted water, drained

1. Place sun-dried tomatoes in small bowl; pour hot water over to cover. Let stand 10 to 15 minutes or until tomatoes are soft. Drain well; cut tomatoes into quarters.

2. Spray medium nonstick skillet with cooking spray; heat over medium heat until hot. Add mushrooms and garlic; cook and stir about 5 minutes or until tender. Add sun-dried tomatoes, parsley and rosemary; cook and stir 1 minute.

3. Stir broth into vegetable mixture; heat to a boil. Combine cornstarch and cold water in small bowl; stir into broth mixture. Boil 1 to 2 minutes, stirring constantly. Pour mixture over warm linguine; toss to coat.
Makes 6 servings

Ricotta-Stuffed Chicken with Sun-Dried Tomato Linguine

Vegetable Lasagna

Tomato-Basil Sauce (recipe follows)
2 tablespoons olive oil
4 medium carrots, sliced
3 medium zucchini, sliced
6 ounces spinach leaves, stemmed
    and chopped
¼ teaspoon salt
¼ teaspoon black pepper
1 egg
3 cups ricotta cheese
½ cup plus 2 tablespoons grated
    Parmesan cheese, divided
12 uncooked lasagna noodles
1½ cups (6 ounces) shredded
    mozzarella cheese
1½ cups (6 ounces) shredded Monterey
    Jack cheese
½ cup water
    Belgian endive leaves, Bibb lettuce
    leaves and fresh basil sprigs for
    garnish

1. Prepare Tomato-Basil Sauce.

2. Heat oil in large skillet over medium heat until hot. Add carrots; cook and stir 4 minutes. Add zucchini; cook and stir 8 minutes or until crisp-tender. Add spinach; cook and stir 1 minute or until spinach is wilted. Stir in salt and pepper.

3. Preheat oven to 350°F. Beat egg in medium bowl. Stir in ricotta cheese and ½ cup Parmesan cheese.

4. Spread 1 cup Tomato-Basil Sauce in bottom of 13×9-inch baking pan; top with 4 lasagna noodles.

5. Spread one-third of ricotta mixture over noodles. Spoon one-third of vegetable mixture over cheese. Top with 1 cup Tomato-Basil Sauce. Sprinkle with ½ cup *each* mozzarella and Monterey Jack cheese. Repeat layers twice, ending with mozzarella and Monterey Jack cheese. Sprinkle with remaining 2 tablespoons Parmesan cheese.

6. Carefully pour water around sides of pan. Cover pan tightly with foil.

7. Bake lasagna 1 hour or until bubbly. Uncover. Let stand 10 to 15 minutes. Garnish, if desired.   *Makes 8 servings*

Tomato-Basil Sauce

2 cans (28 ounces *each*) plum
    tomatoes
1 teaspoon olive oil
1 medium onion, chopped
3 cloves garlic, minced
1 tablespoon sugar
1 tablespoon dried basil leaves
¼ teaspoon salt
¼ teaspoon black pepper

1. Drain tomatoes, reserving ½ cup juice. Seed and chop tomatoes.

2. Heat oil in large skillet over medium heat until hot. Add onion and garlic; cook and stir 5 minutes or until tender. Stir in tomatoes, reserved juice, sugar, basil, salt and pepper.

3. Bring to a boil over high heat. Reduce heat to low. Simmer, uncovered, 25 to 30 minutes or until most of juices have evaporated.
    Makes 4 cups sauce

Vegetable Lasagna

Three Cheese Vegetable Lasagna

1 teaspoon olive oil
1 large onion, chopped
3 cloves garlic, minced
1 can (28 ounces) no-salt-added
    tomato purée
1 can (14½ ounces) no-salt-added
    tomatoes, undrained and
    chopped
2 cups (6 ounces) sliced fresh
    mushrooms
1 medium zucchini, finely chopped
1 large green bell pepper, chopped
2 teaspoons dried basil leaves,
    crushed
1 teaspoon *each* salt and sugar
    (optional)
½ teaspoon *each* red pepper flakes
    and dried oregano leaves, crushed
2 cups (15 ounces) SARGENTO® Light
    Ricotta Cheese
1 package (10 ounces) frozen
    chopped spinach, thawed and
    squeezed dry
2 egg whites
2 tablespoons (½ ounce) SARGENTO®
    Fancy Supreme Shredded
    Parmesan Cheese
8 ounces lasagna noodles, cooked
    according to package directions,
    without oil or salt
¾ cup (3 ounces) *each* SARGENTO®
    Light Fancy Shredded Mozzarella
    and Mild Cheddar Cheese, divided

Preheat oven to 375°F. Spray large skillet with nonstick vegetable spray. Heat oil in large skillet over medium heat; add onion and garlic. Cook until tender, stirring occasionally. Add tomato purée, tomatoes and liquid, mushrooms, zucchini, bell pepper, basil, salt, sugar, if desired, pepper flakes and oregano. Bring to a boil; reduce heat to low. Cover and simmer 10 minutes or until vegetables are crisp-tender.

Combine ricotta cheese, spinach, egg whites and Parmesan cheese in medium bowl; mix well. Spread 1 cup sauce in bottom of 13×9-inch baking dish. Layer 3 lasagna noodles over sauce. Top with half of ricotta cheese mixture and 2 cups sauce. Repeat layering with 3 more lasagna noodles, remaining ricotta mixture and 2 cups sauce. Combine mozzarella and Cheddar cheeses. Sprinkle ¾ cup cheese mixture over sauce. Top with 2 remaining lasagna noodles and sauce. Cover with foil; bake 30 minutes. Uncover; bake 15 minutes more. Sprinkle with remaining ¾ cup cheese mixture. Let stand 10 minutes before serving.

Makes 10 servings

Tortellini Bake Parmesano

1 package (12 ounces) fresh or frozen cheese tortellini or ravioli
½ pound lean ground beef
½ medium onion, finely chopped
2 cloves garlic, minced
½ teaspoon dried oregano, crushed
1 can (26 ounces) DEL MONTE® Chunky Spaghetti Sauce with Garlic & Herb
2 small zucchini, sliced
⅓ cup (about 1½ ounces) grated Parmesan cheese

1. Cook pasta according to package directions; rinse and drain.

2. Meanwhile, brown beef with onion, garlic and oregano in large skillet over medium-high heat; drain. Season with salt and black pepper, if desired.

3. Add spaghetti sauce and zucchini. Cook 15 minutes or until thickened, stirring occasionally.

4. Arrange half of pasta in oiled 2-quart microwavable dish; top with half each of sauce and cheese. Repeat layers ending with cheese; cover.

5. Microwave on HIGH 8 to 10 minutes or until heated through, rotating dish halfway through cooking time.   *Makes 4 servings*

Prep and cook time: 35 minutes

Tip: For convenience, double this recipe and freeze one for later use. The recipe can also be made ahead, refrigerated and heated just before serving (allow extra time in microwave if dish is chilled).

Sonoma Fettuccine Alfredo

½ pound dried fettuccine pasta
1 jar (8 ounces) SONOMA® Marinated Dried Tomatoes
1½ cups whipping cream, divided
1 cup (3 ounces) grated fresh Parmesan cheese, divided
Salt and black pepper to taste
3 tablespoons chopped chives
½ teaspoon nutmeg

Cook pasta in large pot of boiling salted water 5 to 8 minutes until just tender; drain well. Meanwhile, drain tomato marinating oil into large skillet; snip tomatoes in half and reserve. Add ½ cup cream to skillet. Cook over high heat, stirring constantly, about 3 minutes until slightly thickened. Reduce heat to medium; add cooked pasta and mix gently. Add ½ cup cheese, ½ cup cream and reserved tomatoes. Lift and mix pasta gently. Repeat with remaining cheese and cream; mix again. Season with salt and pepper. Transfer to warmed individual pasta bowls or large platter. Sprinkle with chives and nutmeg. Serve immediately.

Makes 4 servings

Stuffed Jumbo Shells with Garlic Vegetables

Garlic Vegetables (recipe follows)
12 uncooked jumbo pasta shells
2 cups ricotta cheese
1 package (10 ounces) frozen chopped spinach, thawed and squeezed dry
¼ cup grated Parmesan cheese
2 cloves garlic, minced
¾ teaspoon dried marjoram leaves
½ teaspoon dried basil leaves
¼ teaspoon dried thyme leaves
½ teaspoon salt
½ teaspoon black pepper
Additional grated Parmesan cheese

1. Prepare Garlic Vegetables. Spoon into bottom of 10-inch round baking dish.

2. Cook shells according to package directions. Drain; cool.

3. Combine ricotta, spinach, ¼ cup Parmesan cheese, garlic, marjoram, basil, thyme, salt and pepper in medium bowl. Spoon cheese mixture into shells.

4. Preheat oven to 350°F. Arrange shells on top of Garlic Vegetables. Carefully spoon sauce from vegetables over shells.

5. Bake, loosely covered with foil, 35 to 40 minutes or until heated through.

6. Sprinkle with additional Parmesan cheese.
Makes 4 servings

Garlic Vegetables

2 tablespoons olive oil, divided
1 large head garlic, peeled and chopped
⅓ cup sun-dried tomatoes (not packed in oil)
2 tablespoons all-purpose flour
1¼ cups canned vegetable broth
2 large carrots, peeled and cut into ¼-inch slices
1 medium zucchini, sliced
1 medium yellow summer squash, sliced
2 tablespoons minced fresh parsley
Salt and black pepper to taste

1. Heat 1 tablespoon oil in small skillet over medium heat until hot. Add garlic; cook and stir 2 to 3 minutes. Reduce heat to low and cook about 15 minutes or until garlic is golden brown, stirring frequently.

2. Add tomatoes; cook over medium heat 2 minutes. Stir in flour. Cook and stir 2 minutes. Gradually stir in broth. Cook 1 to 2 minutes or until sauce thickens, stirring constantly. Set aside.

3. Heat remaining 1 tablespoon oil in medium skillet over medium heat until hot. Add carrots; cook and stir 2 minutes. Add zucchini and squash; cook and stir 3 minutes or until crisp-tender. Remove from heat.

4. Stir garlic mixture and parsley into carrot mixture in skillet. Season to taste with salt and pepper. *Makes 2 cups vegetables*

Stuffed Jumbo Shells with Garlic Vegetables

Rigatoni with Four Cheeses

3 cups milk
1 tablespoon chopped carrot
1 tablespoon chopped celery
1 tablespoon chopped onion
1 tablespoon fresh parsley sprigs
¼ teaspoon black peppercorns
¼ teaspoon hot pepper sauce
½ bay leaf
  Dash nutmeg
¼ cup Wisconsin butter
¼ cup all-purpose flour
½ cup (2 ounces) grated Wisconsin
    Parmesan cheese
¼ cup (1 ounce) grated Wisconsin
    Romano cheese
12 ounces rigatoni, cooked and
    drained
1½ cups (6 ounces) shredded
    Wisconsin Cheddar cheese
1½ cups (6 ounces) shredded
    Wisconsin Mozzarella cheese
¼ teaspoon chili powder

In 2-quart saucepan, combine milk, carrot,
celery, onion, parsley, peppercorns, hot
pepper sauce, bay leaf and nutmeg. Bring to a
boil. Reduce heat to low; simmer 10 minutes.
Strain, reserving liquid. Melt butter in 2-quart
saucepan over low heat. Blend in flour.
Gradually add reserved liquid; cook, stirring
constantly, until thickened. Remove from
heat. Add Parmesan and Romano cheeses; stir
until blended. Pour over pasta; toss well.
Combine Cheddar and Mozzarella cheese. In
buttered 2-quart casserole, layer half of pasta
mixture, Cheddar cheese mixture and

Rigatoni with Four Cheeses

remaining pasta mixture. Sprinkle with chili powder. Bake at 350°F 25 minutes or until hot. *Makes 6 servings*

Favorite recipe from **Wisconsin Milk Marketing Board**

Eggplant Pasta Bake

    4 ounces bow-tie pasta
    1 pound eggplant, diced
    1 clove garlic, minced
    ¼ cup olive oil
1½ cups shredded Monterey Jack cheese, divided
    1 cup sliced green onions
    ½ cup grated Parmesan cheese
    1 can (14½ ounces) DEL MONTE® *FreshCut*™ Brand Diced Tomatoes with Basil, Garlic & Oregano

1. Preheat oven to 350°F. Cook pasta according to package directions; drain.

2. Cook eggplant and garlic in oil in large skillet over medium-high heat until tender.

3. Toss eggplant with cooked pasta, 1 cup Monterey Jack cheese, green onions and Parmesan cheese.

4. Place in greased 9-inch square baking dish. Top with tomatoes and remaining ½ cup Monterey Jack cheese. Bake 15 minutes or until heated through. *Makes 6 servings*

Prep and cook time: 30 minutes

One-Pot Chicken Couscous

    ¼ cup olive oil
    2 pounds boneless, skinless chicken breasts, cut into 1-inch chunks
    4 large carrots, peeled and sliced
    2 medium onions, diced
    2 large cloves garlic, minced
    2 cans (13¾ ounces each) chicken broth
    2 cups uncooked couscous
    2 teaspoons TABASCO® Pepper Sauce
    ½ teaspoon salt
    1 cup raisins or currants
    1 cup slivered almonds, toasted
    ¼ cup chopped fresh parsley or mint

In 12-inch skillet over medium-high heat, in hot oil, cook chicken until well browned on all sides. With slotted spoon, remove chicken to plate. Reduce heat to medium. In drippings remaining in skillet, cook carrots and onions 5 minutes. Add garlic; cook 2 minutes longer, stirring frequently.

Add chicken broth, couscous, TABASCO® Sauce, salt and chicken chunks. Heat to boiling, then reduce heat to low. Cover and simmer 5 minutes. Stir in raisins, almonds and parsley. *Makes 8 servings*

A FISH STORY

Boiled Whole Lobster with Burned Butter Sauce

½ cup butter
2 tablespoons chopped fresh
   parsley

1 tablespoon cider vinegar
1 tablespoon capers
2 live lobsters*

Purchase live lobsters as close to time of cooking as possible. Store in refrigerator.

Fill 8-quart stockpot with enough water to cover lobsters. Cover stockpot; bring water to a boil over high heat. Meanwhile, to make Burned Butter Sauce, melt butter in medium saucepan over medium heat. Cook and stir butter until it turns dark chocolate brown. Remove from heat. Add parsley, vinegar and capers. Pour into 2 individual ramekins; set aside.

(continued on page 152)

Boiled Whole Lobster with Burned Butter Sauce

(Boiled Whole Lobster with Burned Butter Sauce, *continued from page 150***)**

Holding each lobster by its back, submerge head first into boiling water. Cover and continue to heat. When water returns to a boil, cook lobsters from 10 to 18 minutes, according to size:

1 pound—10 minutes
1¼ pounds—12 minutes
1½ pounds—15 minutes
2 pounds—18 minutes

Transfer to 2 large serving platters. Remove bands restraining claws. Cut through underside of shells with kitchen shears and loosen meat from shells. Provide nutcrackers and seafood forks. Serve lobsters with Burned Butter Sauce. *Makes 2 servings*

Chesapeake Crab Strata

4 tablespoons butter or margarine
4 cups unseasoned croutons
2 cups shredded Cheddar cheese
2 cups milk
8 eggs, beaten
½ teaspoon dry mustard
½ teaspoon seafood seasoning
 Salt and black pepper to taste
1 pound crabmeat, picked over to
 remove any shells

Preheat oven to 325°F. Place butter in 11×7-inch baking dish. Heat in oven until melted, tilting to coat dish. Remove dish from oven; spread croutons over melted butter. Top with cheese; set aside.

Combine milk, eggs, dry mustard, seafood seasoning, salt and pepper; mix well. Pour egg mixture over cheese in dish; sprinkle with crabmeat. Bake 50 minutes or until mixture is set. Remove from oven and let stand about 10 minutes. Garnish, if desired.
 Makes 6 to 8 servings

Easy Crab-Asparagus Pie

4 ounces crabmeat, shredded
12 ounces fresh asparagus, cooked
½ cup chopped onion, cooked
1 cup (4 ounces) shredded Monterey
 Jack cheese
¼ cup (1 ounce) grated Parmesan
 cheese
¾ cup all-purpose flour
¾ teaspoon baking powder
½ teaspoon salt
2 tablespoons butter, chilled
1½ cups milk
4 eggs, slightly beaten

1. Preheat oven to 350°F. Lightly grease 10-inch quiche dish or pie plate.

2. Layer crabmeat, asparagus and onion in prepared pie plate; top with cheeses. Season with black pepper to taste.

3. Combine flour, baking powder and salt in large bowl. With pastry blender or 2 knives, cut in butter until mixture forms coarse crumbs. Stir in milk and eggs; pour over vegetables and cheeses.

4. Bake 30 minutes or until knife inserted near center comes out clean. *Makes 6 servings*

Chesapeake Crab Strata

Crab Cakes with Tomato Salsa

CRAB CAKES
1 pound crabmeat
1 tablespoon FILIPPO BERIO® Olive Oil
1 onion, finely chopped
1 cup fresh white bread crumbs, divided
2 eggs, beaten, divided
2 tablespoons drained capers, rinsed and chopped
2 tablespoons mayonnaise
1 tablespoon chopped parsley
1 tablespoon ketchup
Finely grated peel of half a lemon
1 tablespoon lemon juice
Salt and freshly ground black pepper
Additional FILIPPO BERIO® Olive Oil for frying

TOMATO SALSA
3 tablespoons FILIPPO BERIO® Olive Oil
4 large tomatoes, finely chopped
2 cloves garlic, crushed
¼ cup lemon juice
4½ teaspoons sweet or hot chili sauce
1 tablespoon sugar
Salt and freshly ground black pepper

For Crab Cakes, pick out and discard any shell or cartilage from crabmeat. Place crabmeat in medium bowl; flake finely. In small skillet, heat 1 tablespoon olive oil over medium heat until hot. Add onion; cook and stir 3 to 5 minutes or until softened. Add to crabmeat. Gently mix in ½ cup bread crumbs, 1 egg, capers, mayonnaise, parsley, ketchup, lemon peel and lemon juice. Shape mixture into 8 round cakes; cover and refrigerate 30 minutes.

Meanwhile, for Tomato Salsa, in medium skillet, heat olive oil over medium heat until hot. Add tomatoes and garlic; cook and stir 5 minutes. Add lemon juice, chili sauce and sugar; mix well. Season to taste with salt and pepper.

Dip crab cakes into remaining beaten egg, then in remaining ½ cup bread crumbs. Press crumb coating firmly onto crab cakes.

In large nonstick skillet, pour in just enough olive oil to cover bottom. Heat over medium-high heat until hot. Add crab cakes; fry 5 to 8 minutes, turning frequently, until cooked through and golden brown. Drain on paper towels. Season to taste with salt and pepper. Serve hot with Tomato Salsa for dipping.

Makes 8 crab cakes

Crab Cakes with Tomato Salsa

Jazzy Jambalaya

1 package (6.8 ounces) RICE-A-RONI®
    Spanish Rice
1 cup chopped cooked chicken or
    ham
1 cup chopped onion
1 cup chopped green bell pepper
3 tablespoons vegetable oil
2 cloves garlic, minced
1 can (14½ ounces) tomatoes,
    undrained and chopped
    Dash hot pepper sauce (optional)
½ pound raw shrimp, shelled,
    deveined *or* 8 ounces frozen
    cleaned precooked shrimp

1. In large skillet, combine rice-vermicelli mix, chicken, onion, bell pepper, oil and garlic. Sauté over medium heat, stirring frequently, until vermicelli is golden brown.

2. Stir in 2 cups water, tomatoes and juice, hot pepper sauce, if desired, and contents of seasoning packet; bring to a boil over high heat.

3. Cover; reduce heat. Simmer 10 minutes.

4. Stir in shrimp.

5. Cover; continue cooking 8 to 10 minutes or until liquid is absorbed, rice is tender and shrimp turn pink.   *Makes 5 servings*

Jazzy Jambalaya

Hot Shrimp with Cool Salsa

¼ cup prepared salsa
4 tablespoons fresh lime juice,
    divided
1 teaspoon honey
1 clove garlic, minced
2 to 4 drops hot pepper sauce
1 pound large shrimp, peeled and
    deveined, with tails intact
1 cup finely diced honeydew melon
½ cup finely diced unpeeled cucumber
2 tablespoons minced parsley
1 green onion, finely chopped
1½ teaspoons sugar
1 teaspoon olive oil
¼ teaspoon salt

1. To make marinade, combine prepared salsa, 2 tablespoons lime juice, honey, garlic and hot pepper sauce in small bowl. Thread shrimp onto skewers. Brush shrimp with marinade; set aside.

2. To make salsa, combine remaining 2 tablespoons lime juice, melon, cucumber, parsley, green onion, sugar, oil and salt in medium bowl; mix well.

3. Grill shrimp over medium coals 4 to 5 minutes or until shrimp are opaque, turning once. Serve with salsa.   *Makes 4 servings*

Tequila-Lime Prawns

1 pound medium shrimp, peeled and
    deveined
3 tablespoons butter or margarine
1 tablespoon olive oil
2 large cloves garlic, minced
2 tablespoons tequila
1 tablespoon lime juice
¼ teaspoon salt
¼ teaspoon crushed red pepper
3 tablespoons coarsely chopped
    cilantro
Hot cooked rice (optional)

Pat shrimp dry with paper towels. Heat butter and oil in large skillet over medium heat. When butter is melted, add garlic; cook 30 seconds. Add shrimp; cook 2 minutes, stirring occasionally. Stir in tequila, lime juice, salt and crushed red pepper. Cook 2 minutes or until most of liquid evaporates and shrimp are pink and glazed. Add cilantro; cook 10 seconds. Serve over hot cooked rice, if desired. Garnish with lime wedges, if desired.   *Makes 3 to 4 servings*

Shrimp Curry

1¼ pounds raw large shrimp
1 large onion, chopped
½ cup canned light coconut milk
3 cloves garlic, minced
2 tablespoons finely chopped fresh
   ginger
2 to 3 teaspoons hot curry powder
¼ teaspoon salt
1 can (14½ ounces) diced tomatoes
1 teaspoon cornstarch
2 tablespoons chopped fresh cilantro
3 cups hot cooked rice

1. Peel shrimp, leaving tails attached and reserving shells. Place shells in large saucepan; cover with water. Bring to a boil over high heat. Reduce heat to low; simmer 15 to 20 minutes. Strain shrimp stock and set aside. Discard shells.

2. Spray large skillet with nonstick cooking spray; heat over medium heat. Add onion; cover and cook 5 minutes. Add coconut milk, garlic, ginger, curry powder, salt and ½ cup shrimp stock; bring to a boil. Reduce heat to low and simmer 10 to 15 minutes or until onion is tender.

3. Add shrimp and tomatoes to skillet; return mixture to a simmer. Cook 3 minutes.

4. Stir cornstarch into 1 tablespoon cooled shrimp stock until dissolved. Add mixture to skillet with cilantro; simmer 1 to 2 minutes or just until slightly thickened, stirring occasionally. Serve over rice. Garnish with carrot and lime slices, if desired.

Makes 6 servings

Garlic Shrimp with Wilted Spinach

2 teaspoons olive or vegetable oil
¼ cup diagonally sliced green onions
2 tablespoons sherry or dry white
   wine (optional)
1 envelope LIPTON® Recipe Secrets®
   Savory Herb with Garlic Soup
   Mix*
1 cup water
1 pound uncooked medium shrimp,
   peeled and deveined
2 cups fresh trimmed spinach leaves
   (about 4 ounces)
1 large tomato, diced
¼ cup chopped unsalted cashews
   (optional)

Also terrific made with LIPTON® Recipe Secrets® Golden Herb with Lemon or Golden Onion Soup Mix.

In 12-inch skillet, heat oil over medium heat and cook green onions, stirring occasionally, 2 minutes or until slightly soft. Add sherry, if desired, and bring to a boil over high heat, stirring frequently. Stir in savory herb with garlic soup mix blended with water. Bring to a boil over high heat. Reduce heat to low and simmer 2 minutes or until sauce is thickened. Stir in shrimp, spinach, tomato and cashews, if desired. Simmer, stirring occasionally, 2 minutes or until shrimp turn pink.

Makes about 4 servings

Shrimp Curry

Stir-Fried Scallops with Vegetables

1 pound sea scallops
¼ teaspoon salt
⅛ teaspoon black pepper
½ cup vegetable broth
1 tablespoon cornstarch
3 tablespoons butter or margarine, divided
1 package (6 ounces) red radishes, quartered
¼ cup dry white wine
1 package (6 ounces) frozen snow peas, partially thawed
½ cup sliced bamboo shoots
Hot cooked couscous

• Rinse scallops and pat dry with paper towels. Sprinkle with salt and pepper.

• Stir broth into cornstarch in cup until smooth; set aside.

• Heat wok over high heat about 1 minute or until hot. Add 1½ tablespoons butter; swirl to coat bottom and heat 30 seconds. Arrange half the scallops in single layer in wok, leaving ½ inch between. (Scallops should not touch.) Cook scallops until browned on both sides. Remove scallops to large bowl. Repeat with remaining 1½ tablespoons butter and scallops. Reduce heat to medium-high.

• Add radishes to wok; stir-fry about 1 minute or until crisp-tender. Remove radishes to bowl with scallops.

• Add wine to wok. Stir broth mixture; add to wok. Add snow peas and bamboo shoots; stir-fry until heated through.

• Return scallops and radishes to wok; stir-fry until heated through. Serve over couscous. Garnish, if desired. *Makes 4 servings*

Seafood Gumbo

1 bag SUCCESS® Rice
1 tablespoon reduced-calorie margarine
¼ cup chopped onion
¼ cup chopped green bell pepper
2 cloves garlic, minced
1 can (28 ounces) whole tomatoes, cut up, undrained
2 cups chicken broth
½ teaspoon ground red pepper
½ teaspoon dried thyme leaves, crushed
½ teaspoon dried basil leaves, crushed
¾ pound white fish, cut into 1-inch pieces
1 package (10 ounces) frozen cut okra, thawed and drained
½ pound shrimp, peeled and deveined

Prepare rice according to package directions.

Melt margarine in large saucepan over medium-high heat. Add onion, bell pepper and garlic; cook and stir until crisp-tender. Stir in tomatoes, broth, red pepper, thyme and basil. Bring to a boil. Reduce heat to low; simmer, uncovered, until thoroughly heated, 10 to 15 minutes. Stir in fish, okra and shrimp; simmer until fish flakes easily with fork and shrimp curl and turn pink. Add rice; heat thoroughly, stirring occasionally, 5 to 8 minutes. *Makes 4 servings*

Stir-Fried Scallops with Vegetables

Tarragon Scallops & Zucchini

1¼ pounds sea scallops
6 tablespoons butter or margarine
2 small zucchini, thinly sliced
¼ teaspoon onion powder
2 cups instant white rice
3 large green onions including tops, chopped
3 tablespoons chopped fresh tarragon *or* ¾ teaspoon dried tarragon leaves
¼ teaspoon salt
2 tablespoons lemon juice
2 teaspoons cornstarch

1. Rinse scallops; pat dry with paper towels. Cut large scallops in half.

2. Melt butter in large nonstick skillet over medium heat. Stir in scallops, zucchini and onion powder; cook and stir 2 minutes. Cover; reduce heat. Cook 7 minutes.

3. Meanwhile, prepare rice according to package directions. Combine green onions, tarragon and salt in small bowl. Blend lemon juice and cornstarch in another small bowl, stirring until cornstarch dissolves; set aside.

4. Stir green onion and cornstarch mixtures into skillet. Increase heat to medium; cook and stir 1 minute or until sauce thickens and scallops are opaque. Serve over rice.

Makes 4 servings

Prep and cook time: 20 minutes

Tarragon Scallops & Zucchini

Spicy Snapper & Black Beans

1½ pounds fresh red snapper fillets, cut into 4 portions (6 ounces *each*)
Juice of 1 lime
½ teaspoon coarsely ground black pepper
Nonstick cooking spray
1 cup GUILTLESS GOURMET® Spicy Black Bean Dip
½ cup water
½ cup (about 35) crushed GUILTLESS GOURMET® Baked Tortilla Chips (yellow or white corn)
1 cup GUILTLESS GOURMET® Salsa

Wash fish thoroughly; pat dry with paper towels. Place fish in 13×9-inch glass baking dish. Pour lime juice over top; sprinkle with pepper. Cover and refrigerate 1 hour.

Preheat oven to 350°F. Coat 11×7-inch glass baking dish with cooking spray. Combine bean dip and water in small bowl; spread 1 cup bean mixture in bottom of prepared baking dish. Place fish over bean mixture, discarding juice. Spread remaining bean mixture over top of fish; sprinkle with crushed chips.

Bake about 20 minutes or until chips are lightly browned and fish turns opaque and flakes easily when tested with fork. To serve, divide fish among 4 serving plates; spoon ¼ cup salsa over top of each serving.

Makes 4 servings

Note: Make this recipe with 4 boneless skinless chicken breast halves in place of red snapper fillets. Prepare as directed and bake about 40 minutes or until chicken is no longer pink in center. Serve as directed.

Squid Mediterranean

2 pounds cleaned, whole squid (body and tentacles)
1 tablespoon olive oil
¾ cup finely chopped onion
1 clove garlic, minced
2 (16-ounce) cans Italian-style tomatoes, drained and chopped
3 tablespoons sliced black olives
1 tablespoon capers
½ teaspoon dried oregano
¼ teaspoon dried marjoram
⅛ teaspoon crushed red pepper

Cut body of squid into ½-inch slices; set aside. Heat olive oil in large skillet; add onion and garlic. Cook until onion is tender. Add squid and remaining ingredients. Bring to a boil. Cover; reduce heat and simmer 30 minutes or until squid is tender.
Makes 4 servings

Prep time: about 45 minutes

Favorite recipe from **National Fisheries Institute**

Snapper with Pesto Butter

½ cup butter or margarine, softened
1 cup packed fresh basil leaves,
    coarsely chopped *or* ½ cup
    chopped fresh parsley plus
    2 tablespoons dried basil leaves,
    crushed
3 tablespoons finely grated fresh
    Parmesan cheese
1 clove garlic, minced
    Olive oil
2 to 3 teaspoons lemon juice
4 to 6 red snapper, rock cod, salmon
    or other medium-firm fish fillets
    (at least ½ inch thick)
    Salt and black pepper
    Lemon wedges
    Fresh basil or parsley sprigs and
    lemon strips for garnish

To make Pesto Butter, place butter, basil, cheese, garlic and 1 tablespoon oil in a blender or food processor; process until blended. Stir in lemon juice to taste. Rinse fish; pat dry with paper towels. Brush one side of fish lightly with oil; season with salt and pepper.

Oil hot grid to help prevent sticking. Grill fillets, oiled sides down, on a covered grill, over medium **KINGSFORD**® Briquets, 5 to 9 minutes. Halfway through cooking time, brush tops with oil; season with salt and pepper. Turn and continue grilling until fish turns opaque throughout. (Allow 3 to 5 minutes for each ½ inch of thickness.) Serve each fillet with a spoonful of Pesto Butter and a wedge of lemon. Garnish with basil sprigs and lemon strips.

Makes 4 to 6 servings

Baked Fish with Potatoes and Onions

1 pound baking potatoes, very thinly
    sliced
1 large onion, very thinly sliced
1 small red or green bell pepper,
    thinly sliced
    Salt and black pepper
½ teaspoon dried oregano leaves,
    crushed, divided
1 pound lean fish fillets, cut 1 inch
    thick
¼ cup butter or margarine
¼ cup all-purpose flour
2 cups milk
¾ cup (3 ounces) shredded Cheddar
    cheese

Preheat oven to 375°F.

Arrange half of potatoes in buttered 3-quart casserole. Top with half of onion and half of bell pepper. Season with salt and black pepper. Sprinkle with ¼ teaspoon oregano. Arrange fish in single layer over vegetables. Arrange remaining potatoes, onion and bell pepper over fish. Season with salt, black pepper and remaining ¼ teaspoon oregano.

Melt butter in medium saucepan over medium heat. Stir in flour; cook until bubbly, stirring constantly. Gradually stir in milk. Cook until thickened, stirring constantly. Pour white sauce over casserole. Cover and bake at 375°F 40 minutes or until potatoes are tender. Sprinkle with cheese. Bake, uncovered, about 5 minutes more or until cheese is melted.   *Makes 4 servings*

Snapper with Pesto Butter

Blackened Snapper with Red Onion Salsa

Cajun Seasoning Mix
    (recipe follows)
Red Onion Salsa (recipe follows)
4 red snapper fillets (about 6 ounces
    each)
2 tablespoons butter

Prepare Cajun Seasoning Mix and Red Onion Salsa; set aside. Rinse red snapper and pat dry with paper towels. Sprinkle with Cajun Seasoning Mix. Heat large, heavy skillet over high heat until very hot. Add butter and swirl skillet to coat bottom. When butter no longer bubbles, place fish in pan. Cook fish 6 to 8 minutes or until surface is very brown and fish flakes easily when tested with fork, turning halfway through cooking. Serve with Red Onion Salsa. *Makes 4 servings*

Cajun Seasoning Mix

2 tablespoons salt
1 tablespoon paprika
1½ teaspoons garlic powder
1 teaspoon onion powder
1 teaspoon cayenne pepper
½ teaspoon ground white pepper
½ teaspoon dried thyme leaves
½ teaspoon dried oregano leaves
½ teaspoon black pepper

Combine all ingredients in small bowl.
    Makes about ½ cup mix

Red Onion Salsa

1 tablespoon vegetable oil
1 large red onion, chopped
1 clove garlic, minced
½ cup chicken broth
¼ cup dry red wine or red wine
    vinegar
¼ teaspoon dried thyme leaves
    Salt and black pepper to taste

Heat oil in small saucepan over medium-high heat. Add onion; cover and cook 5 minutes. Add garlic; cook 1 minute. Add remaining ingredients. Cover and cook 10 minutes. Uncover; cook until liquid reduces to ¼ cup.
    Makes about 1 cup salsa

Savory Salmon

6 small salmon steaks (about
    6 ounces *each*)
¾ cup prepared HIDDEN VALLEY®
    Original Ranch® Salad Dressing
2 teaspoons chopped fresh dill *or*
    ¼ teaspoon dried dill weed
1 teaspoon chopped fresh parsley
    Lemon wedges
    Fresh dill sprigs (optional)

Preheat oven to 375°F. Arrange salmon in large buttered baking dish; spread 2 tablespoons salad dressing over each steak. Sprinkle with chopped dill and parsley. Bake until fish flakes easily when tested with fork, 10 to 15 minutes. Place under broiler 45 to 60 seconds to brown. Serve with lemon wedges and garnish with dill sprigs, if desired. *Makes 6 servings*

Blackened Snapper with Red Onion Salsa

Broiled Salmon Fillets with Lime Salsa

1½ pounds fresh salmon fillets, quartered
½ cup plus 2 tablespoons lime juice, divided
1 jar chunky green salsa or pico de gallo
⅓ cup finely chopped green onions, including tops
⅓ cup finely chopped fresh cilantro

1. Preheat broiler. Place fillets, skin sides up, in large casserole. Pour ½ cup lime juice over fillets; set aside. Lightly spray broiler pan with nonstick cooking spray; set aside.

2. Pour salsa into small bowl; mix in remaining 2 tablespoons lime juice, green onions and cilantro. Set aside.

3. Arrange fillets, skin sides up, on prepared broiler pan. Broil 6 inches from heat 4 to 5 minutes or until skin has begun to brown and char slightly. Remove pan; turn fillets over. Return to broiler 6 to 8 minutes or until fillets have begun to brown and flake easily with fork. Serve with lime salsa.

Makes 4 servings

Prep and cook time: 23 minutes

Sole Almondine

1 package (6.5 ounces) RICE-A-RONI® Broccoli Au Gratin
1 medium zucchini
4 sole, scrod or orange roughy fillets
1 tablespoon lemon juice
¼ cup grated Parmesan cheese, divided
  Salt and black pepper (optional)
¼ cup sliced almonds
2 tablespoons margarine or butter, melted

1. Prepare Rice-A-Roni® Mix as package directs.

2. While Rice-A-Roni® is simmering, cut zucchini lengthwise into 12 thin slices. Heat oven to 350°F.

3. In 11×7-inch glass baking dish, spread prepared rice evenly. Set aside. Sprinkle fish with lemon juice, 2 tablespoons cheese, salt and pepper, if desired. Place zucchini strips over fish; roll up. Place fish, seam-side down, on rice.

4. Combine almonds and margarine; sprinkle evenly over fish. Top with remaining 2 tablespoons cheese. Bake 20 to 25 minutes or until fish flakes easily with fork.

Makes 4 servings

Broiled Salmon Fillet with Lime Salsa

Catfish with Fresh Corn Relish

4 catfish fillets (*each* about 6 ounces
    and at least ½ inch thick)
2 tablespoons paprika
½ teaspoon salt
½ teaspoon ground red pepper
    Fresh Corn Relish (recipe follows)
    Lime wedges
    Grilled baking potatoes (optional)
    Tarragon sprigs for garnish

Rinse fish; pat dry with paper towels.
Combine paprika, salt and red pepper in cup;
lightly sprinkle on both sides of fish.

Oil hot grid to help prevent sticking. Grill
fish, on a covered grill, over medium
KINGSFORD® Briquets, 5 to 9 minutes.
Halfway through cooking time, turn fish over
and continue grilling until fish turns from
translucent to opaque throughout. (Grilling
time depends on the thickness of fish; allow
3 to 5 minutes for each ½ inch of thickness.)
Serve with Fresh Corn Relish, lime wedges
and potatoes, if desired. Garnish with
tarragon sprigs. *Makes 4 servings*

Fresh Corn Relish

¼ cup cooked fresh corn or thawed
    frozen corn
¼ cup finely diced green bell pepper
¼ cup finely slivered red onion
2 tablespoons seasoned (sweet) rice
    vinegar
1 tablespoon vegetable oil
    Salt and black pepper
½ cup cherry tomatoes, cut into
    quarters

Toss together corn, green pepper, onion,
vinegar and oil in medium bowl. Season with
salt and black pepper. Cover and refrigerate
until ready to serve. Just before serving,
gently mix in tomatoes.
Makes about 1½ cups relish

Southern Breaded Catfish

⅓ cup pecan halves
¼ cup cornmeal
2 tablespoons all-purpose flour
1 teaspoon paprika
¼ teaspoon cayenne pepper
2 egg whites
4 catfish fillets (about 1 pound)
4 cups cooked rice

1. Place pecans in food processor or blender;
process until finely chopped. Combine
pecans, cornmeal, flour, paprika and cayenne
in shallow bowl.

2. Beat egg whites in small bowl with wire
whisk until foamy. Dip catfish fillets in pecan
mixture, then in egg whites, then again in
pecan mixture. Place fillets on plate; cover
and refrigerate at least 15 minutes.

3. Spray large nonstick skillet with nonstick
cooking spray; heat over medium-high heat.
Place catfish fillets in single layer in skillet.

4. Cook fillets 2 minutes per side or until
golden brown. Serve over rice. Serve with
vegetables and garnish, if desired.
Makes 4 servings

Catfish with Fresh Corn Relish

Mahi-Mahi with Fresh Pineapple Salsa

1½ cups diced fresh pineapple
¼ cup finely chopped red bell pepper
¼ cup finely chopped green bell
    pepper
2 tablespoons chopped fresh cilantro
2 tablespoons fresh lime juice,
    divided
½ teaspoon crushed red pepper
½ teaspoon grated lime peel
    Nonstick cooking spray
4 mahi-mahi fillets (4 ounces *each*)
1 tablespoon olive oil
½ teaspoon ground white pepper

To prepare Pineapple Salsa, combine pineapple, bell peppers, cilantro, 1 tablespoon lime juice, crushed red pepper and lime peel in medium bowl.

Preheat broiler. Spray rack of broiler pan with cooking spray. Rinse mahi-mahi and pat dry with paper towels; place on rack. Combine remaining 1 tablespoon lime juice and olive oil; brush on mahi-mahi.

Broil, 4 inches from heat, 2 minutes. Turn and brush second side with olive oil mixture; sprinkle with white pepper. Continue to broil 2 minutes or until fish flakes easily when tested with fork. Serve with Pineapple Salsa.		*Makes 4 servings*

Tip: Pineapple Salsa may be prepared 1 to 2 days ahead and refrigerated.

Mahi-Mahi with Fresh Pineapple Salsa

"Grilled" Tuna with Vegetables in Herb Butter

4 pieces heavy-duty aluminum foil, (12×18 inches *each*)
1 can (12 ounces) STARKIST® Tuna, drained and broken into chunks
1 cup slivered red or green bell pepper
1 cup slivered yellow squash or zucchini
1 cup pea pods, cut crosswise into halves
1 cup slivered carrots
4 green onions, cut into 2-inch slices
Salt and black pepper to taste (optional)

HERB BUTTER
3 tablespoons butter or margarine, melted
1 tablespoon lemon or lime juice
2 teaspoons dried tarragon leaves, crushed
1 clove garlic, minced
1 teaspoon dried dill weed

On each piece of foil, mound tuna, bell pepper, squash, pea pods, carrots and green onions. Sprinkle with salt and black pepper.

For Herb Butter, in small bowl stir together butter, lemon juice, tarragon, garlic and dill. Drizzle over tuna and vegetables. Fold edges of each foil square together to make packets.

TO GRILL
Place foil packets about 4 inches above hot coals. Grill for 10 to 12 minutes or until heated through, turning packets over halfway through grill time.

TO BAKE
Place foil packets on baking sheet. Bake in preheated 450°F oven for 15 to 20 minutes or until heated through.

TO SERVE
Cut an "X" on top of each packet; peel back foil.   *Makes 4 servings*

Nutrients per Serving:

Calories:	235	Cholesterol:	70 mg
Total Fat:	9 g	Sodium:	519 mg

Tuna and Rice Skillet Dinner

1 package (6½ ounces) chicken
    flavored rice mix
½ cup chopped onion
    Water
1½ cups frozen peas and carrots,
    thawed
1 can (10¾ ounces) cream of
    mushroom soup
⅛ teaspoon ground black pepper
1 can (12 ounces) STARKIST® Solid
    White or Chunk Light Tuna,
    drained and chunked
⅓ cup toasted slivered almonds
    (optional)

In medium saucepan, combine rice mix and onion; add water. Prepare rice according to package directions. Stir in vegetables, soup and pepper; blend well. Simmer, covered, 5 to 7 minutes, stirring occasionally. Stir in tuna; top with almonds, if desired.

Makes 4 to 6 servings

Prep time: 30 minutes

Baja Fish Tacos

1 package (12) ORTEGA® Taco Dinner
    Kit (shells, taco seasoning mix
    and taco sauce)
½ cup sour cream
½ cup mayonnaise
¼ cup chopped fresh cilantro
1 pound (about 4) cod or other white
    fish fillets, cut into 1-inch pieces
2 tablespoons vegetable oil
2 tablespoons lemon juice
5 cups (1 small head) shredded red or
    green cabbage
1½ cups (1 medium) chopped tomato
    Lime wedges

COMBINE sour cream, mayonnaise, cilantro and 2 tablespoons taco seasoning mix in small bowl. Combine fish, oil, lemon juice and remaining taco seasoning mix in medium bowl; pour into large skillet. Cook, stirring constantly, over medium-high heat for 4 to 5 minutes or until fish flakes easily when tested with fork.

REMOVE taco shells from freshness pack. Heat shells in microwave at HIGH (100%) for 40 to 60 seconds or heat on baking sheet in preheated 350°F oven for 5 to 6 minutes.

LAYER fish mixture, cabbage and tomato evenly into taco shells. Top with sour cream sauce. Serve with lime wedges and taco sauce.

Makes 6 servings

Tip: Try a variety of fish and seafood such as shark, shrimp, crab or lobster in these fresh-tasting tacos.

Baja Fish Tacos

Pineapple Salsa Topped Halibut

PINEAPPLE SALSA
¾ cup diced fresh pineapple *or* 1 can
(8 ounces) unsweetened
pineapple tidbits, drained
2 tablespoons finely chopped red bell
pepper
2 tablespoons chopped fresh cilantro
2 teaspoons vegetable oil
1 teaspoon minced ginger
1 teaspoon minced jalapeño pepper

HALIBUT
4 halibut or swordfish steaks
(6 ounces *each*), cut ¾ inch thick
1 tablespoon garlic-flavored olive oil
¼ teaspoon salt

1. For salsa, combine pineapple, bell pepper, cilantro, vegetable oil, ginger and jalapeño pepper in small bowl; mix well. Cover; refrigerate.

2. Prepare grill for direct cooking. Brush halibut with garlic-flavored oil; sprinkle with salt.

3. Grill halibut, on uncovered grill, over medium-hot coals 8 minutes or until halibut flakes easily when tested with fork, turning once.

4. Top halibut with salsa; serve immediately.
Makes 4 servings

New England Fisherman's Skillet

4 small red potatoes, diced
1 medium onion, chopped
1 tablespoon olive oil
2 stalks celery, chopped
2 cloves garlic, minced
½ teaspoon dried thyme, crushed
1 can (14½ ounces) DEL MONTE®
Original Recipe Stewed Tomatoes
1 pound firm white fish (such as
halibut, snapper or cod)

1. Brown potatoes and onion in oil over medium-high heat in large skillet, stirring occasionally.

2. Stir in celery, garlic and thyme; cook 4 minutes. Add tomatoes; bring to a boil. Cook 4 minutes or until thickened.

3. Add fish; cover and cook over medium heat 5 to 8 minutes or until fish flakes easily with fork. Garnish with lemon wedges and chopped parsley, if desired.
Makes 4 servings

Prep time: 10 minutes
Cook time: 25 minutes

Pineapple Salsa Topped Halibut

MEMORABLE

MEATS

Veal in Gingered Sweet Bell Pepper Sauce

1 teaspoon olive oil
¾ pound veal cutlets, thinly
   sliced
½ cup fat-free (skim) milk
1 tablespoon chopped tarragon
2 teaspoons crushed capers

1 jar (7 ounces) roasted red
   peppers, drained
1 tablespoon lemon juice
½ teaspoon freshly grated
   ginger
½ teaspoon black pepper

1. Heat oil in medium saucepan over high heat. Add veal; lightly brown both sides. Reduce heat to medium. Add milk, chopped tarragon and capers. Cook, uncovered, 5 minutes or until veal is fork-tender and milk evaporates.

2. Place roasted peppers, lemon juice, ginger and black pepper in food processor or blender; process until smooth. Set aside.

3. Remove veal from pan with slotted spoon; place in serving dish. Spoon roasted pepper sauce over veal. Garnish as desired.   *Makes 4 servings*

Veal in Gingered Sweet Bell Pepper Sauce

Honey-Citrus Glazed Veal Chops

3 tablespoons fresh lime juice
2 tablespoons honey
2 teaspoons grated fresh ginger
½ teaspoon grated lime peel
4 veal rib chops, cut 1 inch thick
 (about 8 ounces *each*)

Stir together lime juice, honey, ginger and lime peel in small bowl. Place veal rib chops in glass dish just large enough to hold chops. Brush lime mixture liberally over both sides of chops. Refrigerate, covered, 30 minutes while preparing coals. Remove chops from dish; brush with any remaining lime mixture. Place chops on grid over medium coals. Grill 12 to 14 minutes for medium (160°F) or to desired doneness, turning once. (Or, broil 4 to 5 inches from heat source 5 to 6 minutes per side for medium or to desired doneness, turning once.) *Makes 4 servings*

Prep time: 10 minutes
Cook time: 12 to 14 minutes

Nutrients per Serving:

Calories:	186	Cholesterol:	97 mg
Total Fat:	6 g	Sodium:	84 mg

Favorite recipe from **National Cattlemen's Beef Association**

Honey-Citrus Glazed Veal Chop

Veal Parmesan

¼ cup egg substitute or 1 large egg
1 large egg white
1 tablespoon water
¾ cup seasoned dry bread crumbs
¼ cup (1 ounce) shredded ALPINE LACE® Fat Free Pasteurized Process Skim Milk Cheese Product—For Parmesan Lovers
6 veal cutlets (3 ounces *each*), pounded thin
2 tablespoons unsalted butter substitute, divided
½ cup chopped yellow onion
2 teaspoons minced garlic
1 can (28 ounces) crushed tomatoes, undrained
½ cup slivered fresh basil leaves
½ teaspoon freshly ground black pepper
2 cups (8 ounces) shredded ALPINE LACE® Reduced Fat Mozzarella Cheese
¼ cup finely chopped fresh parsley

1. Preheat the oven to 425°F. Spray a 13×9-inch baking dish and a large nonstick skillet with nonstick cooking spray.

2. In a pie plate, whisk the egg substitute (or the whole egg) with the egg white and water until foamy. On a separate plate, toss the bread crumbs with the Parmesan. Dip the veal into the egg mixture, letting the excess drip off, then coat with the bread crumb mixture.

3. In the skillet, melt 1 tablespoon of the butter over medium-high heat. Sauté the veal for 2 minutes on each side or until golden brown, turning once. Using a slotted spatula, transfer to a plate.

4. In the same skillet, melt the remaining tablespoon of butter; add the onion and garlic and sauté 5 minutes. Stir in the tomatoes and their juices, the basil and pepper. Lower the heat; simmer, uncovered, for 5 minutes.

5. Spread half of the sauce in the baking dish. Top with the veal, then the remaining sauce and the mozzarella. Bake, uncovered, 10 minutes or until bubbly. Sprinkle with the parsley and serve hot.   *Makes 6 servings*

Mushroom-Stuffed Veal Breast

4 teaspoons olive oil, divided
1½ cups chopped mushrooms
½ cup finely chopped red bell pepper
2 cloves garlic, minced
½ teaspoon dried rosemary, crushed
1 (2½- to 3-pound) boneless veal
    breast
½ teaspoon salt
⅓ cup *each* marsala and water

Heat 2 teaspoons oil in 10-inch nonstick skillet over medium heat until hot. Add mushrooms, bell pepper and garlic; cook and stir about 5 minutes or just until mushrooms are tender. Stir in rosemary. Remove from heat; cool. Unroll boneless veal breast; trim excess surface fat. Sprinkle evenly with salt. Spread cooled mushroom mixture evenly over surface. Roll up veal; tie securely with string. Heat remaining 2 teaspoons oil in Dutch oven over medium heat until hot. Add veal; cook until browned on all sides. Add marsala and water. Cover and simmer over low heat 1 hour and 30 minutes to 1 hour and 45 minutes until veal is tender. Transfer veal to platter; keep warm. Skim fat from pan juices, if necessary. Cook over high heat until reduced by one third. Slice veal; discard strings. Spoon pan juices over each serving.

Makes 8 to 10 servings

Prep time: 20 minutes
Cook time: 1 hour and 45 minutes to 2 hours

Favorite recipe from **National Cattlemen's Beef Association**

Pork Chops with Apples and Stuffing

4 pork chops, ½ inch thick
    Salt and black pepper
1 tablespoon oil
2 medium apples, cored, cut into
    8 wedges
1 cup apple juice
2 cups STOVE TOP® Cornbread
    Stuffing Mix in the Canister
¼ cup chopped pecans

SPRINKLE pork chops with salt and pepper. Heat oil in large skillet on medium-high heat. Add pork and apples; cook until pork is browned on both sides.

STIR in apple juice. Bring to a boil. Reduce heat to low; cover and simmer 8 minutes or until pork is cooked through. Remove pork from skillet.

STIR stuffing mix and pecans into skillet. Return pork to skillet; cover. Remove from heat. Let stand 5 minutes.

Makes 4 servings

Prep time: 10 minutes
Cook time: 20 minutes

Mushroom-Stuffed Veal Breast

Pork Chops in Creamy Garlic Sauce

1 cup fat-free reduced-sodium chicken broth
¼ cup cloves garlic, peeled and crushed (about 12 to 15)
½ teaspoon olive oil
4 boneless pork loin chops, about ¼ inch thick each
1 tablespoon minced fresh parsley
½ teaspoon tarragon
¼ teaspoon salt
¼ teaspoon black pepper
2 tablespoons water
1 tablespoon all-purpose flour
1 tablespoon dry sherry
2 cups cooked white rice

1. Place broth and garlic in small saucepan. Bring to a boil over high heat. Cover; reduce heat to low. Simmer 25 to 30 minutes or until garlic mashes easily with fork. Set aside to cool. Purée in blender or food processor until smooth.

2. Heat olive oil in large nonstick skillet over medium-high heat. Add pork; cook 1 to 1½ minutes on each side or until browned. Pour garlic purée into skillet. Sprinkle with parsley, tarragon, salt and pepper. Bring to a boil; cover. Reduce heat to low; simmer 10 to 15 minutes or until pork is juicy and barely pink in center. Remove pork from skillet; keep warm.

3. Combine water and flour in small cup. Slowly pour flour mixture into skillet; bring to a boil. Cook and stir until mixture thickens. Stir in sherry. Pour sauce over pork and rice. Garnish as desired.

Makes 4 servings

Italian Pork Cutlets

1 teaspoon CRISCO® Vegetable Oil
6 lean, boneless, center-cut pork loin slices (4 ounces *each*), ¾ inch thick
1 can (8 ounces) tomato sauce
1½ cups sliced fresh mushrooms
1 small green bell pepper, cut into strips
½ cup sliced green onions with tops
1 teaspoon Italian herb seasoning
½ teaspoon salt
⅛ teaspoon black pepper
¼ cup water
1 teaspoon cornstarch
½ cup (2 ounces) shredded low moisture part-skim mozzarella cheese
2⅔ cups hot cooked rice (cooked without salt or fat)

1. Heat Crisco® Oil in large skillet over medium heat. Add meat. Cook until browned on both sides.

2. Add tomato sauce, mushrooms, green pepper, onions, Italian herb seasoning, salt and black pepper. Reduce heat to low. Cover. Simmer 30 minutes or until meat is tender.

3. Combine water and cornstarch in small bowl. Stir until well blended. Add to juices in skillet. Cook and stir until thickened.

4. Sprinkle cheese over meat mixture. Cover. Heat until cheese melts. Serve with rice.

Makes 6 servings

Pork Chops in Creamy Garlic Sauce

Pork-Stuffed Peppers

3 large green bell peppers
¼ cup raisins
1 pound ground pork
½ cup chopped onion
½ cup chopped carrot
½ cup chopped celery
¼ teaspoon salt
1 cup cooked brown rice
2 tablespoons sunflower seeds
½ cup plain yogurt

Remove tops, seeds and membranes from bell peppers. Cut in half lengthwise. Cook in boiling salted water 5 minutes; drain.

Soak raisins in water 10 to 15 minutes; drain and set aside. Combine pork, onion, carrot, celery and salt in medium skillet. Cook over low heat until pork is done and vegetables are tender, stirring occasionally. Drain thoroughly. Add rice, sunflower seeds, yogurt and raisins; mix well. Spoon mixture into bell peppers. Place in 12×8×2-inch baking dish. Bake at 350°F 30 to 35 minutes or until heated through. *Makes 6 servings*

Prep time: 20 minutes
Cook time: 30 minutes

Favorite recipe from **National Pork Producers Council**

Southwest Pork and Dressing

1 pound boneless pork, cut into
    1-inch strips
2 teaspoons chili powder
¼ cup margarine or butter
½ cup diagonally sliced green onions
1½ cups water
1 cup frozen sweet corn, thawed
1 can (4 ounces) chopped green
    chilies, drained
3 cups STOVE TOP® Cornbread
    Stuffing Mix in the Canister
1¼ cups (5 ounces) shredded Monterey
    Jack cheese, divided

TOSS meat with chili powder. Melt margarine in large skillet on medium-high heat. Add pork and onions; cook and stir until pork is browned.

STIR in water, corn and chilies. Bring to a boil. Stir in stuffing mix and ¾ cup of the cheese. Remove from heat. Sprinkle with remaining ½ cup cheese. Cover. Let stand 5 minutes. *Makes 4 to 6 servings*

Prep time: 10 minutes
Cook time: 15 minutes

Potato and Pork Frittata

12 ounces (about 3 cups) frozen hash
 brown potatoes
1 teaspoon Cajun seasoning
4 egg whites
2 whole eggs
¼ cup low-fat (1%) milk
1 teaspoon dry mustard
¼ teaspoon coarsely ground black
 pepper
10 ounces (about 3 cups) frozen
 stir-fry vegetables
⅓ cup water
¾ cup chopped cooked lean pork
½ cup (2 ounces) shredded Cheddar
 cheese

1. Preheat oven to 400°F. Spray baking sheet with nonstick cooking spray. Spread potatoes on baking sheet; sprinkle with Cajun seasoning. Bake 15 minutes or until hot. Remove from oven. *Reduce oven temperature to 350°F.*

2. Beat egg whites, eggs, milk, mustard and pepper in small bowl. Place vegetables and water in medium nonstick skillet. Cook over medium heat 5 minutes or until vegetables are crisp-tender; drain.

3. Add pork and potatoes to vegetables in skillet; stir lightly. Add egg mixture. Sprinkle with cheese. Cook over medium-low heat 5 minutes. Place skillet in 350°F oven; bake 5 minutes or until egg mixture is set and cheese is melted. *Makes 4 servings*

Potato and Pork Frittata

Fruited Boneless Pork Loin

1 cup pitted prunes
1 cup dried apricots
1 (3-pound) boneless pork loin roast
1 clove garlic, cut into thin strips
3 tablespoons FILIPPO BERIO® Olive
    Oil, divided
  Salt and freshly ground black
    pepper
2 onions, each cut into 6 wedges
2 tart apples (such as Granny Smith),
    peeled, cored and each cut into
    8 wedges
8 fresh sage leaves, chopped*
1 tablespoon lime or lemon juice
1 cup plus 2 tablespoons chicken
    broth, divided
3 tablespoons all-purpose flour
½ cup reserved prune/apricot liquid
¼ cup Madeira wine

*Omit sage if fresh is unavailable. Do not substitute
dried sage leaves.

Cover prunes and apricots with cold water;
soak at least 2 hours or overnight. Drain,
reserving liquid. Preheat oven to 400°F. With
tip of sharp knife, score pork at 1-inch
intervals. Press garlic into cuts. Place pork in
large shallow roasting pan; insert meat
thermometer into center of thickest part of
roast. Drizzle with 2 tablespoons olive oil;
season with salt and pepper. Roast 1 hour.
Add onions, apples and sage to fruit mixture.
Drizzle with lime juice. Spoon around pork
in roasting pan; baste pork with juices and
remaining 1 tablespoon olive oil. Pour 2
tablespoons broth over pork. Roast 30 to 40
minutes or until meat thermometer registers
160°F turning and basting fruit mixture

frequently with juices. Transfer pork to warm
serving platter. Surround with fruit mixture;
keep warm. Pour drippings from roasting
pan into measuring cup; skim off fat. Return
juices to roasting pan. In roasting pan over
medium heat, gradually stir flour into juices
until smooth. Cook and stir 1 minute. Add
remaining 1 cup broth, ½ cup reserved liquid
and Madeira. Bring to a boil, stirring
frequently. Reduce heat to low; simmer
5 minutes. Serve hot with pork and fruit
mixture. Carve pork into thin slices.

Makes 4 to 6 servings

Shredded Pork Tacos

1 cup chopped onion
1 clove garlic, minced
3 cups shredded cooked roast pork
1 tablespoon diced jalapeño pepper
12 small flour tortillas, warmed
3 cups shredded lettuce
2 cups diced tomatoes
¾ cup (3 ounces) shredded Cheddar
    cheese

In medium nonstick skillet, cook and stir
onion and garlic over medium heat 5 minutes
until soft and translucent. Stir in cooked
pork; heat thoroughly. Stir in jalapeño
pepper. On each tortilla, spoon ¼ cup
shredded pork mixture, lettuce, tomatoes,
cheese and top with salsa, if desired.

Makes 6 servings

Favorite recipe from **National Pork
Producers Council**

Fruited Boneless Pork Loin

Caribbean Jerk-Style Pork

Nutrients per Serving:

Calories:	282	Cholesterol:	79 mg
Total Fat:	5 g	Sodium:	111 mg

¾ cup DOLE® Pineapple Juice or
    Pineapple Orange Juice, divided
1 tablespoon prepared yellow
    mustard
1 teaspoon dried thyme leaves,
    crushed
¼ teaspoon crushed red pepper
12 ounces boneless pork loin chops or
    chicken breasts, cut into strips
½ cup DOLE® Golden or Seedless
    Raisins
½ cup sliced DOLE® Green Onions
2 medium firm DOLE® Bananas, cut
    diagonally into ¼-inch slices
    Hot cooked rice or noodles
    (optional)

• Stir together ½ cup juice, mustard, thyme and red pepper in small bowl; set aside.

• Place pork in large, nonstick skillet sprayed with vegetable cooking spray. Cook and stir pork over medium-high heat 3 to 5 minutes or until pork is no longer pink. Remove pork from skillet.

• Add remaining ¼ cup juice to skillet; stir in raisins and green onions. Cook and stir 1 minute.

• Stir in pork and reserved mustard mixture; cover and cook 2 minutes or until heated through. Stir in bananas. Serve over hot rice.
Makes 4 servings

Prep time: 10 minutes
Cook time: 10 minutes

Vegetable Pork Stir-Fry

¾ pound pork tenderloin
1 tablespoon vegetable oil
1½ cups (about 6 ounces) sliced fresh
    mushrooms
1 large green bell pepper, cut into
    strips
1 zucchini, thinly sliced
2 ribs celery, cut into diagonal slices
1 cup thinly sliced carrots
1 clove garlic, minced
1 cup chicken broth
2 tablespoons reduced-sodium soy
    sauce
1½ tablespoons cornstarch
3 cups hot cooked rice

Slice pork across the grain into ⅛-inch strips. Brown pork strips in oil in large skillet over medium-high heat. Push meat to side of skillet. Add mushrooms, bell pepper, zucchini, celery, carrots and garlic; stir-fry about 3 minutes. Combine broth, soy sauce and cornstarch. Add to skillet and cook, stirring, until thickened; cook 1 minute longer. Serve over rice. *Makes 6 servings*

Nutrients per Serving:

Calories:	257	Cholesterol:	37 mg
Total Fat:	4 g	Sodium:	732 mg

Favorite recipe from **USA Rice Federation**

Vegetable Pork Stir-Fry

Beef & Broccoli Pepper Steak

1 tablespoon margarine or butter
1 pound well-trimmed top round steak, cut into thin strips
1 package (6.8 ounces) RICE-A-RONI® Beef Flavor
2 cups broccoli florets
1 small onion, thinly sliced
½ cup red or green bell pepper strips

1. In large skillet, melt margarine over medium heat. Add meat; sauté just until browned.

2. Remove from skillet; set aside. Keep warm.

3. In same skillet, prepare Rice-A-Roni® Mix as package directs; simmer 10 minutes. Add meat and remaining ingredients; simmer an additional 10 minutes or until most of liquid is absorbed and vegetables are crisp-tender.

Makes 4 servings

Beef & Broccoli Pepper Steak

Herb-Crusted Roast Beef and Potatoes

1 (4½-pound) eye of round or sirloin
    tip beef roast
¾ cup plus 2 tablespoons FILIPPO
    BERIO® Olive Oil, divided
    Salt and freshly ground black
    pepper
2 tablespoons paprika
2 pounds small red skin potatoes, cut
    into halves
1 cup dry bread crumbs
1 teaspoon dried thyme leaves
1 teaspoon dried rosemary
½ teaspoon salt
¼ teaspoon freshly ground black
    pepper

Preheat oven to 325°F. Brush roast with
2 tablespoons olive oil. Season to taste with
salt and pepper. Place in large roasting pan;
insert meat thermometer into center of
thickest part of roast. Roast 45 minutes.

Meanwhile, in large bowl, combine ½ cup
olive oil and paprika. Add potatoes; toss until
lightly coated. In small bowl, combine bread
crumbs, thyme, rosemary, ½ teaspoon salt,
¼ teaspoon pepper and remaining ¼ cup
olive oil.

Carefully remove roast from oven. Place
potatoes around roast. Press bread crumb
mixture onto top of roast to form crust.
Sprinkle any remaining bread crumb mixture
over potatoes. Roast an additional 40 to
45 minutes or until meat thermometer
registers 145°F for medium-rare or until
desired doneness is reached. Transfer roast to
carving board; tent with foil. Let stand 5 to
10 minutes before carving. Cut into ¼-inch-
thick slices. Serve immediately with
potatoes, spooning any bread crumb mixture
from roasting pan onto meat.

Makes 8 servings

Delicious Ground Beef Medley

1 pound ground beef
½ cup chopped onion
¼ cup chopped celery
2 cups uncooked elbow macaroni
1 can (10¾ ounces) condensed cream
    of chicken soup
1 can (10¾ ounces) condensed cream
    of mushroom soup
⅔ cup milk
½ teaspoon salt
    Dash of black pepper
1 can (16 ounces) corn, drained
½ cup chopped green bell pepper

1. Brown ground beef with onion and celery.
Drain.

2. Cook macaroni according to package
directions. Drain.

3. In 2½-quart casserole dish, combine soups
with milk, salt and black pepper. Add beef
mixture, macaroni, corn and bell pepper.
Bake at 350°F for 30 minutes.

Makes 8 servings

Favorite recipe from **North Dakota Beef
Commission**

Beef Pot Roast

3 pounds beef eye of round roast
1 can (14 ounces) fat-free reduced-
  sodium beef broth
2 cloves garlic
1 teaspoon herbes de Provence *or*
  ¼ teaspoon *each* rosemary,
  thyme, sage and savory
4 small turnips, peeled and cut into
  wedges
10 ounces fresh Brussels sprouts,
  trimmed
20 baby carrots
  4 ounces pearl onions, outer skins
  removed
2 teaspoons cornstarch mixed with
  1 tablespoon water

1. Heat large nonstick skillet over medium-high heat. Place roast, fat side down, in skillet. Cook until evenly browned. Remove roast from skillet; place in Dutch oven.

2. Pour broth into Dutch oven; bring to a boil over high heat. Add garlic and herbes de Provence. Cover tightly. Reduce heat; cook 1½ hours.

3. Add turnips, Brussels sprouts, carrots and onions to Dutch oven. Cover; cook 25 to 30 minutes or until vegetables are tender. Remove meat and vegetables from Dutch oven. Arrange on serving platter; cover with foil to keep warm.

4. Strain broth; return to Dutch oven. Stir blended cornstarch mixture into broth. Bring to a boil over medium-high heat; cook and stir 1 minute or until thick and bubbly. Serve immediately with pot roast and vegetables. Garnish as desired.   *Makes 6 servings*

Old-Fashioned Beef Pot Pie

1 pound ground beef
1 can (11 ounces) condensed beef
  with vegetables and barley soup
1 package (10 ounces) frozen peas
  and carrots, thawed and drained
½ cup water
½ teaspoon seasoned salt
⅛ teaspoon garlic powder
⅛ teaspoon ground black pepper
1 cup (4 ounces) shredded Cheddar
  cheese, divided
1⅓ cups (2.8-ounce can) FRENCH'S®
  French Fried Onions, divided
1 package (7.5 ounces) refrigerated
  biscuits

Preheat oven to 350°F. In large skillet, brown ground beef in large chunks; drain. Stir in soup, vegetables, water and seasonings; bring to a boil. Reduce heat and simmer, uncovered, 5 minutes. Remove from heat; stir in ½ *cup* cheese and ⅔ *cup* French Fried Onions.

Pour mixture into 12×8-inch baking dish. Cut each biscuit in half; place, cut side down, around edge of casserole. Bake, uncovered, 15 to 20 minutes or until biscuits are done. Top with remaining ½ *cup* cheese and ⅔ *cup* onions; bake, uncovered, 5 minutes or until onions are golden brown.
          Makes 4 to 6 servings

Beef Pot Roast

Grilled Beef with Two Sauces

1 (1-pound) boneless beef sirloin steak

ROASTED GARLIC SAUCE
¾ **cup mayonnaise***
¼ **cup Roasted Garlic Purée (page 197)**
¼ **cup GREY POUPON® Dijon Mustard**
2 **tablespoons chopped parsley**
1 **tablespoon lemon juice**

SUN–DRIED TOMATO SAUCE
¾ **cup chopped roasted red peppers**
½ **cup sun-dried tomatoes, chopped****
3 **tablespoons GREY POUPON® Dijon Mustard**
2 **tablespoons chopped parsley**
2 **to 3 tablespoons olive oil**
¼ **teaspoon crushed red pepper flakes**

*Low-fat mayonnaise may be substituted for regular mayonnaise.

**If sun-dried tomatoes are very dry, soften in warm water for 15 minutes. Drain before using.

Grill beef over medium heat to desired doneness and chill.

For Roasted Garlic Sauce, in medium bowl, blend all ingredients. Chill at least 1 hour to blend flavors.

For Sun-Dried Tomato Sauce, in medium bowl, combine roasted red peppers, sun-dried tomatoes, mustard and parsley. Slowly add oil as needed to bind. Add red pepper flakes. Chill at least 1 hour to blend flavors. Bring to room temperature before serving.

Grilled Beef with Two Sauces

To serve, slice beef and arrange on 4 serving plates. Spoon about 2 tablespoons of each sauce onto each plate. Serve with sliced tomatoes and cooled steamed asparagus; garnish as desired.　　*Makes 4 servings*

Roasted Garlic Purée
Remove excess papery outside of 1 head garlic and separate into cloves. Place in 8×8×2-inch baking pan. Add 2 to 3 tablespoons olive oil and 1 cup chicken broth. Bake at 350°F for 25 to 30 minutes or until garlic is soft. Cool and squeeze garlic pulp from skins; discard liquid in pan.

Italian Beef and Pasta

1¼ pounds boneless beef round steak
　　(full cut) or boneless beef chuck
　　steak, cut ½ inch thick
1 tablespoon vegetable oil
1 medium onion, chopped
1 large clove garlic, minced
1 teaspoon Italian seasoning
1 can (14½ ounces) Italian-style
　　stewed tomatoes, undrained,
　　chopped
1 can (13¾ ounces) beef broth
¼ cup red wine
½ pound mushrooms, halved
1½ cups (4 ounces) uncooked
　　mostaccioli
2 tablespoons grated Parmesan
　　cheese
1 tablespoon chopped parsley
　　(optional)

Cut steak into 1-inch pieces. Heat oil in large skillet or Dutch oven over medium heat until hot. Add half of steak; cook and stir until browned. Pour off any drippings; discard. Set cooked steak aside. Repeat with remaining steak. Return steak to skillet. Stir in onion, garlic and Italian seasoning; cook 2 minutes. Add tomatoes, broth and wine. Bring to a boil. Reduce heat to low; cover tightly and cook on top of range or in 300°F oven 1½ hours, or until meat is tender. Add mushrooms and mostaccioli, stirring to separate pasta. Cook, covered, 20 minutes. Remove cover; continue cooking 10 minutes or until mostaccioli is tender. Transfer to deep serving dish; stir in Parmesan cheese. Sprinkle with parsley, if desired.

Makes 4 servings

Favorite recipe from **National Cattlemen's Beef Association**

Spicy Beef Stir-Fry

1 boneless beef sirloin, top loin or tenderloin steak, cut 1 inch thick (about 1 pound)
5 tablespoons low-sodium teriyaki sauce, divided
1 teaspoon hot chili oil *or* ½ teaspoon crushed Szechuan peppercorns
1 tablespoon cornstarch
1 tablespoon dry sherry
2 tablespoons peanut oil or vegetable oil, divided
2 cups sliced fresh mushrooms
1 small onion, cut into 1-inch pieces
Hot cooked angel hair pasta

Cut beef across grain into ⅛-inch-thick slices; cut each slice into 1½-inch pieces. Combine 1 tablespoon teriyaki sauce and chili oil in medium bowl. Add beef and toss to coat; set aside.

Combine cornstarch, remaining 4 tablespoons teriyaki sauce and sherry in small bowl; stir until smooth. Set aside.

Heat wok over high heat until hot. Drizzle 1 tablespoon peanut oil into wok and heat 30 seconds. Add half of beef mixture; stir-fry 2 minutes or until beef is barely pink in center. Remove beef to large bowl. Repeat with remaining beef mixture. Reduce heat to medium-high.

Add remaining 1 tablespoon peanut oil to wok and heat 30 seconds. Add mushrooms and onion; stir-fry 5 minutes or until vegetables are tender.

Stir cornstarch mixture; add to wok. Stir-fry 30 seconds or until sauce thickens. Return beef to wok; cook until heated through. Serve over pasta.   *Makes 4 servings*

Beef with Snow Peas & Baby Corn

¾ pound ground beef
1 clove garlic, minced
1 teaspoon vegetable oil
6 ounces snow peas, halved lengthwise
1 red bell pepper, cut into strips
1 can (15 ounces) baby corn, drained, rinsed
1 tablespoon soy sauce
1 teaspoon sesame oil
Salt and freshly ground black pepper
2 cups cooked rice

Brown ground beef in wok or large skillet. Drain. Add garlic; cook until tender. Set aside. Wipe out wok with paper towel.

Heat vegetable oil in wok over medium-high heat. Add snow peas and bell pepper; stir-fry 2 to 3 minutes or until vegetables are crisp-tender. Stir in ground beef mixture, baby corn, soy sauce and sesame oil. Season with salt and black pepper to taste. Serve over rice.   *Makes 4 servings*

Spicy Beef Stir-Fry

Teriyaki Beef

¾ **pound sirloin tip steak, cut into thin
    strips**
½ **cup teriyaki sauce**
¼ **cup water**
1 **tablespoon cornstarch**
1 **teaspoon sugar**
1 **bag (16 ounces) BIRDS EYE® frozen
    Farm Fresh Mixtures Broccoli,
    Carrots and Water Chestnuts**

• Spray large skillet with nonstick cooking
spray; cook beef strips over medium-high
heat 7 to 8 minutes, stirring occasionally.

• Combine teriyaki sauce, water, cornstarch
and sugar; mix well.

• Add teriyaki sauce mixture and vegetables
to beef. Bring to a boil; quickly reduce heat
to medium.

• Cook 7 to 10 minutes or until broccoli is
heated through, stirring occasionally.

Makes 4 to 6 servings

Prep time: 5 to 10 minutes
Cook time: 20 minutes

Serving Suggestion: Serve over hot cooked
rice.

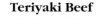

Teriyaki Beef

Fix-It-Fast Corned Beef & Cabbage

**1 small head cabbage (about
1½ pounds), cored and cut into
6 wedges
1 can (12 ounces) corned beef, sliced,
or ½ pound sliced deli corned
beef
1 can (16 ounces) sliced potatoes,
drained
1 can (14 ounces) sliced carrots,
drained
1⅓ cups (2.8-ounce can) FRENCH'S®
French Fried Onions, divided
1 can (10¾ ounces) condensed cream
of celery soup
¾ cup water**

Preheat oven to 375°F. Arrange cabbage
wedges and corned beef slices alternately
down center of 13×9-inch baking dish. Place
potatoes, carrots and ⅔ *cup* French Fried
Onions along sides of dish. In small bowl,
combine soup and water; pour over meat and
vegetables. Bake, covered, at 375°F 40
minutes or until cabbage is tender. Top with
remaining ⅔ *cup* onions; bake, uncovered, 3
minutes or until onions are golden brown.

Makes 4 to 6 servings

Microwave Directions: Arrange cabbage
wedges down center of 12×8-inch
microwave-safe dish; add 2 tablespoons
water. Cook, covered, on HIGH 10 to 12
minutes or until fork-tender. Rotate dish
halfway through cooking time. Drain.
Arrange cabbage, corned beef, potatoes,
carrots and ⅔ *cup* onions in dish as directed.
Reduce water to ¼ cup. In small bowl,
combine soup and water; pour over meat and
vegetables. Cook, covered, 8 to 10 minutes or
until vegetables are heated through. Rotate
dish halfway through cooking time. Top with
remaining ⅔ *cup* onions; cook, uncovered,
1 minute. Let stand 5 minutes.

Quick Beef Stroganoff

**1 pound ground beef
2¼ cups water
1 package LIPTON® Noodles &
Sauce–Butter
1 jar (4½ ounces) sliced mushrooms,
drained
2 tablespoons finely chopped
pimiento
⅛ teaspoon garlic powder
½ cup sour cream**

In 10-inch skillet, brown ground beef; drain.
Stir in remaining ingredients *except* sour
cream. Bring to a boil, then simmer, stirring
frequently, 7 minutes or until noodles are
tender. Stir in sour cream; heat through but
do not boil. *Makes about 2 servings*

Microwave Directions: In 2-quart casserole,
cook ground beef at HIGH (100% power) 4 to
6 minutes. Add water, noodles & sauce–butter,
mushrooms, pimiento and garlic powder.
Heat at HIGH 10 minutes or until noodles are
tender, stirring occasionally. Stir in sour
cream.

PERFECT

POULTRY

Chicken Vesuvio

1 whole chicken (about
   3¾ pounds)
¼ cup olive oil
3 tablespoons lemon juice

4 cloves garlic, minced
3 large baking potatoes
Salt and lemon pepper
   seasoning

Preheat oven to 375°F. Place chicken, breast side down, on rack in large shallow roasting pan. Combine olive oil, lemon juice and garlic; brush half of oil mixture over chicken. Set aside remaining oil mixture. Roast chicken, uncovered, 30 minutes.

Meanwhile, peel potatoes; cut lengthwise into quarters. Turn chicken, breast side up. Arrange potatoes around chicken in roasting pan. Brush chicken and potatoes with remaining oil mixture; sprinkle with salt and lemon pepper seasoning to taste. Roast chicken and potatoes, basting occasionally with pan juices, 50 minutes or until meat thermometer inserted into thickest part of thigh, not touching bone, registers 180°F and potatoes are tender.

Makes 4 to 6 servings

Chicken Vesuvio

Barbecue Chicken with Cornbread Topper

1½ pounds boneless skinless chicken breasts and thighs, cut into ¾-inch pieces
1 can (15 ounces) red beans, drained and rinsed
1 can (8 ounces) tomato sauce
1 cup chopped green bell pepper
½ cup barbecue sauce
1 envelope (6.5 ounces) cornbread mix
Ingredients for cornbread mix

1. Heat nonstick skillet over medium heat. Add chicken; cook and stir 5 minutes or until cooked through.

2. Combine chicken, beans, tomato sauce, bell pepper and barbecue sauce in 8-inch microwavable ovenproof dish.

3. Preheat oven to 375°F. Loosely cover chicken mixture with plastic wrap or waxed paper. Microwave on MEDIUM-HIGH (70% power) 8 minutes or until heated through, stirring after 4 minutes.

4. While chicken mixture is heating, prepare cornbread mix according to package directions. Spoon batter over chicken mixture. Bake 15 to 18 minutes or until toothpick inserted in center of cornbread layer comes out clean. *Makes 8 servings*

Chicken Breasts Florentine

2 pounds boneless skinless chicken breasts
¼ cup all-purpose flour
2 eggs, well beaten
⅔ cup seasoned dry bread crumbs
1 envelope LIPTON® Recipe Secrets® Golden Onion Soup Mix
1½ cups water
¼ cup dry white wine
1 clove garlic, finely chopped
2 tablespoons finely chopped fresh parsley
⅛ teaspoon black pepper
Hot cooked rice pilaf or white rice
Hot cooked spinach

Microwave Directions: Dip chicken in flour, then eggs, then bread crumbs. In 3-quart microwave-safe casserole, microwave chicken, uncovered, at HIGH (100% power) 4 minutes, rearranging chicken once. Combine golden onion soup mix, water, wine and garlic in small bowl; add to chicken. Microwave, uncovered, at HIGH 5 minutes or until boiling, stirring once. Microwave, uncovered, at MEDIUM (50% power), stirring occasionally, 7 minutes or until chicken is no longer pink in center and sauce is slightly thickened. Stir in parsley and pepper. Let stand, covered, 5 minutes. To serve, arrange chicken over hot rice and spinach; garnish as desired. *Makes about 6 servings*

Barbecue Chicken with Cornbread Topper

Crispy Oven-Baked Chicken

**4 boneless skinless chicken breast
halves (about 4 ounces *each*)**
**¾ cup GUILTLESS GOURMET® Salsa
Nonstick cooking spray**
**1 cup (3.5 ounces) crushed*
GUILTLESS GOURMET® Baked
Tortilla Chips (yellow corn, white
corn or chili & lime)**
**Cherry tomatoes and pineapple
sage leaves (optional)**

**Crush tortilla chips in the original bag or between
two pieces of waxed paper with a rolling pin.*

Wash chicken; pat dry with paper towels.
Place chicken in shallow nonmetal pan or
place in large resealable plastic food storage
bag. Pour salsa over chicken. Cover with foil
or seal bag; marinate in refrigerator 8 hours
or overnight.

Preheat oven to 350°F. Coat baking sheet
with cooking spray. Place crushed chips on
waxed paper. Remove chicken from salsa,
discarding salsa; roll chicken in crushed
chips. Place on prepared baking sheet; bake
45 minutes or until chicken is no longer pink
in center and chips are crisp. Serve hot.
Garnish with tomatoes and sage, if desired.

Makes 4 servings

Nutrients per Serving:

Calories:	237	Cholesterol:	69 mg
Total Fat:	5 g	Sodium:	272 mg

Crispy Oven-Baked Chicken

Country Chicken Pot Pie

1 package (1.8 ounces) white sauce mix
2¼ cups milk
3 cups BIRDS EYE® frozen Mixed Vegetables
2 to 3 cups diced cooked chicken*
1½ cups seasoned croutons**

*No leftover cooked chicken handy? Before beginning recipe, cut 1 pound boneless skinless chicken into 1-inch cubes. Brown chicken in 1 tablespoon butter or margarine in large skillet, then proceed with recipe.

**For a quick homemade touch, substitute 4 bakery-bought biscuits for croutons. Split and add to skillet, cut side down.

• Prepare white sauce mix with milk in large skillet according to package directions.

• Add vegetables and chicken. Bring to boil over medium-high heat; cook 3 minutes or until heated through, stirring occasionally.

• Top with croutons; cover and let stand 5 minutes.   *Makes about 4 servings*

Prep time: 5 minutes
Cook time: 15 minutes

Serving Suggestion: Serve with a green salad.

Country Chicken Dinner

¼ cup milk
2 tablespoons margarine or butter
1 package (4.7 ounces) PASTA RONI® Chicken & Broccoli with Linguine
2 cups frozen mixed broccoli, cauliflower and carrots vegetable medley
2 cups chopped cooked chicken or turkey
1 teaspoon dried basil leaves

1. In round 3-quart microwavable glass casserole, combine 1¾ cups water, milk and margarine. Microwave, uncovered, at HIGH 4 to 5 minutes or until boiling.

2. Gradually add pasta while stirring.

3. Stir in contents of seasoning packet, frozen vegetables, chicken and basil.

4. Microwave, uncovered, at HIGH 14 to 15 minutes, stirring gently after 7 minutes. Sauce will be thin, but will thicken upon standing.

5. Let stand 4 to 5 minutes or until desired consistency. Stir before serving.
Makes 4 servings

Lemon-Garlic Roasted Chicken

1 chicken (3½ to 4 pounds)
   Salt and black pepper
2 tablespoons butter or margarine,
   softened
2 lemons, cut into halves
4 to 6 cloves garlic, peeled and left
   whole
5 to 6 sprigs fresh rosemary
   Garlic Sauce (recipe follows)
   Additional rosemary sprigs and
   lemon wedges

Rinse chicken; pat dry with paper towels. Season with salt and pepper, then rub the skin with butter. Place lemons, garlic and rosemary in cavity of chicken. Tuck wings under back and tie legs together with cotton string.

Arrange medium-low **KINGSFORD**® Briquets on each side of a rectangular metal or foil drip pan. Pour in hot tap water to fill pan half full. Place chicken, breast side up, on grid, directly above the drip pan. Grill chicken, on a covered grill, about 1 hour or until a meat thermometer inserted in the thigh registers 175° to 180°F or until the joints move easily and juices run clear when chicken is pierced. Add a few briquets to both sides of the fire, if necessary, to maintain a constant temperature.

While chicken is cooking, prepare Garlic Sauce. When chicken is done, carefully lift it from the grill to a wide shallow bowl so that all the juices from the cavity run into the bowl. Transfer juices to a small bowl or gravy boat. Carve chicken; serve with Garlic Sauce and cooking juices. Garnish with rosemary sprigs and lemon wedges.

Makes 4 servings

Garlic Sauce

2 tablespoons olive oil
1 large head of garlic, cloves
   separated and peeled
2 (1-inch-wide) strips lemon peel
1 can (14½ ounces) low-salt chicken
   broth
½ cup water
1 sprig each sage and oregano *or* 2 to
   3 sprigs parsley
¼ cup butter, softened

Heat oil in a saucepan; add garlic cloves and lemon peel. Sauté over medium-low heat, stirring frequently, until garlic just starts to brown in a few spots. Add broth, water and herbs; simmer to reduce mixture by about half. Discard herb sprigs and lemon peel. Transfer broth mixture to a blender or food processor; process until smooth. Return garlic purée to the saucepan and whisk in butter over very low heat until smooth. Sauce can be rewarmed before serving.

Makes about 1 cup sauce

Tip: The chicken is delicious served simply with its own juices, but the Garlic Sauce is so good you may want to double the recipe.

Lemon-Garlic Roasted Chicken

Chicken Fajitas

4 boneless, skinless chicken breast
 halves
2 teaspoons ground cumin
1½ teaspoons TABASCO® Pepper Sauce
1 teaspoon chili powder
½ teaspoon salt
 Spicy Tomato Salsa (recipe follows)
 Corn Relish (recipe follows)
8 flour tortillas
1 tablespoon vegetable oil
3 large green onions, cut into 2-inch
 pieces
½ cup shredded Cheddar cheese
½ cup guacamole or sliced avocado
 Sour cream

Cut chicken breasts into ½-inch strips. In
large bowl toss chicken strips with cumin,
TABASCO® Sauce, chili powder and salt; set
aside. Prepare Spicy Tomato Salsa and Corn
Relish. Wrap tortillas in foil; heat in preheated
350°F oven 10 minutes or until warm.
Meanwhile, in large skillet, heat vegetable oil
over medium-high heat. Add chicken
mixture; cook 4 minutes, stirring frequently.
Add green onions; cook 1 minute longer or
until chicken is browned and tender.

To serve, arrange warmed tortillas with
chicken, Spicy Tomato Salsa, Corn Relish,
Cheddar cheese, guacamole and sour cream.
To eat, place chicken in center of each
tortilla; add Salsa, Relish, cheese, guacamole
and sour cream. Fold bottom quarter and
both sides of tortilla to cover filling.

Makes 4 servings

Spicy Tomato Salsa

1 large ripe tomato, diced
1 tablespoon chopped fresh cilantro
1 tablespoon lime juice
¼ teaspoon salt
¼ teaspoon TABASCO® Pepper Sauce

In medium bowl toss tomato, cilantro, lime
juice, salt and TABASCO® Sauce.

Corn Relish

1 can (11 ounces) corn, drained
½ cup diced green bell pepper
1 tablespoon lime juice
¼ teaspoon salt
¼ teaspoon TABASCO® Pepper Sauce

In medium bowl toss corn, bell pepper, lime
juice, salt and TABASCO® Sauce.

Creamy Chicken Broccoli Skillet

½ cup MIRACLE WHIP® Salad Dressing
1 pound boneless skinless chicken
 breasts, cubed
1 package (10 ounces) frozen
 chopped broccoli, thawed *or*
 2 cups fresh broccoli florets
½ pound (8 ounces) VELVEETA®
 Process Cheese Spread, cut up
 Hot cooked MINUTE® Original Rice

HEAT salad dressing in large skillet on
medium heat. Add chicken; cook and stir
about 8 minutes or until cooked through.

STIR in broccoli; heat thoroughly.

ADD process cheese spread. Stir until
thoroughly melted. Serve over rice.

Makes 4 serving

Savory Chicken & Biscuits

2 tablespoons olive or vegetable oil
1 pound boneless skinless chicken
    breasts, cut into 1-inch pieces
    (about 2 cups)
1 medium onion, chopped
1 cup thinly sliced carrots
1 cup thinly sliced celery
1 envelope LIPTON® Recipe Secrets®
    Savory Herb with Garlic Soup
    Mix*
1 cup milk
1 package (10 ounces) refrigerated
    flaky buttermilk biscuits

*Also terrific made with LIPTON® Recipe Secrets®
Golden Onion or Golden Herb with Lemon
Soup Mix.*

Preheat oven to 400°F.

In 12-inch skillet, heat oil over medium-high
heat and cook chicken, stirring occasionally,
5 minutes or until almost done. Stir in onion,
carrots and celery; cook, stirring occasionally,
3 minutes. Stir in savory herb with garlic
soup mix blended with milk. Bring to boiling
point over medium-high heat, stirring
occasionally; cook 1 minute. Turn into lightly
greased 2-quart casserole; arrange biscuits on
top of chicken mixture with edges touching.
Bake 10 minutes or until biscuits are golden
brown.   *Makes about 4 servings*

Menu Suggestion: Serve with a mixed green
salad and LIPTON® Iced Tea.

Savory Chicken & Biscuits

Thai Chicken with Basil

1 small bunch fresh basil
2 cups vegetable oil
6 large shallots, chopped
5 cloves garlic, minced
1 piece fresh ginger (about 1-inch square), cut into very thin strips
1 pound ground chicken or turkey
2 fresh Thai or jalapeño chilies, seeded and cut into thin slices*
2 teaspoons brown sugar
½ teaspoon salt
   Boston lettuce leaves

Chili peppers can sting and irritate the skin; wear rubber gloves when handling peppers and do not touch eyes. Wash hands after handling.

Set aside 8 basil sprigs. Stem remaining basil leaves and cut into ¼-inch-thick strips to equal ½ cup; set aside. Heat oil in wok over medium-high heat until oil registers 375°F on deep-fry thermometer. Add 1 basil sprig** and deep-fry about 15 seconds or until basil is glossy and crisp. Remove fried sprig with slotted spoon to paper towels; drain. Repeat with remaining 7 sprigs, reheating oil between batches.

Let oil cool slightly. Pour off oil, reserving ¼ cup. Return ¼ cup oil to wok and heat over medium-high heat 30 seconds or until hot. Add shallots, garlic and ginger; cook and stir 1 minute. Add chicken and stir-fry about 4 minutes or until lightly browned. Push chicken up side of wok, letting juices remain in bottom.

Continue to cook about 5 to 7 minutes until all juices evaporate. Add chili slices, brown sugar and salt to chicken and cook 1 minute. Stir in reserved basil strips. Remove from heat.

Line serving plate with lettuce. Spoon chicken mixture on top. Garnish as desired. Top with fried basil and serve immediately.
Makes 4 servings

**Use long-handled tongs since oil may splatter.*

Double-Coated Chicken

7 cups KELLOGG'S CORN FLAKES® cereal, crushed to 1¾ cups
1 egg
1 cup skim milk
½ cup all-purpose flour
½ teaspoon salt
¼ teaspoon black pepper
3 pounds broiler-fryer chicken pieces, washed and patted dry
3 tablespoons margarine, melted

1. Measure crushed Kellogg's Corn Flakes® cereal into shallow dish or pan. Set aside.

2. In small mixing bowl, beat egg and milk slightly. Add flour, salt and pepper. Mix until smooth. Dip chicken in batter. Coat in crumbs. Place in single layer, skin side up, in foil-lined, shallow baking pan. Drizzle with margarine.

3. Bake in preheated 350°F oven about 1 hour or until chicken is tender and juices run clear. Do not cover pan or turn chicken while baking.
Makes 6 servings

Thai Chicken with Basil

Walnut Chicken

1 pound boneless skinless chicken
   thighs
1 tablespoon cornstarch
3 tablespoons soy sauce
1 tablespoon rice wine
2 tablespoons minced fresh ginger
2 cloves garlic, minced
¼ to ½ teaspoon crushed red pepper
3 tablespoons vegetable oil
½ cup walnut halves or pieces
1 cup frozen cut green beans, thawed
½ cup sliced water chestnuts
2 green onions with tops, cut into
   1-inch pieces
¼ cup water
   Hot cooked rice

• Rinse chicken and pat dry with paper towels. Cut into 1-inch cubes. Combine cornstarch, soy sauce, wine, ginger, garlic and crushed red pepper in large bowl; stir until smooth. Add chicken; toss. Marinate 10 minutes.

• Heat wok or large skillet over high heat about 1 minute or until hot. Drizzle oil into wok and heat 30 seconds. Add walnuts; stir-fry about 1 minute or until lightly browned. Remove to small bowl. Add chicken mixture to wok; stir-fry about 5 to 7 minutes or until chicken is no longer pink in center. Add green beans, water chestnuts, green onions and water; stir-fry until heated through. Serve over rice. Sprinkle with walnuts.

Makes 4 servings

Chicken Diablo

2 tablespoons fresh lemon juice
1 tablespoon olive oil
2 cloves garlic, crushed
½ to ¾ teaspoon crushed red pepper
½ to ¾ teaspoon ground black pepper
   Salt (optional)
1 package (about 1 pound) PERDUE®
   FIT 'N EASY® Fresh Skinless &
   Boneless Chicken Breasts
1 lemon, sliced

In shallow bowl, combine lemon juice, oil, garlic, peppers and salt, if desired. Add chicken to marinade, turning to coat both sides. Cover and marinate in refrigerator 1 hour or longer.

Preheat broiler. Drain chicken, reserving marinade. Broil 6 to 8 inches from heat source 6 to 8 minutes on each side until cooked through. Meanwhile in small saucepan, bring marinade to a boil. Turn chicken 2 or 3 times during cooking and brush with boiled marinade. To serve, garnish with lemon slices. *Makes 4 servings*

Nutrients per Serving:

Calories:	192	Cholesterol:	82 mg
Total Fat:	5 g	Sodium:	93 mg

Walnut Chicken

Turkey Cottage Pie

¼ cup butter or margarine
¼ cup all-purpose flour
1 envelope LIPTON® Recipe Secrets®
   Golden Onion Soup Mix
2 cups water
2 cups cut-up cooked turkey or
   chicken
1 package (10 ounces) frozen mixed
   vegetables, thawed
1¼ cups shredded Swiss cheese (about
   5 ounces), divided
⅛ teaspoon black pepper
5 cups hot mashed potatoes

Preheat oven to 375°F.

In large saucepan, melt butter and add flour; cook, stirring constantly, 5 minutes or until golden. Stir in golden onion soup mix thoroughly blended with water. Bring to a boil, then simmer 15 minutes or until thickened. Stir in turkey, vegetables, 1 cup cheese and pepper. Turn into lightly greased 2-quart casserole; top with potatoes, then remaining ¼ cup cheese. Bake 30 minutes or until bubbling. *Makes about 8 servings*

Microwave Directions: In 2-quart casserole, heat butter at HIGH (100% power) 1 minute. Stir in flour and heat, uncovered, stirring frequently, 2 minutes. Stir in golden onion soup mix thoroughly blended with water. Heat, uncovered, stirring occasionally, 4 minutes or until thickened. Stir in turkey, vegetables, 1 cup cheese and pepper. Top with potatoes, then remaining ¼ cup cheese. Heat, uncovered, turning casserole occasionally, 5 minutes or until bubbling. Let stand uncovered 5 minutes. For additional color, sprinkle, if desired, with paprika.

Buffalo Turkey Kabobs

⅔ cup HELLMANN'S® or BEST FOODS®
   Real or Light Mayonnaise or Low
   Fat Mayonnaise Dressing, divided
1 teaspoon hot pepper sauce
1½ pounds boneless turkey breast, cut
   into 1-inch cubes
2 red bell peppers or 1 red and
   1 yellow bell pepper, cut into
   1-inch squares
2 medium onions, cut into wedges
¼ cup (1 ounce) crumbled blue cheese
2 tablespoons milk
1 medium stalk celery, minced
1 medium carrot, minced

1. In medium bowl combine ⅓ cup of the mayonnaise and hot pepper sauce. Stir in turkey. Let stand at room temperature 20 minutes.

2. On 6 skewers, alternately thread turkey, bell peppers and onions. Grill or broil 5 inches from heat, brushing with remaining mayonnaise mixture and turning frequently, 12 to 15 minutes.

3. Meanwhile, in small bowl blend remaining ⅓ cup mayonnaise with the blue cheese and milk. Stir in celery and carrot. Serve with kabobs. *Makes 6 servings*

Turkey Cottage Pie

Turkey Chili with Black Beans

1 pound ground turkey breast
1 can (about 14½ ounces) reduced-
    sodium chicken broth
1 large onion, finely chopped
1 green bell pepper, seeded and diced
2 teaspoons chili powder
½ teaspoon ground allspice
¼ teaspoon ground cinnamon
¼ teaspoon paprika
1 can (15 ounces) black beans, rinsed
    and drained
1 can (14 ounces) crushed tomatoes
    in tomato purée, undrained
2 teaspoons apple cider vinegar

1. Heat large nonstick skillet over high heat. Add turkey, chicken broth, onion and bell pepper. Cook and stir, breaking up turkey. Cook until turkey is no longer pink.

2. Add chili powder, allspice, cinnamon and paprika. Reduce heat to medium-low; simmer 10 minutes. Add black beans, tomatoes and vinegar; bring to a boil.

3. Reduce heat to low; simmer 20 to 25 minutes or until thickened to desired consistency. Garnish as desired.

Makes 4 servings

Turkey Chili with Black Beans

Turkey Parmesan

²/₃ cup milk
2 tablespoons margarine or butter
2 cups zucchini slices, halved
1 package (5.1 ounces) PASTA RONI®
    Angel Hair Pasta with Parmesan
    Cheese
2 cups cooked turkey strips
1 jar (2 ounces) chopped pimientos,
    drained
2 tablespoons grated Parmesan
    cheese

1. In round 3-quart microwavable glass casserole, combine 1½ cups water, milk, margarine and zucchini. Microwave, uncovered, on HIGH 6 minutes.

2. Stir in pasta, contents of seasoning packet and turkey. Separate pasta with fork, if needed.

3. Microwave, uncovered, on HIGH 7 to 8 minutes, stirring after 2 minutes. Separate pasta with fork, if needed.

4. Sauce will be very thin, but will thicken upon standing. Stir in pimientos and cheese.

5. Let stand 3 to 4 minutes or until desired consistency. Stir before serving.

Makes 4 servings

Turkey Tetrazzini

2 tablespoons cornstarch
1¼ cups skim milk
  ¾ cup turkey broth or chicken
    bouillon
  ½ teaspoon salt
  ½ teaspoon garlic powder
  ⅛ teaspoon black pepper
  2 cups cubed cooked turkey
  4 ounces spaghetti, cooked according
    to package instructions and
    drained
  1 can (4 ounces) mushrooms, drained
  1 jar (2 ounces) chopped pimiento,
    drained
  ¼ cup grated Parmesan cheese
  2 tablespoons dry white wine
  2 tablespoons sliced almonds

1. Preheat oven to 375°F.

2. In 3-quart saucepan, over medium heat, combine cornstarch, milk, broth, salt, garlic powder and pepper. Bring mixture to boil, stirring constantly. Remove from heat and stir in turkey, spaghetti, mushrooms, pimiento, cheese and wine.

3. Pour turkey mixture into lightly greased 9-inch square casserole. Top with almonds. Bake 25 minutes or until mixture bubbles and top is browned. *Makes 4 servings*

Favorite recipe from **National Turkey Federation**

Soft Turkey Tacos

8 corn tortillas (6 inches)*
1½ teaspoons vegetable oil
1 pound ground turkey
1 small onion, chopped
1 teaspoon dried oregano leaves
Salt and black pepper
Chopped tomatoes
Shredded lettuce
Salsa
Refried beans (optional)

*Substitute 8 (10-inch) flour tortillas for corn tortillas, if desired.

1. Wrap tortillas in foil. Place in cold oven; set temperature to 350°F.

2. Heat oil in large skillet over medium heat. Add turkey and onion; cook until turkey is no longer pink, stirring occasionally. Stir in oregano. Season with salt and pepper to taste. Keep warm.

3. For each taco, fill warm tortilla with turkey mixture; top with tomatoes, lettuce and salsa. Serve with refried beans, if desired.

Makes 4 servings

Note: To warm tortillas in microwave oven, wrap loosely in damp paper towel. Microwave on HIGH (100% power) 2 minutes or until hot.

Manhattan Turkey à la King

8 ounces wide egg noodles
1 pound boneless turkey or chicken, cut into strips
1 tablespoon vegetable oil
1 can (14½ ounces) DEL MONTE® Pasta Style Chunky Tomatoes
1 can (10¾ ounces) condensed cream of celery soup
1 medium onion, chopped
2 stalks celery, sliced
1 cup sliced mushrooms

1. Cook noodles according to package directions; drain. In large skillet, brown turkey in oil over medium-high heat. Season with salt and pepper, if desired.

2. Add remaining ingredients, *except* noodles. Cover and cook over medium heat 5 minutes.

3. Remove cover; cook 5 minutes or until thickened, stirring occasionally. Serve over hot noodles. Garnish with chopped parsley, if desired.
Makes 6 servings

Prep time: 7 minutes
Cook time: 20 minutes

Hint: Cook pasta ahead; rinse and drain. Cover and refrigerate. Just before serving, heat in microwave or dip in boiling water.

Soft Turkey Tacos

Sautéed Turkey Medallions

2 tablespoons chopped shallots
¼ cup margarine or butter, divided
2 cups COLLEGE INN® Lower Sodium
 Chicken Broth
2 tablespoons reduced sodium soy
 sauce
2 tablespoons balsamic vinegar
½ cup GREY POUPON® Dijon Mustard
¼ cup heavy cream
6 (4-ounce) turkey cutlets
1 medium red onion, sliced
6 sun-dried tomatoes, cut into thin
 slices (about ⅓ cup)*
⅓ cup seedless raisins, soaked in
 1 tablespoon cognac for 1 hour

If sun-dried tomatoes are very dry, soften in warm water for 15 minutes. Drain before using.

In medium skillet, over medium heat, sauté shallots in 1 tablespoon margarine until tender. Add chicken broth, soy sauce and vinegar; heat to a boil. Reduce heat; simmer until liquid is reduced by half. Stir in mustard and cream; heat through. Remove from heat; keep warm.

In another skillet, over medium heat, brown turkey on both sides in 2 tablespoons margarine, about 5 to 7 minutes; remove from skillet and keep warm. In same skillet, sauté red onion in remaining margarine until tender. Add tomatoes and drained raisins; cook 2 minutes more. To serve, top turkey cutlets with onion mixture and warm sauce. Garnish as desired.   *Makes 6 servings*

Easy Turkey and Rice

1 bag SUCCESS® Rice
 Vegetable cooking spray
1 tablespoon olive oil
½ pound fresh mushrooms, sliced
¾ cup sliced celery
¼ cup chopped green onion
¼ cup chopped red bell pepper
2 cups chopped cooked turkey
1 can (10¾ ounces) condensed cream
 of chicken soup
½ cup fat-free mayonnaise
½ cup peanuts (optional)

Prepare rice according to package directions.

Preheat oven to 350°F.

Spray 1½-quart casserole with cooking spray; set aside. Heat oil in large skillet over medium heat. Add vegetables; cook and stir until crisp-tender. Add rice and all remaining ingredients *except* peanuts; mix lightly. Spoon into prepared casserole. Bake until thoroughly heated, about 25 minutes. Sprinkle with peanuts and garnish, if desired.
          Makes 4 servings

Sautéed Turkey Medallion

Plentiful Pizzas

Artichoke Heart, Olive and Goat Cheese Pizza

New York-Style Pizza Crust (page 226)
2 teaspoons olive oil
2 teaspoons minced fresh rosemary leaves *or* 1 teaspoon dried rosemary leaves
3 cloves garlic, minced
½ cup (2 ounces) shredded reduced-fat Monterey Jack cheese, divided

1 jar (14 ounces) water-packed artichoke hearts, drained and cut into quarters
3 oil-packed sun-dried tomatoes, drained and cut into slices
2½ ounces soft ripe goat cheese such as Montrachet, sliced or crumbled
10 kalamata olives, pitted and cut into halves

(continued on page 226)

Artichoke Heart, Olive and Goat Cheese Pizza

(**Artichoke Heart, Olive and Goat Cheese Pizza,** *continued from page 224*)

1. Prepare New York-Style Pizza Crust. Preheat oven to 500°F. Brush surface of prepared crust with olive oil. Sprinkle with rosemary and garlic and brush again to coat with oil. Bake about 4 minutes or until crust begins to turn golden.

2. Sprinkle with ¼ cup Monterey Jack cheese, leaving 1-inch border. Top with artichokes, tomatoes, goat cheese and olives. Sprinkle with remaining ¼ cup Monterey Jack cheese. Return to oven and bake 3 to 4 minutes more or until crust is deep golden and Monterey Jack cheese is melted. Cut into 8 wedges.

Makes 4 servings

New York-Style Pizza Crust

⅔ cup warm water (110° to 115°F)
1 teaspoon sugar
½ of ¼-ounce package rapid-rise yeast
    or active dry yeast
1¾ cups all-purpose or bread flour
½ teaspoon salt
1 tablespoon cornmeal (optional)

1. Combine water and sugar in small bowl; stir to dissolve sugar. Sprinkle yeast on top; stir to combine. Let stand 5 minutes until foamy.

2. Combine flour and salt in large bowl. Stir in yeast mixture. Stir until mixture forms soft dough. Remove dough to lightly floured surface. Knead dough 5 minutes or until smooth and elastic, adding additional flour as needed. Place in bowl coated with nonstick cooking spray. Turn dough in bowl so top is coated with cooking spray; cover with towel. Let rise in warm place 30 minutes or until doubled in bulk.

3. Punch dough down; place on lightly floured surface and knead 2 minutes or until smooth. Pat dough into 7-inch disk. Let rest 2 to 3 minutes. Pat and gently stretch dough from edges until dough seems to not stretch anymore. Let rest 2 to 3 minutes. Continue patting and stretching until dough is 12 to 14 inches in diameter. Spray 12- to 14-inch pizza pan with cooking spray; sprinkle with cornmeal, if desired. Press dough into pan. Follow topping and baking directions for individual recipes.

Makes 1 thin 14-inch crust

Grilled Vegetable Pizza

1 teaspoon salt
2 cups (¼-inch) zucchini slices
10 (¼-inch) eggplant slices
2 tablespoons olive oil
1 (12-inch) BOBOLI® Brand Italian
    Bread Shell
1 cup KRAFT® Shredded Low-Moisture
    Part-Skim Mozzarella Cheese,
    divided
¼ cup (¼-inch) roasted red pepper
    slices
1 tablespoon coarsely chopped fresh
    basil leaves

Preheat grill. Lightly salt zucchini and eggplant. Brush with oil. Grill on both sides until tender. Sprinkle Boboli® Italian bread shell with ½ cup cheese. Top with grilled vegetables, roasted red peppers, basil and remaining ½ cup cheese. Place bread shell on grill 5 inches from coals. Cover and grill for 3 to 4 minutes or until cheese is melted.

Makes 4 to 6 servings

BBQ Beef Pizza

½ pound lean ground beef
1 medium green bell pepper
⅔ cup prepared barbecue sauce
1 (14-inch) prepared pizza crust
3 to 4 onion slices, rings separated
½ (2¼-ounce) can sliced black olives, drained
1 cup (4 ounces) shredded cheese (colby and Monterey Jack mix)

1. Preheat oven to 400°F. Brown ground beef in large skillet over high heat 6 to 8 minutes or until beef is no longer pink. Pour off drippings; remove from heat.

2. Meanwhile, seed bell pepper and slice into ¼-inch-thick rings. Add barbecue sauce to beef in skillet. Place pizza crust on baking pan. Spread beef mixture over pizza crust to within ½ inch of edge. Arrange onion slices and pepper rings over beef. Sprinkle with olives and cheese. Bake 8 minutes or until cheese is melted. Cut into 8 wedges.

Makes 3 to 4 servings

Prep and cook time: 20 minutes

BBQ Beef Pizza

Stir-Fry Chicken Pizza with Wisconsin Mozzarella Cheese

2 skinned, boned chicken breast
    halves, cut into thin julienne
    strips
2 tablespoons plus 2 teaspoons oil,
    divided
2 teaspoons minced ginger
1 red bell pepper, seeded, cut into
    matchstick pieces
4 green onions, cut into 1-inch pieces
2 tablespoons unsalted peanuts
    (optional)
½ teaspoon crushed red pepper flakes
2 tablespoons water
1 tablespoon soy sauce
1 tablespoon lemon juice
2 teaspoons cornstarch
4 pita bread rounds
1 clove garlic, minced
2 cups (8 ounces) shredded Part-Skim
    Wisconsin Mozzarella Cheese

In medium skillet or wok, stir-fry chicken in 1 tablespoon hot oil until tender. Remove from skillet. Heat 1 tablespoon oil in skillet. Add ginger; cook 30 seconds. Add bell pepper, onions, peanuts and crushed red pepper; stir-fry until vegetables are crisp-tender. Combine water, soy sauce, lemon juice and cornstarch. Add chicken and soy sauce mixture to skillet. Stir until thickened. Remove from heat.

Brush one side of each bread round with remaining 2 teaspoons oil; sprinkle with garlic. Toast under broiler. Place ¼ chicken mixture on each bread round; sprinkle each with ½ cup cheese. Broil until cheese is melted. *Makes 4 servings*

Favorite recipe from **Wisconsin Milk Marketing Board**

Chicken-Pesto Pizza

8 ounces chicken tenders, cut into
    bite-sized pieces
1 medium onion, thinly sliced
⅓ cup prepared pesto
3 medium plum tomatoes, thinly
    sliced
1 (14-inch) prepared pizza crust
1 cup (4 ounces) shredded mozzarella
    cheese

1. Preheat oven to 450°F. Coat medium nonstick skillet with nonstick cooking spray; cook and stir chicken over medium heat 2 minutes. Add onion and pesto; cook and stir about 3 minutes or until chicken is cooked through.

2. Arrange tomato slices and chicken mixture on pizza crust to within 1 inch of edge. Sprinkle cheese over topping. Bake 8 minutes or until pizza is hot and cheese is melted and bubbly. *Makes 6 servings*

Prep and cook time: 22 minutes

Chicken-Pesto Pizza

Fresh Tomato Pizza

New York-Style Pizza Crust
   (page 226)
1 to 1¼ pounds ripe tomatoes, cored
1 tablespoon olive oil
3 to 4 cloves garlic, minced
½ cup (2 ounces) shredded Monterey
   Jack cheese or part-skim
   mozzarella cheese
2 tablespoons grated Parmesan
   cheese
Cracked black pepper
10 to 12 fresh basil leaves

1. Prepare New York-Style Pizza Crust.
Preheat oven to 500°F.

2. Slice tomatoes and place between double
layers of paper towels. Press gently to
remove juice.

3. Combine oil and garlic in small bowl.
Brush oil mixture over entire surface of
prepared crust. Pierce surface with fork
12 to 14 times. Sprinkle with Monterey Jack
cheese leaving 1-inch border. Bake 3 to
4 minutes or until crust is light golden and
cheese is melted.

4. Arrange tomato slices over cheese.
Sprinkle with Parmesan cheese and pepper.
Bake 4 to 6 minutes or until crust is dark
golden. Cut into 8 wedges. Top with whole
or slivered basil leaves.   *Makes 4 servings*

Grilled Beef 'n' Vegetable-Topped Pizzas

1 pound ground beef
¾ cup prepared spaghetti sauce
½ cup A.1.® Bold & Spicy Steak Sauce
1 pound frozen bread or pizza dough,
   thawed
2 tablespoons olive oil
2 cups shredded mozzarella cheese
   (8 ounces)
¼ cup chopped tomato
¼ cup sliced green onions
¼ cup sliced ripe olives

In medium skillet, over medium-high heat,
brown ground beef until no longer pink,
stirring to separate; drain. Stir in spaghetti
sauce and steak sauce; cook and stir until
heated through. Keep warm.

Divide dough in half; shape each piece into
8-inch round. Brush one side of each dough
round with oil. Grill pizza dough rounds,
oiled side down, over low heat for 5 to 7
minutes or until dough is firm and brown.
Brush tops of dough rounds with oil; turn
over on grill surface. Top each with half of
beef mixture, cheese, tomato, green onions
and olives. Grill, covered with lid or foil, for
5 to 7 minutes or until bottoms are golden
and cheese melts. Serve immediately.
   Makes 2 (8-inch) pizza rounds

Fresh Tomato Pizza

Sausage Pizza Piena

1 tablespoon olive oil
1 onion, chopped
1 red bell pepper, diced
1 green bell pepper, diced
1 pound turkey sausage, casing removed
1 teaspoon dried marjoram leaves
1 pound thawed frozen bread dough, at room temperature
2 cups (8 ounces) shredded mozzarella cheese
2 eggs, lightly beaten
3 tablespoons FRANK'S® Original REDHOT® Cayenne Pepper Sauce
1 tablespoon milk
Grated Parmesan cheese
Sesame seeds

1. Heat oil in large nonstick skillet. Add onion and bell peppers; cook 5 minutes or until tender. Add sausage and marjoram. Cook and stir 5 minutes or until meat is no longer pink. Drain well; cool.

2. Preheat oven to 375°F. Cut dough in half. Roll half of dough into 14×10-inch rectangle on lightly floured board. (Let dough rest 5 minutes if dough springs back when rolling.) Pat onto bottom and 1 inch up sides of greased 13×9×2-inch baking pan. Roll out remaining half of dough to 13×9-inch rectangle; keep covered.

3. Stir cheese, eggs and RedHot® sauce into sausage mixture; toss to coat evenly. Spoon evenly over bottom dough. Cover sausage mixture with top half of dough. Pinch top and bottom edges of dough to seal. Brush top lightly with milk. Sprinkle with Parmesan cheese and sesame seeds.

4. Bake 25 minutes or until golden and bread sounds hollow when tapped. Let stand 10 minutes. Cut into squares to serve.

Makes 6 to 8 servings

Prep time: 30 minutes
Bake time: 25 minutes

Greek Grilled Pizza Wedges

⅓ cup prepared pizza sauce
¼ cup A.1.® Steak Sauce
4 (6-inch) whole wheat pita breads
2 tablespoons olive oil
4 ounces deli sliced roast beef, coarsely chopped
½ cup chopped tomato
⅓ cup sliced pitted ripe olives
½ cup crumbled feta cheese* (2 ounces)

*¾ cup shredded mozzarella cheese may be substituted.

In small bowl, combine pizza sauce and steak sauce; set aside. Brush both sides of pita bread with oil. Spread sauce mixture on one side of each pita; top with roast beef, tomato, olives and feta cheese.

Grill prepared pita, topping side up, over medium heat for 4 to 5 minutes or until topping is hot and pita is crisp. Cut each pita into 4 wedges to serve.

Makes 8 appetizer servings

Sausage Pizza Piena

Deep Dish All-American Pizza

SAUCE
- 1 pound lean ground beef
- ½ cup chopped onion
- ½ cup chopped green bell pepper
- 1 cup ketchup
- 1 tablespoon Worcestershire sauce
- 1 teaspoon dry mustard
- 1 teaspoon garlic salt
- ¼ teaspoon black pepper

CRUST
- 3 to 3½ cups all-purpose flour, divided
- 1 package RED STAR® Active Dry Yeast or QUICK•RISE™ Yeast
- 1½ teaspoons salt
- 1 cup warm water
- 3 tablespoons oil

TOPPINGS
- 2 medium firm, ripe tomatoes, sliced
- 1 cup sliced fresh mushrooms
- 2 cups (8 ounces) shredded Cheddar cheese

Preheat oven to 425°F.

Cook and stir beef, onion and green bell pepper in skillet until meat is lightly browned; drain if necessary. Add ketchup, Worcestershire sauce, mustard, garlic salt and black pepper. Simmer 15 minutes.

In large mixer bowl, combine 1½ cups flour, yeast and salt; mix well. Add warm water (120° to 130°F) and oil to flour mixture. Blend at low speed until moistened; beat 3 minutes at medium speed. Gradually stir in enough remaining flour to make a firm dough. Knead 3 to 5 minutes on floured surface. Lightly re-flour surface and roll dough into 16-inch circle or 15×11-inch rectangle. Place in greased 14-inch round deep-dish pizza pan or 13×9-inch baking pan, pushing dough halfway up sides of pan. Cover; let rise in warm place about 15 minutes.

Spread sauce over dough. Arrange tomatoes on sauce. Sprinkle with mushrooms and cheese. Bake 20 to 25 minutes until edge is crisp and golden brown. Serve immediately.

Makes 1 (14-inch) round or 1 (13×9-inch) deep-dish pizza

Fresh Vegetable Pizza

- 1 envelope active dry yeast
- 1 teaspoon sugar
- ½ cup warm water
- 3 large cloves CHRISTOPHER RANCH Garlic, divided
- 1¾ cups sifted all-purpose flour, divided
- 1 tablespoon oil
- 1 teaspoon salt, divided
- 3 small firm ripe tomatoes
- 1 cup thinly sliced zucchini
- 1 cup sliced fresh mushrooms
- ¼ cup sliced green onion
- 1½ cups (6 ounces) shredded Monterey Jack cheese, divided
- ½ teaspoon dried basil, crushed
- ½ teaspoon dried Italian herbs
- 2 tablespoons grated Parmesan cheese

Sprinkle yeast and sugar over warm water; let stand 5 minutes to soften. Peel 1 clove garlic; press through garlic press. Add garlic and ¾ cup flour to yeast; beat until smooth. Stir in oil and ½ teaspoon salt. Gradually stir in remaining 1 cup flour to make moderately stiff dough. Turn out onto floured board and knead about 2 minutes until smooth. Place in greased 10-inch pizza pan and press out to cover pan. Let dough stand while preparing remaining ingredients.

Preheat oven to 375°F. Blanch tomatoes in boiling water to cover. Let stand 10 seconds. Lift out and peel off skins. Remove cores and slice tomatoes about ¼ inch thick to measure about 2 cups. Blanch zucchini slices in boiling water; cook 1 minute and drain well. Combine with mushrooms and green onion. Press remaining 2 cloves garlic; add to vegetables and mix well. Sprinkle 1 cup Monterey Jack cheese over dough. Spoon half of vegetable mixture over cheese. Arrange tomato slices on top, overlapping if necessary. Top with remaining vegetable mixture. Sprinkle with herbs, remaining ½ teaspoon salt, remaining ½ cup Monterey Jack cheese and Parmesan cheese. Let stand about 15 minutes until edge of dough springs back when lightly touched. Bake below center of oven about 40 minutes or until edge of crust is nicely browned. Serve warm.

Makes 1 (10-inch) pizza

Shrimp and Feta Mini Pita Pizzas

1 package (7 ounces) mini pita breads
_or_ 24 (2-inch) pita breads
½ cup spaghetti or tomato sauce
¼ cup chopped fresh parsley
2 tablespoons FRANK'S® Original
REDHOT® Cayenne Pepper Sauce
½ teaspoon dried oregano leaves
24 cooked medium shrimp, shelled
and deveined (about 6 ounces)
½ cup (2 ounces) crumbled feta
cheese
½ cup (2 ounces) shredded mozzarella
cheese

1. Preheat oven to 450°F. Line baking sheet with foil. Grease foil. Arrange pitas on prepared baking sheet. Combine spaghetti sauce, parsley, RedHot® sauce and oregano in small bowl. Spoon evenly over pitas.

2. Place 1 shrimp on each pita. Sprinkle evenly with cheeses. Bake 8 to 10 minutes or until heated through. Serve warm.

Makes 6 to 8 servings

Prep time: 20 minutes
Cook time: 8 minutes

Salad Pizza

Whole-Wheat Crust (recipe follows)
¼ cup balsamic vinegar
1 tablespoon Dijon mustard
1 tablespoon minced shallot
1 clove garlic, minced
1 teaspoon sugar
½ teaspoon dried basil leaves
½ teaspoon dried oregano leaves
½ teaspoon black pepper
2 tablespoons olive oil
¾ cup (3 ounces) reduced-fat part-skim mozzarella cheese or reduced-fat Swiss cheese
2 tablespoons grated Parmesan cheese
4 cups assorted gourmet mixed salad greens, washed and torn
½ cup cherry tomato halves
½ cup sliced red onion
¼ cup chopped yellow bell pepper

Preheat oven to 450°F. Prepare Whole-Wheat Crust, baking 10 to 12 minutes.

Combine balsamic vinegar, mustard, shallot, garlic, sugar, basil, oregano and black pepper in small bowl; whisk to combine. Gradually whisk in olive oil.

Sprinkle cheeses on prepared crust. Bake 10 to 15 minutes or until crust is golden brown and cheese is melted.

Meanwhile, combine salad greens, tomatoes, onion and bell pepper in large bowl. Pour vinegar mixture over top; toss to combine.

Remove crust from oven and top with salad mixture. Cut into 8 wedges; serve immediately. *Makes 8 servings*

Whole-Wheat Crust

1¼ cups warm water (110° to 115°F)
2 tablespoons honey or sugar
1 package (¼ ounce) active dry yeast
2 to 2½ cups all-purpose flour, divided
1 cup whole-wheat flour
¼ teaspoon salt (optional)
1 tablespoon cornmeal

Combine water and honey in small bowl; stir to dissolve honey. Sprinkle yeast on top; stir to combine. Let stand 5 minutes until foamy.

Combine 2 cups all-purpose flour, whole-wheat flour and salt, if desired, in large bowl. Stir in yeast mixture. Mix until mixture forms soft dough. Remove dough to lightly floured surface. Knead 5 to 10 minutes, adding remaining ½ cup all-purpose flour, if necessary, until dough is smooth and elastic.

Place dough in large bowl coated with nonstick cooking spray. Turn dough in bowl so top is coated with cooking spray; cover with towel or plastic wrap. Let rise in warm place about 1½ hours or until doubled in bulk. Punch down dough and pat into disk. Gently stretch dough into 14- to 15-inch circle.

Spray 14-inch pizza pan with cooking spray; sprinkle with cornmeal. Press dough into pan. Follow topping and baking directions for individual recipes.
Makes 1 thick 14-inch crust

Salad Pizza

Niçoise Pizza

4 ounces goat cheese
½ cup ricotta cheese
½ cup minced fresh basil
1 teaspoon black pepper
1 purchased bread or pizza crust
    (16-ounce size)
2 tablespoons olive oil, divided
1 large red onion, cut into thin slices
¼ pound fresh young green beans,
    rinsed, stemmed and cut into
    ½-inch pieces
1 yellow or red bell pepper, seeded
    and cut into thin strips
3 tablespoons sliced ripe olives
½ cup freshly grated Parmesan cheese

1. Preheat oven to 450°F. Combine goat cheese, ricotta cheese, basil and black pepper until blended. Spread on bread crust to within ½ inch of edge. Set aside.

2. Heat 1 tablespoon oil in large skillet over medium heat until hot. Add onion to skillet; cook and stir 8 to 10 minutes or until onion is very tender and brown. Arrange on top of cheese mixture.

3. Heat remaining 1 tablespoon olive oil in same skillet over medium heat until hot. Add beans; cook and stir 1 minute. Add bell pepper; cook and stir 1 minute or until crisp-tender. Arrange on top of onion.

4. Top with olives; sprinkle with Parmesan cheese. Bake 8 to 10 minutes or until bread crust is heated through. Garnish, if desired.

Makes 4 servings

Mexicali Pizza

Vegetable oil
2 large flour tortillas *or* 4 small flour
    tortillas
1 pound ground beef
1 package (1.0 ounce) LAWRY'S® Taco
    Spices & Seasonings
¾ cup water
1½ cups (6 ounces) shredded Monterey
    Jack or Cheddar cheese
3 tablespoons diced green chiles
2 medium tomatoes, sliced
1 can (2¼ ounces) sliced black olives,
    drained
½ cup salsa

In large skillet, pour oil to ¼-inch depth; heat. (For small tortillas, use small skillet.) Fry each flour tortilla about 5 seconds. While still pliable, turn tortilla over. Fry until golden brown. (Edges of tortilla should turn up about ½ inch.) Drain well on paper towels. In medium skillet, brown ground beef until crumbly; drain fat. Add Taco Spices & Seasonings and water; mix well. Bring to a boil over medium-high heat; reduce heat to low and cook, uncovered, 5 minutes. Place fried tortillas on pizza pan. Layer taco meat, ½ of cheese, chiles, tomatoes, remaining ½ of cheese, olives and salsa on each fried tortilla. Bake, uncovered, in 425°F oven 15 minutes for large pizzas or 7 to 8 minutes for small pizzas. *Makes 4 servings*

Serving Suggestion: Serve with fresh fruit kabobs.

Hint: One pound ground turkey or 1½ cups shredded cooked chicken can be used in place of beef.

Niçoise Pizza

Beef Tortilla Pizza

1 pound lean ground beef
1 medium onion, chopped
1 teaspoon *each* dried oregano leaves
  and salt
4 large (10-inch) flour tortillas
  Vegetable oil
1 medium tomato, seeded and
  chopped
1 tablespoon thinly sliced fresh basil
  leaves
1 cup shredded mozzarella cheese
¼ cup grated Parmesan cheese

Heat oven to 400°F. Brown ground beef and onion in skillet over medium heat 8 to 10 minutes or until beef is no longer pink. Pour off drippings. Stir oregano and salt into beef. Lightly brush tortillas with oil. Bake tortillas on 2 large baking sheets 3 minutes. Spoon beef mixture evenly over top of each tortilla; top with an equal amount of tomato. Sprinkle with basil and cheeses. Return to oven and bake 12 to 14 minutes or until tortillas are lightly browned.

Makes 4 servings

Prep and cook time: 27 minutes

Serving Suggestion: Serve Beef Tortilla Pizza with a mixed green salad with Italian dressing.

Favorite recipe from **National Cattlemen's Beef Association**

Caramelized Onion and Olive Pizza

2 tablespoons olive oil
1½ pounds onions, thinly sliced
2 teaspoons fresh rosemary *or*
  1 teaspoon dried rosemary
1 tablespoon balsamic vinegar
1 cup California ripe olives, sliced
1 (12-inch) prebaked thick pizza crust
2 cups (8 ounces) shredded
  mozzarella cheese

Preheat oven to 450°F. Heat oil in medium nonstick skillet until hot. Add onions and rosemary. Cook, stirring frequently, about 15 minutes or until onions begin to brown. Stir in ¼ cup water; scrape up any browned bits. Reduce heat to medium-low and continue to cook, stirring occasionally, 15 to 30 minutes or until onions are golden. Add water, 1 tablespoon at a time, if pan appears dry.

Remove pan from heat and stir in vinegar, scraping up any browned bits from pan. Gently stir in olives. Place pizza crust on pizza pan or baking sheet. Spoon onion mixture into center of crust. Sprinkle with cheese. Bake about 15 minutes or until cheese is melted. Cut into wedges and serve warm. *Makes 8 to 10 servings*

Prep time: 15 minutes
Cook time: About 1 hour

Favorite recipe from **California Olive Industry**

Thai Chicken Pizzas

2 boneless skinless chicken breast
  halves (½ pound)
2 teaspoons Thai seasoning
2 tablespoons pineapple juice
1 tablespoon peanut butter
1 tablespoon oyster sauce
1 teaspoon Thai chili paste*
2 (10-inch) flour tortillas
½ cup shredded carrot
½ cup sliced green onions
½ cup red bell pepper slices
¼ cup chopped cilantro
½ cup (2 ounces) shredded mozzarella
  cheese

*Thai chili paste is available at some larger
supermarkets and at Asian markets.*

1. Preheat oven to 400°F. Cut chicken breasts
crosswise into thin slices, each about 1½×½
inch. Sprinkle with Thai seasoning. Let stand
5 minutes. Spray large nonstick skillet with
cooking spray; heat over medium heat until
hot. Add chicken; cook and stir 3 minutes or
until chicken is lightly browned and no
longer pink in center.

2. Combine pineapple juice, peanut butter,
oyster sauce and chili paste in small bowl
until smooth.

3. Place tortillas on baking sheets. Spread
peanut butter mixture over tortillas. Divide
chicken, carrot, green onions, bell pepper and
cilantro evenly between tortillas. Sprinkle
with cheese. Bake 5 minutes or until tortillas
are crisp and cheese is melted. Cut into
wedges. *Makes 4 servings*

Thai Chicken Pizzas

Zucchini, Black Bean and Sun-Dried Tomato Pizza

½ cup sun-dried tomato halves
1 large seeded peeled tomato, cut into quarters
1 (12-inch) prepared pizza crust
1 cup drained canned black beans
¾ cup grated carrots
1 tablespoon olive oil
1½ cups thinly sliced zucchini
1 small onion, cut into thin slices
¼ teaspoon crushed red pepper
⅔ cup part-skim mozzarella cheese

1. Preheat oven to 425°F. Place sun-dried tomatoes in small bowl; cover with boiling water. Let stand 15 minutes; drain. Coarsely chop.

2. Place tomato and sun-dried tomatoes in food processor. Process using on/off pulsing action until tomatoes are finely chopped.

3. Place crust on baking sheet. Spread with tomato mixture. Top with beans and carrots.

4. Heat oil in medium skillet over medium heat until hot. Add zucchini, onion and crushed red pepper. Cook and stir 5 minutes or just until zucchini and onion are soft. Arrange on pizza. Sprinkle with cheese.

5. Bake 12 to 15 minutes or until cheese is melted and pizza is hot. Cut into 8 slices.

Makes 4 servings

Pesto Dijon Pizzas

½ cup chopped parsley*
⅓ cup GREY POUPON® Dijon Mustard
¼ cup PLANTERS® Walnuts, chopped*
1 tablespoon olive oil*
2 tablespoons grated Parmesan cheese, divided*
1½ teaspoons dried basil leaves, divided*
2 (8-ounce) packages small prepared pizza crusts
4 ounces thinly sliced deli baked ham
3 plum tomatoes, sliced
1 cup shredded mozzarella cheese (4 ounces)

*1 (7-ounce) container prepared pesto sauce may be substituted for parsley, walnuts, olive oil, 1 tablespoon Parmesan cheese and 1 teaspoon basil. Stir mustard into prepared pesto sauce.

In small bowl, combine parsley, mustard, walnuts, oil, 1 tablespoon Parmesan cheese and 1 teaspoon basil. Divide mixture and spread evenly onto each pizza crust. Top each crust with 2 ounces ham, tomato slices and mozzarella cheese. Sprinkle with remaining Parmesan cheese and basil. Place on baking sheet. Bake at 450°F for 8 to 10 minutes or until cheese melts. Cut into wedges; serve warm.

Makes 4 main-dish servings

Zucchini, Black Bean and Sun-Dried Tomato Pizza

GLORIOUS

SIDES

Apple & Carrot Casserole

6 large carrots, sliced
4 large apples, peeled, halved,
    cored and sliced
5 tablespoons all-purpose
    flour
1 tablespoon packed brown
    sugar

½ teaspoon salt (optional)
½ teaspoon ground nutmeg
1 tablespoon margarine
½ cup orange juice

Preheat oven to 350°F. Cook carrots in large saucepan in boiling water
5 minutes; drain. Layer carrots and apples in large casserole. Combine flour,
brown sugar, salt, if desired, and nutmeg; sprinkle over top. Dot with margarine;
pour orange juice over flour mixture. Bake 30 minutes or until carrots are
tender.   *Makes 6 servings*

Apple & Carrot Casserole

Chile Relleno Casserole

12 ounces pork sausage
1 small onion, chopped
⅔ cup chunky salsa
¾ cup milk
4 eggs
¼ cup all-purpose flour
½ teaspoon LAWRY'S® Seasoned
    Pepper
¼ teaspoon LAWRY'S® Garlic Powder
    with Parsley
2 cups (8 ounces) shredded Monterey
    Jack cheese
2 cans (7 ounces each) whole green
    chiles, seeded

In medium skillet, brown pork until crumbly and well done. Add onion and cook over medium-high heat until tender; drain fat. Add salsa; reduce heat to low and cook, uncovered, until mixture thickens. In separate bowl, beat together milk, eggs, flour, Seasoned Pepper and Garlic Powder with Parsley; add cheese. In lightly greased 8×8×2-inch baking dish, layer half of chiles, half of pork mixture and half of cheese-egg mixture; repeat layers. Bake, uncovered, in 350°F. oven 35 minutes. Let stand 10 minutes before serving. *Makes 6 to 8 servings*

Microwave Directions: In medium glass bowl, combine pork and onion. Microwave on HIGH 6 minutes; stirring once. Drain fat. Stir in salsa. Continue and layer as stated above. Microwave at MEDIUM (50% power) 20 minutes, rotating after 7 minutes. Let stand 10 minutes before serving.

Serving Suggestion: Serve with stuffed green bell peppers and chilled gazpacho soup.

Creamy Spam™ Broccoli Casserole

Nonstick cooking spray
1 (7-ounce) package elbow macaroni
2 cups frozen cut broccoli, thawed
    and drained
1 (12-ounce) can SPAM® Lite
    Luncheon Meat, cubed
½ cup chopped red bell pepper
2 cups skim milk
2 tablespoons cornstarch
¼ teaspoon black pepper
1 cup (4 ounces) shredded fat-free
    Cheddar cheese
¾ cup soft bread crumbs
2 teaspoons margarine, melted

Heat oven to 350°F. Spray 2-quart casserole with nonstick cooking spray. Cook macaroni according to package directions; drain. In prepared casserole, combine macaroni, broccoli, Spam® and bell pepper. In small saucepan, stir together milk, cornstarch and black pepper until cornstarch is dissolved. Bring to a boil, stirring constantly, until thickened. Reduce heat to low. Add cheese; stir until melted. Stir sauce into Spam™ mixture. Combine bread crumbs and margarine; sprinkle on top of casserole. Bake 40 minutes or until thoroughly heated. *Makes 8 servings*

Creamy Spam™ Broccoli Casserole

Hot Three-Bean Casserole

2 tablespoons olive oil
1 cup coarsely chopped onion
1 cup chopped celery
2 cloves garlic, minced
1 can (15 ounces) chick-peas, drained
   and rinsed
1 can (15 ounces) kidney beans,
   drained and rinsed
1 cup coarsely chopped tomato
1 can (8 ounces) tomato sauce
1 cup water
1 to 2 jalapeño peppers, minced*
1 tablespoon chili powder
2 teaspoons sugar
1½ teaspoons ground cumin
1 teaspoon salt
1 teaspoon dried oregano
¼ teaspoon black pepper
2½ cups (10 ounces) frozen cut green
   beans
   Fresh oregano for garnish

*Jalapeño peppers can sting and irritate the skin;
wear rubber gloves when handling peppers and do
not touch eyes. Wash hands after handling.

1. Heat olive oil in large skillet over medium
heat until hot. Add onion, celery and garlic.
Cook and stir **5** minutes or until onion is
translucent.

2. Add remaining ingredients *except* green
beans. Bring to a boil; reduce heat to low.
Simmer, uncovered, 20 minutes. Add green
beans. Simmer, uncovered, 10 minutes or
until green beans are just tender. Garnish
with fresh oregano, if desired.

Makes 12 (½-cup) servings

Sweet 'n' Sassy Potato Casserole

3 pounds sweet potatoes, peeled and
   cut into 1-inch pieces
3 Anjou pears or tart apples, peeled
   and cut into 1-inch pieces
½ cup packed light brown sugar
½ cup maple or pancake syrup
2 tablespoons FRANK'S® Original
   REDHOT® Cayenne Pepper Sauce
2 teaspoons ground cinnamon
¼ teaspoon ground allspice
2 tablespoons unsalted butter

1. Place sweet potatoes in large saucepan;
cover with water. Bring to a boil. Cook 10 to
15 minutes or until tender. Drain. Place
potatoes and pears in greased 3-quart baking
dish.

2. Preheat oven to 400°F. Combine sugar,
maple syrup, RedHot® sauce and spices in
medium bowl. Pour over potatoes and pears.
Dot with butter. Cover tightly.

3. Bake 30 to 35 minutes or until heated
through and pears are tender. Baste mixture
with sauce occasionally. Sprinkle with
chopped toasted almonds, if desired.

Makes 8 servings

Prep time: 25 minutes
Cook time: 35 minutes

Hot Three-Bean Casserole

Fresh Vegetable Casserole

8 small new potatoes
8 baby carrots
1 small head cauliflower, broken into florets
4 stalks asparagus, cut into 1-inch pieces
3 tablespoons butter or margarine
3 tablespoons all-purpose flour
2 cups milk
  Salt and black pepper
¾ cup (3 ounces) shredded Cheddar cheese
  Chopped fresh cilantro

Preheat oven to 350°F. Cook vegetables until crisp-tender. Butter 2-quart casserole. Arrange vegetables in prepared casserole. Melt butter in medium saucepan over medium heat. Stir in flour until smooth. Gradually stir in milk. Cook until thickened, stirring constantly. Season to taste with salt and pepper. Add cheese, stirring until cheese is melted. Pour cheese sauce over vegetables and sprinkle with cilantro. Bake 15 minutes or until heated through.

Makes 4 to 6 servings

Fresh Vegetable Casserole

Baked Apple & Sweet Potato Casserole

6 sweet potatoes
3 apples
2 tablespoons melted butter, divided
½ cup orange juice
¼ cup packed dark brown sugar
¼ cup rum
⅛ teaspoon ground cinnamon
⅛ teaspoon ground allspice

Preheat oven to 350°F. Boil or steam potatoes until tender. Remove skin and cut lengthwise into slices. Peel and core apples; slice into rings. Grease 9×6-inch baking dish with 1 tablespoon butter. Layer potatoes and apples in dish. Combine orange juice, brown sugar, rum, cinnamon and allspice. Pour juice mixture over potato-apple layers. Top with remaining 1 tablespoon butter. Bake 30 minutes or until brown and liquid is absorbed. *Makes 6 servings*

Favorite recipe from **Michigan Apple Committee**

Easy Veg-All® Potato Casserole

1 (15-ounce) can VEG-ALL® Mixed Vegetables, drained
1 cup cooked, cubed ham, turkey or chicken
1 (5.5-ounce) package au gratin potatoes
2 tablespoons bread crumbs

Combine vegetables, ham and au gratin potatoes in medium casserole. Sprinkle with bread crumbs. Cook according to au gratin potatoes package directions. Cool 5 minutes before serving. *Makes 6 servings*

Original Green Bean Casserole

1 can (10¾ ounces) condensed cream of mushroom soup
¾ cup milk
⅛ teaspoon ground black pepper
2 packages (9 ounces each) frozen cut green beans, thawed and drained *or* 2 cans (14.5 ounces each) cut green beans, drained
1⅓ cups (2.8-ounce can) FRENCH'S® French Fried Onions, divided

Preheat oven to 350°F. Combine soup, milk and black pepper in 1½-quart casserole; stir until well blended. Stir in beans and ⅔ *cup* French Fried Onions.

Bake, uncovered, 30 minutes or until hot. Stir; sprinkle with remaining ⅔ *cup* onions. Bake 5 minutes or until onions are golden.
Makes 6 servings

Prep time: 5 minutes
Cook time: 35 minutes

Microwave Directions: Prepare green bean mixture as directed; pour into 1½-quart microwave-safe casserole. Cook, covered, on HIGH 8 to 10 minutes or until heated through. Stir beans halfway through cooking time. Top with remaining onions; cook, uncovered, 1 minute. Let stand 5 minutes.

Harvest Casserole

2 cups USA lentils, rinsed and cooked
2 cups fresh or frozen broccoli, chopped
1½ cups cooked rice
1¼ cups (6 ounces) shredded Cheddar cheese
1 tablespoon soy sauce
½ teaspoon salt (optional)
¼ teaspoon dried thyme
¼ teaspoon dried marjoram
¼ teaspoon dried rosemary
4 eggs
1 cup milk
Additional shredded Cheddar cheese (optional)

Preheat oven to 350°F.

Mix lentils, broccoli, rice, cheese, soy sauce, salt, if desired, thyme, marjoram and rosemary in large bowl. Place mixture in greased 9-inch casserole.

Combine eggs and milk in medium bowl. Pour egg mixture over lentil mixture. Bake 45 minutes or until lightly browned. Top with additional shredded Cheddar cheese, if desired. *Makes 8 servings*

Favorite recipe from **USA Dry Pea & Lentil Council**

Fiesta Corn Casserole

1 tablespoon butter
3 cups corn flakes, divided
1 pound ground beef
1 can (8 ounces) tomato sauce
1 package (1.0 ounce) LAWRY'S® Taco Spices & Seasonings
½ teaspoon LAWRY'S® Seasoned Salt
1 can (17 ounces) whole kernel corn, drained (reserve ¼ cup liquid)
2 cups (8 ounces) shredded cheddar cheese

Microwave Directions: In 1½-quart shallow glass casserole, place butter and microwave on HIGH 30 seconds. Sprinkle 2 cups corn flakes over butter. Crush remaining 1 cup corn flakes and set aside. In separate microwave-safe dish, microwave ground beef on HIGH 5 minutes, stirring to crumble after 3 minutes. Drain fat and crumble beef. Add tomato sauce, Taco Spices & Seasonings, Seasoned Salt and reserved ¼ cup corn liquid; blend well. Layer half of corn, meat mixture and cheese over buttered corn flakes; repeat layers. Sprinkle remaining 1 cup crushed corn flakes over top in diagonal strips. Microwave on HIGH 12 to 15 minutes. *Makes 4 to 6 servings*

Serving Suggestion: Serve with sliced tomatoes and cucumbers.

Green Rice

2 Anaheim chilies
1 jalapeño pepper
1 tablespoon margarine or olive oil
¼ cup sliced green onions
¼ cup snipped cilantro
Arroz Blanco (recipe follows)
¼ teaspoon dried oregano leaves

Chop chilies and jalapeño pepper in food processor. Melt margarine in large skillet over low heat. Add chili mixture; cook 1 minute over medium heat. Stir in green onions and cilantro; cook 15 to 30 seconds. Stir in Arroz Blanco and oregano; cook until heated through. *Makes 6 servings*

Arroz Blanco

1 tablespoon margarine
½ cup chopped onion
2 cloves garlic, minced
1 cup uncooked rice*
2 cups chicken broth

*Use regular-milled long-grain white rice.

Melt margarine in 2- to 3-quart saucepan over medium heat. Add onion and garlic; cook until onion is tender. Add rice and broth. Bring to a boil; stir. Reduce heat; cover and simmer 15 minutes or until rice is tender and liquid is absorbed. Fluff with fork.
Makes 6 servings

Favorite recipe from **USA Rice Federation**

Risi Bisi

1½ cups uncooked converted long-grain white rice
¾ cup chopped onion
2 cloves garlic, minced
2 cans (about 14 ounces *each*) reduced-sodium chicken broth
⅓ cup water
¾ teaspoon Italian seasoning
½ teaspoon dried basil leaves
½ cup frozen peas, thawed
¼ cup grated Parmesan cheese
¼ cup toasted pine nuts (optional)

Combine rice, onion and garlic in slow cooker. Bring broth and water to a boil in small saucepan. Stir boiling liquid, Italian seasoning and basil into rice mixture. Cover and cook on low 2 to 3 hours or until liquid is absorbed. Add peas. Cover and cook 1 hour. Stir in cheese. Spoon rice into serving bowl. Sprinkle with pine nuts, if desired. *Makes 6 servings*

Spicy Spanish Rice

1 teaspoon canola oil
1 cup uncooked white rice
1 medium onion, chopped
2 cups chicken stock or canned
   low-sodium chicken broth,
   defatted
1 cup GUILTLESS GOURMET® Salsa
   Green chili pepper strips (optional)

Heat large skillet over medium-high heat until hot. Add oil; swirl to coat skillet. Add rice; cook and stir until lightly browned. Remove rice to small bowl. Add onion to same skillet; cook and stir until onion is translucent. Add chicken stock and salsa to skillet; return rice to skillet. Bring to a boil. Reduce heat to low; cover and simmer until liquid is absorbed and rice is tender. Serve hot. Garnish with pepper strips, if desired.

Makes 4 servings

Almond Brown Rice Stuffing

⅓ cup slivered almonds
2 teaspoons margarine
2 medium tart apples, cored and
   diced
½ cup chopped onion
½ cup chopped celery
½ teaspoon poultry seasoning
¼ teaspoon dried thyme leaves
¼ teaspoon ground white pepper
3 cups cooked brown rice (cooked in
   chicken broth)

Cook almonds in margarine in large skillet over medium-high heat until brown. Add apples, onion, celery, poultry seasoning, thyme and white pepper; cook until vegetables are tender-crisp. Stir in rice; cook until thoroughly heated. Serve or use as stuffing for poultry or pork roast. Stuffing may be baked in covered baking dish at 375°F for 15 to 20 minutes.

Makes 6 servings

Microwave Directions: Combine almonds and margarine in 2- to 3-quart microwavable baking dish. Cook on HIGH (100% power) 2 to 3 minutes or until browned. Add apples, onion, celery, poultry seasoning, thyme and pepper. Cover with waxed paper and cook on HIGH 2 minutes. Stir in rice; cook on HIGH 2 to 3 minutes, stirring after 1½ minutes, or until thoroughly heated. Serve as directed above.

Raisin Stuffing: Add ½ cup raisins; cook with apples, onion, celery and seasonings.

Mushroom Stuffing: Add 2 cups (about 8 ounces) sliced mushrooms; cook with apples, onion, celery and seasonings.

Nutrients per Serving:

Calories:	198	Cholesterol:	0 mg
Total Fat:	6 g	Sodium:	30 mg

Favorite recipe from **USA Rice Federation**

Spicy Spanish Rice

Sausage-Cornbread Stuffing

8 ounces bulk pork sausage
½ cup butter or margarine
2 medium onions, chopped
2 cloves garlic, minced
2 teaspoons dried sage
1 teaspoon poultry seasoning
1 package (16 ounces) prepared dry cornbread crumbs
¾ to 1¼ cups chicken broth
Sage leaves for garnish

Brown sausage in large skillet over medium-high heat until no longer pink, stirring to crumble meat. Drain; set aside. Wipe skillet with paper towels.

Melt butter in same skillet over medium heat. Cook onions and garlic in butter 10 minutes or until softened. Stir in sage and poultry seasoning; cook 1 minute.

Combine cornbread crumbs, sausage and onion mixture in large bowl.

If stuffing is to be cooked in a turkey, drizzle ¾ cup broth over stuffing; toss lightly until moistened. Stuff body and neck cavities loosely with stuffing. Stuffing may be prepared up to 1 day before using. Do not stuff turkey until just before roasting. Roast according to instructions given with turkey.

If stuffing is to be cooked separately, drizzle 1¼ cups broth over stuffing; toss stuffing lightly until moistened. Transfer to 3-quart casserole. (May be covered and refrigerated up to 1 day before baking.)

Preheat oven to 350°F. Bake stuffing 45 minutes (55 to 60 minutes if refrigerated) or until heated through. For a drier stuffing, uncover during last 15 minutes of baking. Garnish, if desired.

Makes 12 cups stuffing

Mashed Potatoes

2 pounds medium red boiling potatoes, peeled and cut into pieces
4 large cloves garlic, peeled
¾ cup buttermilk
1 tablespoon butter
½ teaspoon salt
¼ teaspoon black pepper
2 tablespoons chopped chives for garnish

Place potatoes and garlic in large saucepan. Add enough water to cover; bring to a boil over high heat. Reduce heat; simmer, uncovered, 20 to 30 minutes or until potatoes are fork-tender. Drain.

Place potatoes and garlic in medium bowl. Mash until smooth. Add buttermilk, butter, salt and pepper. Stir with fork until combined. Garnish, if desired.

Makes 8 servings

Sausage-Cornbread Stuffing

Broccoli with Red Pepper and Shallots

2 bunches fresh broccoli (about
    2¼ pounds), trimmed and cut into
    1-inch pieces
2 teaspoons margarine or butter
3 large shallots, thinly sliced
1 large red bell pepper, seeded and
    thinly sliced
½ teaspoon salt
¼ teaspoon black pepper
¼ cup sliced almonds, toasted for
    garnish

Bring 2-quarts water to a boil in large saucepan. Add broccoli; return to a boil. Boil, uncovered, 3 to 5 minutes or until bright green and tender. Drain. Rinse and drain again.

Melt margarine in large nonstick skillet over medium heat. Add shallots and bell pepper. Cook 3 minutes, stirring occasionally. Add broccoli to skillet. Cook 4 to 6 minutes, stirring occasionally. Sprinkle with salt and black pepper; mix well. Garnish with almonds, if desired.

Makes 6 to 8 servings

Orange-Glazed Carrots

1 pound fresh or frozen baby carrots,
    thawed
⅓ cup orange marmalade
2 tablespoons butter
2 teaspoons Dijon mustard
½ teaspoon grated fresh ginger

Bring ½ cup water to a boil in 2-quart saucepan. Add carrots, reduce heat. Cover; simmer 10 to 12 minutes for fresh carrots or 8 to 10 minutes for frozen carrots or until crisp-tender.

Drain well; return carrots to saucepan.

Stir in marmalade, butter, mustard and ginger. Simmer, uncovered, over medium heat 3 minutes or until carrots are glazed, stirring occasionally. Serve immediately.

Makes 6 servings

Broccoli with Red Pepper and Shallots

Cranberry-Apple Chutney

1 package (12 ounces) fresh or frozen cranberries
1¼ cups granulated sugar
½ cup water
2 medium Granny Smith apples, peeled, cored and cut into ¼-inch pieces
1 medium onion, chopped
½ cup golden raisins
½ cup packed light brown sugar
¼ cup cider vinegar
1 teaspoon ground ginger
1 teaspoon ground cinnamon
⅛ teaspoon ground allspice
⅛ teaspoon ground cloves
½ cup walnuts or pecans, toasted and chopped (optional)

Wash cranberries and discard any stems or withered cranberries.

Bring granulated sugar and water to a boil in heavy 2-quart saucepan over high heat. Boil gently 3 minutes. Add cranberries, apples, onion, raisins, brown sugar, vinegar, ginger, cinnamon, allspice and cloves. Bring to a boil. Reduce heat; simmer, uncovered, 20 to 25 minutes or until mixture is very thick, stirring occasionally. Cool; stir in walnuts, if desired.

Makes 3½ cups chutney

Chutney-Squash Circles

2 acorn squash (1 pound *each*), seeded
2 tablespoons butter or margarine
½ cup prepared chutney
2 tablespoons water

Preheat oven to 400°F. Cut squash into ¾-inch circles.

Tear off 18-inch square of foil; center in 13×9-inch baking pan. Dot foil with butter and place squash on butter, slightly overlapping circles. Spoon chutney over slices and sprinkle with water. Seal foil.

Bake 20 to 30 minutes or until squash is fork-tender. Transfer to warm serving plate; pour drippings over squash. Garnish, as desired. Serve immediately. *Makes 4 servings*

Cranberry-Apple Chutney

LUSCIOUS

PIES & TARTS

Cranberry Apple Nut Pie

Rich Pie Pastry (page 264)
1 cup sugar
3 tablespoons all-purpose
   flour
¼ teaspoon salt
4 cups sliced peeled tart apples
2 cups fresh cranberries
½ cup golden raisins

½ cup coarsely chopped
   pecans
1 tablespoon grated lemon
   peel
2 tablespoons butter or
   margarine
1 egg, beaten

Preheat oven to 425°F. Divide pie pastry in half. Roll one half on lightly floured surface to form 13-inch circle. Fit into 9-inch pie plate; trim edges. Reroll scraps and cut into decorative shapes for garnish; set aside.

(continued on page 264)

Cranberry Apple Nut Pie

(Cranberry Apple Nut Pie, *continued from* **page 262)**

Combine sugar, flour and salt in large bowl. Stir in apples, cranberries, raisins, pecans and lemon peel; toss well. Spoon fruit mixture into unbaked pie crust. Dot with butter. Roll remaining half of pie pastry on lightly floured surface to form 11-inch circle. Place over filling. Trim and seal edges; flute. Cut 3 slits in center of top crust. Moisten pastry cutouts and decorate as desired. Lightly brush top crust with egg.

Bake 35 to 40 minutes or until apples are tender when pierced with fork and pastry is golden brown. Cool in pan on wire rack. Serve warm. *Makes 1 (9-inch) pie*

Rich Pie Pastry

  2 cups all-purpose flour
  ¼ teaspoon salt
  6 tablespoons butter
  6 tablespoons lard
  6 to 8 tablespoons cold water

Combine flour and salt in medium bowl. Cut in butter and lard with pastry blender or 2 knives until mixture resembles coarse crumbs. Sprinkle water, 1 tablespoon at a time, over flour mixture, mixing until flour is moistened. Shape dough into a ball. Roll, fill and bake as recipe directs.
Makes 1 (9-inch) double pie crust

Note: For single crust, cut recipe in half.

Cranberry Apple Pie with Soft Gingersnap Crust

 20 gingersnaps
 1½ tablespoons margarine
  2 McIntosh apples
  1 cup fresh cranberries
  5 tablespoons dark brown sugar
  ¼ teaspoon cinnamon
  ¼ teaspoon vanilla
  1 teaspoon granulated sugar

Preheat oven to 375°F. Combine gingersnaps and margarine in food processor; process until well combined. Press gingersnap mixture evenly into 8-inch pie plate. Bake 5 to 8 minutes; remove crust from oven and let cool. Slice apples in food processor. Add cranberries, brown sugar, cinnamon and vanilla; blend just until mixed. Spoon apple-cranberry filling into separate pie plate or casserole. Sprinkle with granulated sugar. Bake 35 minutes or until tender. Spoon over gingersnap crust and serve immediately.
Makes 8 servings

Nutrients per Serving:

Calories:	124	Sodium:	90 mg
Cholesterol:	0 mg		

Favorite recipe from **The Sugar Association, Inc.**

Cranberry Apple Pie with Soft Gingersnap Crust

Butterscotch Crumb Apple Pie

FILLING

4 cups pared, cored and thinly sliced tart cooking apples (about 1½ pounds)

2 cups (12-ounce package) NESTLÉ® TOLL HOUSE® Butterscotch Flavored Morsels, divided

2 tablespoons all-purpose flour

1 teaspoon ground cinnamon

1 (9-inch) unbaked pie shell

TOPPING

1 cup (½ of 12-ounce package) NESTLÉ® TOLL HOUSE® Butterscotch Flavored Morsels, reserved from above

¼ cup (½ stick) butter

¾ cup all-purpose flour

⅛ teaspoon salt

Whipped cream or ice cream (optional)

For filling, preheat oven to 350°F. In large bowl, stir apples, 1 cup morsels, flour and cinnamon until apples are coated. Spoon into pie shell.* Bake 20 minutes.

For topping, combine over hot (not boiling) water, 1 cup morsels and butter; stir until morsels are melted and mixture is smooth. Remove from heat. Add flour and salt; blend until mixture forms large crumbs. Crumble topping over hot apple mixture. Bake an additional 30 minutes or until apples are tender. Serve warm with whipped cream or ice cream, if desired.

Makes 1 (9-inch) pie

If using frozen pie shell, use deep-dish style, thawed. Bake pie on cookie sheet.

Quick 'n Lean Golden Apple Pie

7 Golden Delicious apples, cored

3 tablespoons sugar

2 tablespoons unsifted all-purpose flour

1½ teaspoons vanilla extract

½ teaspoon ground cinnamon

¼ teaspoon ground ginger

Canola Pastry (recipe follows)

1. Peel apples, if desired, and thinly slice. In large bowl, combine apples, sugar, flour, vanilla, cinnamon and ginger; toss to blend. Transfer apple mixture to lightly-oiled glass pie dish. Prepare Canola Pastry.

2. Roll pastry between two 12-inch squares of waxed paper to an 11-inch round. Cut round into ¾-inch strips. On waxed paper, weave a lattice top with strips of pastry; slide lattice on to apple filling to cover. Trim edges of lattice.

3. Microwave on High (100%) 10 to 12 minutes or until pie filling is bubbly. Meanwhile, heat oven to 425°F. Bake pie 10 to 15 minutes or until pastry is golden.

Makes 8 servings

Canola Pastry

In medium bowl, combine 1⅓ cups unsifted all-purpose flour and ½ teaspoon salt; stir in ¼ cup canola oil until thoroughly blended. Add 3 tablespoons water to flour mixture, stirring until pastry is moistened. Form into ball and flatten slightly.

Favorite recipe from **Washington Apple Commission**

Freestyle Apple Pie

Crumb Topping (recipe follows)
½ cup sugar
1 tablespoon ARGO® or
   KINGSFORD'S® Corn Starch
½ teaspoon cinnamon
4 cups peeled, sliced apples (about
   4 medium)
1 tablespoon lemon juice
1 refrigerated prepared pie crust for
   (9-inch) pie

1. Preheat oven to 400°F. Prepare Crumb Topping; set aside.

2. In large bowl combine sugar, corn starch and cinnamon. Add apples and lemon juice; toss to coat.

3. Unfold crust; place on foil-lined cookie sheet. Spoon apples into center of crust, leaving 2-inch edge. Sprinkle Crumb Topping over apples. Fold up edge of crust, pinching at 2-inch intervals.

4. Bake 15 minutes. Reduce temperature to 350°F; bake 35 minutes longer or until apples are tender.   *Makes 6 servings*

Crumb Topping

In small bowl combine ½ cup flour and ⅓ cup packed brown sugar. With pastry blender or 2 knives, cut in ½ cup cold MAZOLA® Margarine just until coarse crumbs form. If desired, stir in ½ cup coarsely chopped nuts.

Grasshopper Pie

2 cups graham cracker crumbs
4 tablespoons unsweetened cocoa
   powder
¼ cup margarine, melted
8 ounces nonfat cream cheese,
   softened
1 cup low-fat (1%) milk
2 tablespoons green crème de menthe
   liqueur
2 tablespoons white crème de menthe
   liqueur
1½ teaspoons vanilla
1 container (4 ounces) frozen
   whipped topping, thawed

Spray 9-inch pie plate with nonstick cooking spray. Combine cracker crumbs, cocoa and margarine in medium bowl. Press onto bottom and up side of prepared pie plate. Refrigerate. Beat cream cheese in large bowl with electric mixer until fluffy. Gradually beat in milk until smooth. Stir in both liqueurs and vanilla. Fold in whipped topping. Refrigerate 20 minutes or until chilled, but not set. Pour into chilled crust. Freeze 4 hours or until set.

Makes 8 servings

Pineapple Sweet Potato Pie

1 (9-inch) pastry shell, unbaked
2 cups mashed cooked sweet potatoes
⅔ cup firmly packed brown sugar
¼ cup half-and-half
2 tablespoons butter or margarine, melted
1 teaspoon vanilla extract, divided
½ teaspoon ground cinnamon
¼ teaspoon ground nutmeg
¼ teaspoon salt
1 egg, beaten
1 can (15¼ ounces) DEL MONTE® *FreshCut*™ Brand Sliced Pineapple In Its Own Juice, undrained
1 teaspoon cornstarch
1 teaspoon minced candied ginger

1. Prepare pastry shell; set aside.

2. Combine sweet potatoes, brown sugar, half-and-half, butter, ½ teaspoon vanilla, cinnamon, nutmeg, salt and egg; mix well. Pour into pastry shell.

3. Bake at 425°F 25 to 30 minutes or until set in center; cool.

4. Drain pineapple, reserving ½ cup juice. Pour reserved juice into small saucepan. Add cornstarch; stir until dissolved. Cook, stirring constantly, until thickened and translucent. Stir in ginger and remaining ½ teaspoon vanilla.

5. Cut pineapple slices in half; arrange pineapple over pie. Spoon topping over pineapple. Garnish, if desired.

Makes 8 servings

Early American Pumpkin Pie

1½ cups cooked pumpkin, canned or fresh
1 cup whole or 2% milk
2 eggs, beaten
1 cup sugar
½ teaspoon ground cinnamon
¼ teaspoon salt
¼ teaspoon ground ginger
¼ teaspoon ground nutmeg
1 tablespoon butter or margarine, melted
1 (9-inch) unbaked pie shell
Sweetened whipped cream or whipped topping (optional)
Fresh currants (optional)

Preheat oven to 425°F. Combine all ingredients except pie shell, cream and currants in large bowl; blend well. Pour into pie shell. Bake 45 to 50 minutes or until knife inserted into filling comes out clean. Cool completely. Serve with whipped cream and garnish with currants, if desired. Refrigerate leftovers. *Makes 6 to 8 servings*

Favorite recipe from **Bob Evans**®

Early American Pumpkin Pie

Pumpkin Pecan Pie

3 eggs, divided
1 cup canned solid pack pumpkin
1 cup sugar, divided
½ teaspoon ground cinnamon
¼ teaspoon ground ginger
⅛ teaspoon ground cloves
   Easy-As-Pie Crust (recipe follows) *or*
      1 (9-inch) frozen deep-dish pie
      crust*
⅔ cup KARO® Light or Dark Corn
      Syrup
2 tablespoons MAZOLA® Margarine *or*
      butter, melted
1 teaspoon vanilla
1 cup coarsely chopped pecans or
      walnuts

To use prepared frozen pie crust: Do not thaw. Preheat oven and a cookie sheet. Pour filling into frozen crust. Bake on cookie sheet.

1. Preheat oven to 350°F.

2. In small bowl, combine 1 egg, pumpkin, ⅓ cup sugar, cinnamon, ginger and cloves. Spread evenly in bottom of pie crust.

3. In medium bowl, beat remaining 2 eggs slightly. Stir in corn syrup, remaining ⅔ cup sugar, margarine and vanilla until blended. Stir in pecans; carefully spoon over pumpkin mixture.

4. Bake 50 to 60 minutes or until filling is set around edge. Cool completely on wire rack.
Makes 8 servings

Prep time: 15 minutes
Bake time: 50 minutes, plus cooling

Easy-As-Pie Crust

1¼ cups unsifted flour
⅛ teaspoon salt
½ cup MAZOLA® Margarine
2 to 3 tablespoons cold water

1. In medium bowl, combine flour and salt. With pastry blender or 2 knives, cut in margarine until mixture is crumbly.

2. Sprinkle water over mixture while tossing to blend well. Press dough firmly into ball. On lightly floured surface, roll into 12-inch circle. Fit into 9-inch pie plate. Trim and flute edge. Fill and bake according to recipe.
Makes 1 (9-inch) crust

Traditional Cherry Pie

4 cups frozen tart cherries
1⅓ cup granulated sugar
3 tablespoons quick-cooking tapioca
½ teaspoon almond extract
   Pastry for double-crust 9-inch pie
2 tablespoons butter or margarine

Preheat oven to 400°F. In medium bowl, combine cherries, sugar, tapioca and almond extract; mix well. (It is not necessary to thaw cherries before using.) Let cherry mixture stand 15 minutes. Line 9-inch pie plate with pastry; fill with cherry mixture. Dot with butter. Cover with top crust, cutting slits for steam to escape. Bake 50 to 55 minutes, or until crust is golden brown and filling is bubbly. *Makes 6 to 8 servings*

Favorite recipe from **Cherry Marketing Institute, Inc.**

Pumpkin Pecan Pie

Amaretto Coconut Cream Pie

1 container (8 ounces) thawed
    nondairy whipped topping,
    divided
1 container (8 ounces) coconut
    cream-flavored or vanilla-flavored
    yogurt
¼ cup amaretto liqueur
1 package (4-serving size) instant
    coconut pudding and pie filling
    mix
1 prepared (9-inch) graham cracker
    pie crust
¼ cup flaked coconut, toasted
    Fresh strawberries and mint leaves
    (optional)

Place 2 cups whipped topping, yogurt and
amaretto in large bowl. Add pudding mix.
Beat with wire whisk or electric mixer on
low speed, 1 to 2 minutes or until thickened.

Pour pudding mixture into crust; spread
remaining whipped topping over filling.
Sprinkle with toasted coconut. Garnish with
fresh strawberries and mint leaves, if desired.
Refrigerate until ready to serve.

Makes 8 servings

Light Banana Cream Pie

1 package (1.9 ounces) sugar-free
    vanilla instant pudding and pie
    filling (four ½-cup servings)
2¾ cups low-fat milk
4 ripe, medium DOLE® Bananas, sliced
1 (9-inch) ready-made graham
    cracker pie crust
1 firm, medium DOLE® Banana
    (optional)
    Light frozen non-dairy whipped
    topping, thawed (optional)

• **Prepare** pudding as directed using
2¾ cups low-fat milk. Stir in 4 sliced ripe
bananas.

• **Spoon** banana mixture into pie crust.
Place plastic wrap over pie, lightly pressing
plastic to completely cover filling. Chill
1 hour or until filling is set. Remove plastic
wrap.

• **Cut** firm banana into ½-inch slices. Garnish
pie with whipped topping and banana slices.

Makes 8 servings

Prep time: 10 minutes
Chill time: 1 hour

Nutrients per Serving:

Calories:	199	Cholesterol:	3 mg
Total Fat:	6 g	Sodium:	242 mg

Amaretto Coconut Cream Pie

Mocha Ice Cream Pie

2 cups coffee or vanilla ice cream, softened
1 prepared (9-inch) chocolate crumb pie crust
1 jar (12 ounces) hot caramel ice cream topping, divided
2 cups chocolate ice cream, softened
2 cups thawed nondairy whipped topping
1 English toffee bar (1.4 ounces), chopped

Spread coffee ice cream in bottom of pie crust. Freeze 10 minutes or until semi-firm.

Spread half of caramel topping over coffee ice cream. Spread chocolate ice cream over caramel. Freeze 10 minutes or until semi-firm.

Spread remaining caramel topping over chocolate ice cream. Spoon whipped topping into pastry bag fitted with star decorating tip. Pipe rosettes on top of pie. Sprinkle toffee over topping.

Freeze pie until firm, 6 hours or overnight. Remove from freezer. Allow pie to stand at room temperature 15 minutes before serving.

Makes 8 servings

Chocolate Cream Pie with Skim Milk

⅓ cup sugar
¼ cup cornstarch
3 tablespoons HERSHEY'S Cocoa or HERSHEY'S Dutch Processed Cocoa
2 cups skim milk
1 teaspoon vanilla extract
1 packaged graham cracker crumb crust (6 ounces)
Frozen light non-dairy whipped topping, thawed (optional)
Assorted fresh fruit (optional)

Microwave Directions: In large microwave-safe bowl, stir together sugar, cornstarch and cocoa; gradually stir in milk. Microwave at HIGH (100%) 2 minutes; stir well. Microwave at HIGH 2 to 5 minutes or until mixture just begins to boil; stir well. Microwave at HIGH 30 seconds to 1 minute or until mixture is very hot and thickened. Stir in vanilla. Pour into crust. Press plastic wrap directly onto surface; refrigerate several hours or until set. Garnish with whipped topping and fruit, if desired. Store, covered, in refrigerator.

Makes 10 servings

Nutrients per Serving:

Calories:	120	Cholesterol:	0 mg
Total Fat:	4.5 g	Sodium:	120 mg

Peanut Butter Cream Pie

¾ cup powdered sugar
⅓ cup creamy peanut butter
1 baked (9-inch) pie crust
1 cup milk
1 cup sour cream
1 package (4-serving size) instant French vanilla pudding and pie filling mix
5 peanut butter candy cups, divided
2 cups thawed nondairy whipped topping

Combine powdered sugar and peanut butter with fork in medium bowl until blended. Place evenly in bottom of pie crust.

Place milk and sour cream in large bowl. Add pudding mix. Beat with wire whisk or electric mixer 1 to 2 minutes or until thickened.

Pour half of filling over peanut butter mixture. Coarsely chop 4 candy cups; sprinkle over filling. Top with remaining filling.

Spread whipped topping over filling. Cut remaining candy cup into 8 pieces; place on top of pie. Refrigerate.   *Makes 8 servings*

Peanut Butter Cream Pie

Fudgy Bittersweet Brownie Pie

12 squares (1 ounce *each*) bittersweet
    chocolate*
½ cup margarine or butter
2 eggs
½ cup sugar
1 cup all-purpose flour
½ teaspoon salt
    Vanilla ice cream
    Prepared hot fudge sauce, divided

*Substitute 4 squares unsweetened chocolate plus
8 squares semisweet chocolate, if desired.*

Preheat oven to 350°F. Grease 10-inch tart
pan with removable bottom or 9-inch square
baking pan; set aside.

Melt chocolate and margarine in small heavy
saucepan over low heat, stirring constantly;
set aside.

Beat eggs in medium bowl with electric
mixer at medium speed 30 seconds.
Gradually beat in sugar; beat 1 minute. Beat
in chocolate mixture. Beat in flour and salt at
low speed until just combined. Spread
mixture evenly in prepared pan.

Bake 25 minutes or until center is just set.
Cool pie completely in pan on wire rack. Cut
pie into 12 wedges, or 12 squares if using
square pan. Top each piece with a scoop of
ice cream. Place fudge sauce in small
microwavable bowl. Microwave at HIGH
until hot, stirring once. Spoon fudge sauce
over each serving.   *Makes 12 servings*

Chocolate Mudslide Frozen Pie

1 cup (6 ounces) NESTLÉ® TOLL
    HOUSE® Semi-Sweet Chocolate
    Morsels
1 teaspoon TASTER'S CHOICE®
    Original Freeze-Dried Coffee
1 teaspoon hot water
¾ cup sour cream
½ cup granulated sugar
1 teaspoon vanilla extract
1 prepared (9-inch) chocolate crumb
    crust
1½ cups heavy whipping cream
1 cup powdered sugar
¼ cup NESTLÉ® TOLL HOUSE® Baking
    Cocoa
2 tablespoons NESTLÉ® TOLL HOUSE®
    Semi-Sweet Chocolate Mini
    Morsels

MELT 1 cup morsels in small, heavy-duty
saucepan over lowest possible heat. When
morsels begin to melt, remove from heat; stir.
Return to heat for a few seconds at a time,
stirring until smooth. Remove from heat; cool
for 10 minutes.

COMBINE coffee and water in medium
bowl. Add sour cream, granulated sugar and
vanilla; stir until sugar is dissolved. Stir in
melted chocolate until smooth. Spread into
crust; chill.

BEAT cream, powdered sugar and cocoa in
small mixer bowl until stiff peaks form.
Spread or pipe over chocolate layer. Sprinkle
with mini morsels. Freeze for at least 6 hours
or until firm.   *Makes 8 servings*

Fudgy Bittersweet Brownie Pie

Raspberry Chocolate Mousse Pie

40 chocolate wafer cookies
½ cup butter, melted
½ cup water
7 tablespoons sugar
5 egg yolks
6 squares (1 ounce *each*) semisweet
   chocolate, melted, cooled slightly
3 tablespoons raspberry-flavored
   liqueur (optional)
3½ cups thawed nondairy whipped
   topping
   Sweetened whipped cream, fresh
   raspberries and mint leaves
   (optional)

Place cookies in food processor or blender; process with on/off pulses until finely crushed. Combine cookie crumbs and butter in medium bowl; mix well. Press onto bottom and 1 inch up side of 9-inch springform pan.

Combine water and sugar in medium saucepan. Bring to a boil over medium-high heat. Boil 1 minute.

Place egg yolks in large bowl. Gradually whisk in hot sugar mixture. Return mixture to medium saucepan; whisk over low heat 1 to 2 minutes or until mixture is thick and creamy. Remove from heat; pour mixture back into large bowl.

Raspberry Chocolate Mousse Pie

Whisk in melted chocolate and liqueur, if desired. Beat mixture until cool. Fold in whipped topping. Pour mixture into prepared crust. Freeze until firm. Allow pie to stand at room temperature 20 minutes before serving. Remove side of pan. Garnish, if desired. *Makes 10 servings*

Elegant and Easy Pear Tart

1 can (29 ounces) USA Bartlett pears, undrained
2 packages (3⅛ to 3½ ounces each) vanilla pudding mix
Milk
¼ cup almond-flavored liqueur*
1 (8-inch) pastry shell, baked and cooled
Apricot Glaze (recipe follows)

½ teaspoon almond extract can be substituted.

Drain pears; reserve 1 cup liquid. Prepare pudding according to package directions substituting reserved pear liquid for part of milk; stir in liqueur. Pour into pastry shell; chill until set. Slice pears and arrange over pudding. Brush with warm Apricot Glaze; refrigerate until cold.

Makes 1 (8-inch) tart

Apricot Glaze
Heat ½ cup apricot or peach preserves and 1 tablespoon almond-flavored liqueur or pear liquid. Press through sieve; discard pulp.

Makes about ⅓ cup glaze

Favorite recipe from **Pacific Coast Canned Pear Service**

Pineapple Fruit Tart

¼ cup ground almonds (about 2 tablespoons whole almonds)
¼ cup butter or margarine, softened
¼ cup sugar
2 tablespoons milk
½ teaspoon almond extract
¾ cup all-purpose flour
2 packages (3 ounces each) cream cheese, softened
2 tablespoons sour cream
¼ cup apricot preserves, divided
1 teaspoon vanilla extract
1 can (15¼ ounces) DEL MONTE® *FreshCut*™ Brand Pineapple Spears In Its Own Juice, drained
2 kiwifruits, peeled, sliced and cut into halves
1 cup sliced strawberries

1. Combine almonds, butter, sugar, milk and almond extract; mix well. Blend in flour. Chill dough 1 hour.

2. Press dough evenly onto bottom and up side of tart pan with removable bottom.

3. Bake at 350°F 15 to 18 minutes or until golden brown. Cool.

4. Combine cream cheese, sour cream, 1 tablespoon apricot preserves and vanilla. Spread onto crust. Arrange pineapple, kiwi and strawberries over cream cheese mixture.

5. Heat remaining 3 tablespoons apricot preserves in small saucepan over low heat. Spoon over fruit. *Makes 8 servings*

Pumpkin Apple Tart

CRUST

  1 cup plain dry bread crumbs
  1 cup crunchy nut-like cereal nuggets
  ½ cup sugar
  ½ teaspoon ground cinnamon
  ½ teaspoon ground nutmeg
  ¼ cup MOTT'S® Natural Apple Sauce
  2 tablespoons margarine, melted
  1 egg white

FILLING

  12 ounces evaporated skim milk
  1½ cups solid-pack pumpkin
  ⅔ cup sugar
  ½ cup MOTT'S® Chunky Apple Sauce
  ⅓ cup GRANDMA'S® Molasses
  2 egg whites
  1 whole egg
  ½ teaspoon ground ginger
  ½ teaspoon ground cinnamon
  ½ teaspoon ground nutmeg
  Frozen light nondairy whipped
    topping, thawed (optional)

For crust, preheat oven to 375°F. Spray 9- or 10-inch springform pan with nonstick cooking spray.

In medium bowl, combine bread crumbs, cereal, ½ cup sugar, ½ teaspoon cinnamon and ½ teaspoon nutmeg.

Add ¼ cup apple sauce, margarine and egg white; mix until moistened. Press onto bottom of prepared pan. Bake 8 minutes.

For filling, place evaporated milk in small saucepan. Cook over medium heat until milk almost boils, stirring occasionally.

In large bowl, combine evaporated milk, pumpkin, ⅔ cup sugar, ½ cup chunky apple sauce, molasses, 2 egg whites, whole egg, ginger, ½ teaspoon cinnamon and ½ teaspoon nutmeg. Pour into baked crust.

Increase oven temperature to 400°F. Bake 35 to 40 minutes or until center is set.

Cool 20 minutes on wire rack. Remove side of pan. Spoon or pipe whipped topping onto tart, if desired. Cut into 12 slices. Refrigerate leftovers. *Makes 12 servings*

Nutrients per Serving:

Calories:	210	Cholesterol:	20 mg
Total Fat:	3 g	Sodium:	170 mg

Pumpkin Apple Tart

Hazelnut Plum Tart

1 cup hazelnuts
¼ cup firmly packed light brown
    sugar
1 cup all-purpose flour
⅓ cup **FILIPPO BERIO**® Olive Oil
1 egg, separated
    Pinch salt
3 tablespoons granulated sugar
2 teaspoons cornstarch
½ teaspoon grated lime peel
    Pinch ground nutmeg
    Pinch ground cloves
1¼ pounds plums (about 5 large), cut
    into halves and pitted
3 tablespoons currant jelly
    Sweetened whipped cream
    (optional)

Preheat oven to 375°F. Grease 9-inch tart pan with removable bottom with olive oil. Place hazelnuts in food processor; process until coarsely chopped. Remove ¼ cup for garnish; set aside. Add brown sugar; process until nuts are finely ground. Add flour, olive oil, egg yolk and salt; process until combined.

Spoon mixture into prepared pan. Press firmly in even layer on bottom and up side. Brush inside of crust with egg white. Place in freezer 10 minutes.

In large bowl, combine granulated sugar, cornstarch, lime peel, nutmeg and cloves. Cut each plum half into 4 wedges. Add to sugar mixture; toss until coated. Arrange plums in overlapping circles in crust; spoon any remaining sugar mixture over plums. Place tart on baking sheet.

Bake 45 to 50 minutes or until fruit is tender and juices are thickened. Cool 30 minutes.

Hazelnut Plum Tart

Place currant jelly in small saucepan; heat over low heat, stirring frequently, until melted. Brush over plums; sprinkle with reserved hazelnuts. Serve tart warm or at room temperature with whipped cream, if desired. *Makes 6 servings*

Orange Pumpkin Tart

1½ cups all-purpose flour
1 cup uncooked QUAKER® Oats (quick or old fashioned), divided
1 cup plus 2 tablespoons granulated sugar, divided
¾ cup (1½ sticks) margarine
2 tablespoons water
1 can (16 ounces) pumpkin (1¾ cups)
1 egg white
1 teaspoon pumpkin pie spice
½ cup powdered sugar
2 teaspoons orange juice
½ teaspoon grated orange peel

Preheat oven to 400°F. Combine flour, ¾ cup oats and ½ cup granulated sugar; cut in margarine until crumbly. Reserve ¾ cup oat mixture. Mix remaining oat mixture with water until dough is moistened. Divide into 2 parts; press each onto cookie sheet to form two 12×5-inch tarts. Combine pumpkin, egg white, ½ cup granulated sugar and pumpkin pie spice. Spread over tarts. Top with combined remaining ¼ cup oats, remaining 2 tablespoons granulated sugar and reserved oat mixture. Bake 25 minutes or until golden. Cool. Drizzle with combined powdered sugar, orange juice and orange peel. Refrigerate leftovers. *Makes 12 servings*

Wisconsin Ricotta Tart with Kiwi and Raspberry Sauce

⅓ cup all-purpose flour
⅓ cup packed brown sugar
3 tablespoons butter
1 cup flaked coconut
½ cup chopped pecans or macadamia nuts
2 cups (16 ounces) Wisconsin Ricotta cheese
½ cup powdered sugar
1 teaspoon vanilla
1 teaspoon grated lime peel
1 package (10 ounces) frozen raspberries, thawed
1 kiwifruit

Preheat oven to 350°F. Combine flour and brown sugar; cut in butter until mixture resembles coarse crumbs. Stir in coconut and nuts. Press into 10-inch tart pan or pie plate. Bake crust 15 minutes. Remove from oven and cool.

Combine cheese, powdered sugar, vanilla and lime peel in food processor or blender; process until smooth. Spoon mixture into prepared crust. Refrigerate 1 hour. Before serving, place raspberries in food processor or blender; process until sauce forms. Cut kiwi into slices and arrange in circle on top of tart.* Drizzle tart with ½ of the raspberry sauce. Serve with remaining sauce. *Makes 8 to 10 servings*

Recipe can be prepared to this point and refrigerated until ready to serve.

Favorite recipe from **Wisconsin Milk Marketing Board**

Cherry-Cheese Tart Jubilee

1 container (15 ounces) Wisconsin Ricotta cheese

⅓ cup sour cream

⅓ cup sugar

3 tablespoons almond-flavored liqueur

2 tablespoons all-purpose flour

1 teaspoon grated orange peel

¼ teaspoon salt

2 eggs, separated

1 Tart Shell (recipe follows)

3 cups Northwest frozen pitted dark sweet cherries, partially thawed

2 tablespoons red currant jelly, melted

2 to 3 tablespoons toasted sliced almonds

Preheat oven to 350°F.

Press cheese through sieve into large bowl. Mix in sour cream, sugar, liqueur, flour, orange peel and salt. Beat in egg yolks. In another bowl beat egg whites to form soft peaks; fold into cheese mixture. Pour into prepared Tart Shell. Bake 50 to 60 minutes until lightly browned, puffy and set. Cool on rack. Just before serving arrange partially thawed cherries on tart. Brush cherries with jelly. Garnish with almonds. Serve immediately.

Makes 8 servings

Tart Shell

Preheat oven to 425°F. In large bowl, mix 1 cup flour, 1 tablespoon sugar and ¼ teaspoon salt. Add 6 tablespoons cold butter, cut into pieces. Cut in with pastry blender or 2 knives until coarse crumbs form. Beat 1 egg yolk with 2 tablespoons ice water. Add to flour mixture. Mix with fork and gather into ball. Roll out dough on lightly floured surface into 11-inch circle. Fit into 9½-inch tart pan with removable bottom. Fold pastry overhang back toward inside and press firmly against side of pan, allowing pastry to extend slightly above top. Refrigerate 10 minutes. Prick tart shell all over with fork; line with foil. Fill with pie weights, dried beans or rice. Bake 14 minutes. Remove foil and weights; bake 10 to 15 minutes longer until lightly browned and cooked through. Cool on wire rack.

Favorite recipe from **Wisconsin Milk Marketing Board**

Cherry-Cheese Tart Jubilee

Fruit Lover's Tart

1¼ cups uncooked QUAKER® Oats
    (quick or old fashioned)
⅓ cup firmly packed brown sugar
¼ cup all-purpose flour
2 tablespoons margarine, melted
2 egg whites
1 cup part-skim ricotta cheese
¼ cup Neufchâtel cheese, softened
2 tablespoons powdered sugar
½ teaspoon grated lemon peel
4½ cups any combination sliced fresh
    or frozen fruit, thawed and well
    drained

Heat oven to 350°F. Lightly spray 9-inch pie plate with nonstick cooking spray, or oil lightly. Combine oats, brown sugar, flour, margarine and egg whites, mixing until moistened. Press mixture onto bottom and up side of prepared plate. Bake 15 to 18 minutes or until light golden brown. Remove to wire rack; cool completely. Combine cheeses, powdered sugar and lemon peel. Spread onto oat base; top with fruit. Refrigerate 2 hours. *Makes 1 (9-inch) pie*

Microwave Directions: Combine oats, brown sugar, flour, margarine and egg whites, mixing until moistened. Press mixture onto bottom and up side of 9-inch microwavable pie plate. Microwave at HIGH 2½ to 3 minutes or until top springs back when lightly touched. Cool completely. Proceed as directed.

Nutrients per Serving:

Calories:	240	Cholesterol:	15 mg
Total Fat:	8 g	Sodium:	110 mg

Easy Fruit Tarts

12 wonton skins
    Vegetable cooking spray
2 tablespoons apple jelly or apricot
    fruit spread
1½ cups sliced or cut-up fruit such as
    DOLE® Bananas, Strawberries,
    Raspberries or Red or Green
    Seedless Grapes
1 cup nonfat or low-fat yogurt, any
    flavor

• Press wonton skins into 12 muffin cups sprayed with vegetable cooking spray, allowing corners to stand over edges of muffin cups.

• Bake at 375°F 5 minutes or until lightly browned. Carefully remove wonton cups to wire rack; cool.

• Cook and stir jelly in small saucepan over low heat until jelly melts.

• Brush bottoms of cooled wonton cups with melted jelly. Place two fruit slices in each cup; spoon rounded tablespoon of yogurt on top of fruit. Garnish with fruit slice and mint leaves, if desired. Serve immediately.
Makes 12 servings

Prep time: 20 minutes
Bake time: 5 minutes

Nutrients per Serving:

Calories:	55	Cholesterol:	1 mg
Total Fat:	0 g	Sodium:	60 mg

Easy Fruit Tarts

Nectarine Pecan Tart

PECAN CRUST
  1 cup wafer crumbs
  ½ cup pecan pieces
  2 tablespoons sugar
  3 tablespoons unsalted butter, melted

CREAM CHEESE FILLING
  1 package (8 ounces) plus 1 package
    (3 ounces) cream cheese,
    softened
  3 tablespoons sugar
  2 tablespoons orange juice
  ½ teaspoon vanilla

FRUIT TOPPING
  2 ripe nectarines, cut into halves and
    pitted
  4 tablespoons apricot jelly

1. For crust, preheat oven to 350°F. Process wafer crumbs, pecans and sugar in food processor until coarse crumbs form. Transfer to small bowl; stir in butter. Pat evenly on bottom and 1 inch up side of 8-inch springform pan.

2. Bake 15 minutes or until lightly browned. Cool completely on wire rack.

3. For filling, beat cream cheese, sugar, juice and vanilla in medium bowl with electric mixer at low speed until blended. Increase speed to high; beat 2 minutes or until fluffy. Pour into crust, spreading evenly to side. Cover; refrigerate 3 hours or until set.

Nectarine Pecan Tart

4. For topping, slice nectarines. Arrange over cream cheese mixture. Remove side of springform pan from tart; place on serving platter. Melt jelly in small saucepan, whisking constantly, over low heat. Cool 1 minute. Drizzle jelly over nectarines. Refrigerate, uncovered, 20 minutes or until set.

Makes 6 servings

Note: For best results, serve tart same day as assembled.

Rice Pudding Pear Tart

½ **(15-ounce) package refrigerated pie crust**
2 cups dry red wine
1 teaspoon ground cinnamon
2 large pears, peeled, halved and cored
2 cups cooked rice
2 cups half-and-half
½ **cup plus 1 tablespoon sugar, divided**
2 tablespoons butter or margarine
¼ **teaspoon salt**
2 eggs, beaten
1 teaspoon vanilla extract

Preheat oven to 450°F. Prepare pie crust according to package directions. Place in 10-inch tart pan. Bake 8 to 10 minutes or until lightly browned; set aside. *Reduce oven temperature to 350°F.*

Place wine and cinnamon in 10-inch skillet; bring to a boil. Add pears; reduce heat, cover and poach 10 minutes. Carefully turn pears in liquid; poach 5 to 10 minutes or until tender. Remove from wine; set aside.

Combine rice, half-and-half, ½ cup sugar, butter and salt in 3-quart saucepan. Cook over medium heat 12 to 15 minutes or until slightly thickened. Gradually stir ¼ of hot rice pudding mixture into eggs; return mixture to saucepan, stirring constantly. Continue to cook 1 to 2 minutes. Stir in vanilla. Pour rice pudding mixture into prepared crust. Place pears, cut sides down, on cutting surface. Cut thin lengthwise slices into each pear one third of the way down from stem end. Fan pears over pudding mixture.

Bake 30 minutes or until pudding is set. Remove from oven; sprinkle with remaining 1 tablespoon sugar. Place tart in oven about 4 to 5 inches from heat; broil 1 to 2 minutes or until top is browned. Cool before serving. Garnish as desired. Tart can be made ahead, if desired. *Makes 1 (10-inch) tart*

Favorite recipe from **USA Rice Federation**

CLASSIC COOKIES

Mocha Crinkles

1¾ cups all-purpose flour
¾ cup unsweetened cocoa
    powder
2 teaspoons coffee granules
1 teaspoon baking soda
¼ teaspoon salt
⅛ teaspoon black pepper

1⅓ cups packed light brown
    sugar
½ cup vegetable oil
¼ cup low-fat sour cream
1 egg
1 teaspoon vanilla
½ cup powdered sugar

Mix flour, cocoa, coffee, baking soda, salt and pepper in medium bowl; set aside. Combine brown sugar and oil in another medium bowl with electric mixer. Beat in sour cream, egg and vanilla. Beat in flour mixture until soft dough forms. Form dough into disc; cover. Refrigerate dough until firm, 3 to 4 hours. Preheat oven to 350°F. Place powdered sugar in shallow bowl. Cut dough into 1-inch pieces; roll into balls. Coat with powdered sugar. Place on ungreased cookie sheets. Bake 10 to 12 minutes or until tops of cookies are firm to the touch. Do not overbake. Cool on wire rack. *Makes 6 dozen cookies*

Mocha Crinkles

Original Nestlé® Toll House® Chocolate Chip Cookies

2¼ cups all-purpose flour
1 teaspoon baking soda
1 teaspoon salt
1 cup (2 sticks) butter, softened
¾ cup granulated sugar
¾ cup packed brown sugar
1 teaspoon vanilla extract
2 eggs
2 cups (12-ounce package) NESTLÉ®
 TOLL HOUSE® Semi-Sweet
 Chocolate Morsels
1 cup chopped nuts

COMBINE flour, baking soda and salt in small bowl. Beat butter, granulated sugar, brown sugar and vanilla in large mixer bowl. Add eggs, one at a time, beating well after each addition. Gradually beat in flour mixture. Stir in morsels and nuts. Drop by rounded tablespoons onto ungreased baking sheets.

BAKE in preheated 375°F oven for 9 to 11 minutes or until golden brown. Cool on baking sheets for 2 minutes; remove to wire racks to cool completely.

Makes about 5 dozen cookies

Pan Cookies: PREPARE dough as directed. Spread into greased 15½×10½-inch jelly-roll pan. Bake in preheated 375°F oven for 20 to 25 minutes or until golden brown. Cool in pan on wire rack. *Makes 4 dozen bars*

Slice and Bake Cookies: PREPARE dough as directed. Divide in half; wrap in wax paper. Chill for 1 hour or until firm. Shape each half into 15-inch log; wrap in wax paper.

Chill for 30 minutes.* Cut into ½-inch-thick slices; place on ungreased baking sheets. Bake in preheated 375°F oven for 8 to 10 minutes or until golden brown. Cool on baking sheets for 2 minutes; remove to wire racks to cool.

Makes about 5 dozen cookies

May be stored in refrigerator for up to 1 week or in freezer for up to 8 weeks.

Chocolate-Dipped Oat Cookies

2 cups uncooked rolled oats
¾ cup firmly packed brown sugar
½ cup finely chopped walnuts
½ cup vegetable oil
1 egg
2 teaspoons grated orange peel
¼ teaspoon salt
1 package (12 ounces) milk chocolate chips

Combine oats, sugar, walnuts, oil, egg, orange peel and salt in large bowl until blended. Cover; refrigerate overnight. Preheat oven to 350°F. Lightly grease cookie sheets or line with parchment paper. Melt chocolate chips in top of double boiler over hot, not boiling, water; keep warm. Shape oat mixture into large marble-sized balls. Place 2 inches apart on prepared cookie sheets. Bake 10 to 12 minutes or until golden and crisp. Cool 10 minutes on wire racks. Dip tops of cookies, one at a time, into melted chocolate. Place on waxed paper; cool until chocolate is set.

Makes about 6 dozen cookies

**Original Nestlé® Toll House®
Chocolate Chip Cookies**

Chocolate Chip Caramel Nut Cookies

18 caramels, unwrapped
1 cup Butter Flavor* CRISCO®
 all-vegetable shortening
1 cup granulated sugar
½ cup firmly packed brown sugar
2 eggs, beaten
2¾ cups all-purpose flour
1 teaspoon baking soda
1 teaspoon salt
1 teaspoon vanilla
½ teaspoon hot water
1 cup HERSHEY'S MINICHIPS
 Semi-Sweet Chocolate
½ cup coarsely chopped unsalted
 peanuts

Butter Flavor Crisco is artificially flavored.

1. Preheat oven to 400°F.

2. Cut each caramel into 4 pieces. Cut each piece into 6 pieces.

3. Combine shortening, granulated sugar and brown sugar in large bowl. Beat at medium speed of electric mixer until well blended and creamy. Beat in eggs.

4. Combine flour, baking soda and salt. Add gradually to shortening mixture at low speed of electric mixer. Mix until well blended. Beat in vanilla and hot water. Stir in caramels, small chocolate chips and nuts with spoon. Drop two slightly rounded tablespoonfuls 3 inches apart on ungreased cookie sheets for each cookie. Shape dough into circles, 2 inches in diameter and 1 inch high.

5. Bake at 400°F for 7 to 9 minutes or until light golden brown. Cool 5 minutes on cookie sheets before removing to wire racks.
Makes 2 to 2½ dozen cookies

Chocolate Peanut Butter Cookies

1 package DUNCAN HINES® Moist
 Deluxe Devil's Food Cake Mix
¾ cup JIF® Extra Crunchy Peanut
 Butter
2 eggs
2 tablespoons milk
1 cup candy-coated peanut butter
 pieces

1. Preheat oven to 350°F. Grease cookie sheets.

2. Combine cake mix, peanut butter, eggs and milk in large bowl. Mix at low speed with electric mixer until blended. Stir in peanut butter pieces.

3. Drop dough by slightly rounded tablespoonfuls onto prepared cookie sheets. Bake 7 to 9 minutes or until lightly browned. Cool 2 minutes on cookie sheets. Remove to cooling racks.
Makes about 3½ dozen cookies

Tip: Substitute 1 cup peanut butter chips for peanut butter pieces.

Chocolate Peanut Butter Cookies

Cocoa Crinkle Sandwiches

1¾ cups all-purpose flour
½ cup unsweetened cocoa
1 teaspoon baking soda
¼ teaspoon salt
½ cup butter
1¾ cups sugar, divided
2 eggs
2 teaspoons vanilla
1 can (16 ounces) chocolate or
favorite flavor frosting
½ cup crushed candy canes (optional)

Combine flour, cocoa, baking soda and salt in medium bowl. Melt butter in large saucepan over medium heat; cool slightly. Add 1¼ cups sugar; whisk until smooth. Whisk in eggs, one at a time, until blended. Stir in vanilla until smooth. Stir in flour mixture just until combined. Wrap dough in plastic wrap; refrigerate 2 hours.

Preheat oven to 350°F. Grease cookie sheets. Shape dough into 1-inch balls. Place remaining ½ cup sugar in shallow bowl; roll balls in sugar. Place 1½ inches apart on cookie sheets. Bake 12 minutes or until cookies are set. Let cookies stand on cookie sheets 5 minutes; cool completely on wire racks.

Stir frosting until soft and smooth. Place crushed candy canes on waxed paper. Spread about 2 teaspoons frosting over flat side of one cookie. Place second cookie, flat side down, over frosting, pressing down to allow frosting to squeeze out slightly between cookies. Press exposed frosting into crushed candy canes. Repeat with remaining cookies.
Makes about 20 sandwich cookies

Macaroon Kiss Cookies

⅓ cup butter or margarine, softened
1 package (3 ounces) cream cheese,
softened
¾ cup sugar
1 egg yolk
2 teaspoons almond extract
2 teaspoons orange juice
1¼ cups all-purpose flour
2 teaspoons baking powder
¼ teaspoon salt
1 package (14 ounces) MOUNDS™
Sweetened Coconut Flakes,
divided
1 bag (9 ounces) HERSHEY®'S KISSES™
Milk Chocolates (about 54)

In large bowl, beat together butter, cream cheese and sugar. Add egg yolk, almond extract and orange juice; beat well. Stir together flour, baking powder and salt; gradually add to butter mixture. Stir in 3 cups coconut. Cover tightly; refrigerate 1 hour or until firm enough to handle.

Preheat oven to 350°F. Shape dough into 1-inch balls; roll in remaining coconut. Place on ungreased cookie sheets. Bake 10 to 12 minutes or until lightly browned. Meanwhile, remove wrappers from chocolate pieces. Remove cookies from oven; immediately press chocolate piece in center of each cookie. Cool 1 minute. Carefully remove from cookie sheets; cool completely on wire racks.
Makes about 4½ dozen cookies

Cocoa Crinkle Sandwiches

Double-Dipped Chocolate Peanut Butter Cookies

1¼ cups all-purpose flour
½ teaspoon baking powder
½ teaspoon baking soda
½ teaspoon salt
½ cup butter, softened
½ cup granulated sugar
½ cup packed light brown sugar
½ cup creamy or chunky peanut
   butter
1 egg
1 teaspoon vanilla
   Additional granulated sugar
1½ cups semisweet chocolate chips
3 teaspoons shortening, divided
1½ cups milk chocolate chips

Preheat oven to 350°F. Combine flour, baking powder, baking soda and salt in small bowl.

Beat butter, granulated sugar and brown sugar in large bowl with electric mixer at medium speed until light and fluffy. Beat in peanut butter, egg and vanilla. Gradually stir in flour mixture until blended.

Shape heaping tablespoonfuls of dough into 1½-inch balls. Place balls 2 inches apart on ungreased cookie sheets. (If dough is too soft, refrigerate 30 minutes.)

Dip table fork into granulated sugar; press criss-cross fashion onto each ball, flattening to ½-inch thickness.

Bake 12 minutes or until set. Cool on cookie sheets 2 minutes. Cool completely on wire racks.

Double-Dipped Chocolate Peanut Butter Cookies

Melt semisweet chocolate chips and 1½ teaspoons shortening in heavy small saucepan over low heat. Dip one end of each cookie in mixture; place on waxed paper. Let stand until chocolate is set, about 30 minutes. Repeat with milk chocolate chips and remaining 1½ teaspoons shortening, dipping opposite ends of cookies.

Makes 2 dozen cookies

Chocolate Sugar Cookies

3 squares BAKER'S® Unsweetened Chocolate
1 cup (2 sticks) margarine or butter
1 cup sugar
1 egg
1 teaspoon vanilla
2 cups all-purpose flour
1 teaspoon baking soda
¼ teaspoon salt
Additional sugar

Microwave chocolate and margarine in large microwavable bowl on HIGH 2 minutes or until margarine is melted. Stir until chocolate is completely melted.

Stir 1 cup sugar into melted chocolate mixture until well blended. Stir in egg and vanilla until completely blended. Mix in flour, baking soda and salt. Refrigerate 30 minutes.

Heat oven to 375°F. Shape dough into 1-inch balls; roll in additional sugar. Place 2 inches apart on ungreased cookie sheets. (If thinner, crisper cookies are desired, flatten balls with bottom of drinking glass.)

Bake 8 to 10 minutes or until set. Remove from cookie sheets to cool on wire racks.

Makes about 3½ dozen cookies

Prep time: 15 minutes
Chill time: 30 minutes
Bake time: 8 to 10 minutes

Jam-Filled Chocolate Sugar Cookies: Prepare Chocolate Sugar Cookie dough as directed. Roll in finely chopped nuts in place of sugar. Make indentation in each ball; fill center with your favorite jam. Bake as directed.

Chocolate-Caramel Sugar Cookies: Prepare Chocolate Sugar Cookie dough as directed. Roll in finely chopped nuts in place of sugar. Make indentation in each ball; bake as directed. Microwave 1 package (14 ounces) KRAFT® Caramels with 2 tablespoons milk in microwavable bowl on HIGH 3 minutes or until melted, stirring after 2 minutes. Fill centers of cookies with caramel mixture. Drizzle with melted BAKER'S® Semi-Sweet Chocolate.

Chocolate Chip Brownies

¾ cup granulated sugar
½ cup butter
2 tablespoons water
2 cups semisweet chocolate chips or
    mini chocolate chips, divided
1½ teaspoons vanilla
1¼ cups all-purpose flour
½ teaspoon baking soda
½ teaspoon salt
2 eggs
    Powdered sugar for garnish

Preheat oven to 350°F. Grease 9-inch square baking pan.

Combine sugar, butter and water in medium microwavable bowl. Microwave on HIGH (100% power) 2½ to 3 minutes or until butter is melted. Stir in 1 cup chocolate chips; stir gently until chips are melted and mixture is well blended. Stir in vanilla; let stand 5 minutes to cool.

Combine flour, baking soda and salt in small bowl. Beat eggs into chocolate mixture, one at a time. Add flour mixture; mix well. Stir in remaining 1 cup chocolate chips. Spread batter evenly into prepared pan.

Bake 25 minutes for fudgy brownies or 30 to 35 minutes for cakelike brownies. Remove pan to wire rack to cool completely. Cut into 2¼-inch squares. Place powdered sugar in fine-mesh strainer and sprinkle over brownies, if desired.   *Makes 16 brownies*

Chocolate Chip Brownies

Fudgy Raisin Pixies

½ cup butter
2 cups granulated sugar
4 eggs
2 cups all-purpose flour, divided
¾ cup unsweetened cocoa powder
2 teaspoons baking powder
½ teaspoon salt
½ cup chocolate-covered raisins
    Powdered sugar

Beat butter and sugar in large bowl until light and fluffy. Add eggs; mix until well blended. Combine 1 cup flour, cocoa, baking powder and salt in small bowl; add to butter mixture. Mix until well blended. Stir in remaining 1 cup flour and chocolate-covered raisins. Cover; refrigerate until firm, 2 hours or overnight.

Preheat oven to 350°F. Grease cookie sheets. Coat hands with powdered sugar. Shape rounded teaspoonfuls of dough into 1-inch balls; roll in powdered sugar. Place 2 inches apart on prepared cookie sheets. Bake 14 to 17 minutes or until firm to the touch. Remove immediately from cookie sheets; cool completely on wire racks.

Makes about 4 dozen cookies

Minted Chocolate Chip Brownies

¾ cup granulated sugar
½ cup butter
2 tablespoons water
1 cup semisweet chocolate chips or
    mini semisweet chocolate chips
1½ teaspoons vanilla
2 eggs
1¼ cups all-purpose flour
½ teaspoon baking soda
½ teaspoon salt
1 cup mint chocolate chips
    Powdered sugar for garnish

Preheat oven to 350°F. Grease 9-inch square baking pan. Combine sugar, butter and water in medium microwavable bowl. Microwave on HIGH 2½ to 3 minutes or until butter is melted. Stir in semisweet chips; stir gently until chips are melted and mixture is well blended. Stir in vanilla; let stand 5 minutes to cool.

Beat eggs into chocolate mixture, 1 at a time. Combine flour, baking soda and salt in small bowl; add to chocolate mixture. Stir in mint chocolate chips. Spread into prepared pan.

Bake 25 minutes for fudgy brownies or 30 minutes for cakelike brownies.

Remove to wire rack; cool completely. Cut into 2¼-inch squares. Sprinkle with powdered sugar, if desired.

Makes about 16 brownies

Chocolate Malted Cookies

½ cup butter, softened
½ cup shortening
1¾ cups powdered sugar, divided
1 teaspoon vanilla
2 cups all-purpose flour
1 cup malted milk powder, divided
¼ cup unsweetened cocoa powder

1. Beat butter, shortening, ¾ cup powdered sugar and vanilla in large bowl at high speed of electric mixer.

2. Add flour, ½ cup malted milk powder and cocoa; beat at low speed until well blended. Refrigerate several hours or overnight.

3. Preheat oven to 350°F. Shape slightly mounded teaspoonfuls of dough into balls.

4. Place dough balls about 2 inches apart on ungreased cookie sheets. Bake 14 to 16 minutes or until lightly browned.

5. Meanwhile, combine remaining 1 cup powdered sugar and ½ cup malted milk powder in medium bowl.

6. Remove cookies to wire racks; cool 5 minutes. Roll cookies in powdered sugar mixture.   *Makes about 4 dozen cookies*

Variation: Substitute 6 ounces melted semisweet chocolate for 1 cup powdered sugar and ½ cup malted milk powder used to roll the cookies. Dip cookies in melted chocolate and let dry on wire racks until coating is set.

Cocoa Hazelnut Macaroons

⅓ cup hazelnuts
¾ cup quick oats
⅓ cup brown sugar
6 tablespoons unsweetened cocoa powder
2 tablespoons all-purpose flour
4 egg whites
1 teaspoon vanilla
½ teaspoon salt
⅓ cup plus 1 tablespoon granulated sugar

Preheat oven to 375°F. Bake hazelnuts 8 minutes or until lightly browned. Quickly transfer nuts to clean dry dish towel. Fold towel; rub vigorously to remove as much of the skins as possible. Finely chop hazelnuts. Combine hazelnuts, oats, brown sugar, cocoa and flour in medium bowl; mix well. Set aside.

Reduce oven temperature to 325°F. Combine egg whites, vanilla and salt in clean dry medium bowl. Beat with electric mixer on high until soft peaks form. Gradually add granulated sugar, continuing to beat on high until stiff peaks form. Gently fold in hazelnut mixture with rubber spatula.

Drop level tablespoonfuls of dough onto cookie sheet. Bake 15 to 17 minutes or until tops of cookies no longer appear wet. Cool completely on wire rack.

Makes 3 dozen cookies

Chocolate Malted Cookies

Molded Scotch Shortbread

1½ cups all-purpose flour
¼ teaspoon salt
¾ cup butter, softened
⅓ cup sugar
 1 egg
   10-inch diameter ceramic
   shortbread mold

Preheat oven to temperature recommended by shortbread mold manufacturer. Combine flour and salt in medium bowl.

Beat butter and sugar in large bowl with electric mixer at medium speed until light and fluffy. Beat in egg. Gradually add flour mixture. Beat at low speed until well blended.

Spray shortbread mold with nonstick cooking spray. Press dough firmly into mold. Bake, cool and remove from mold according to manufacturer's directions.

If mold is not available, preheat oven to 350°F. Shape tablespoonfuls of dough into 1-inch balls. Place 2 inches apart on ungreased cookie sheet; press with fork to flatten. Bake 18 to 20 minutes or until edges are lightly browned. Let cookies stand on cookie sheet 2 minutes; transfer to wire rack to cool completely.

Makes 1 shortbread mold or
2 dozen cookies

Spiced Wafers

½ cup butter, softened
1 cup sugar
1 egg
2 tablespoons milk
1 teaspoon vanilla
1¾ cups all-purpose flour
2 teaspoon baking powder
1 teaspoon ground cinnamon
½ teaspoon ground nutmeg
¼ teaspoon ground cloves
   Red hot candies or red colored
   sugar for garnish (optional)

Beat butter in large bowl with electric mixer at medium speed until smooth. Add sugar; beat until well blended. Add egg, milk and vanilla; beat until well blended.

Combine flour, baking powder, cinnamon, nutmeg and cloves in large bowl. Gradually add flour mixture to butter mixture at low speed; blending well after each addition.

Shape dough into 2 logs, each about 2 inches in diameter and 6 inches long. Wrap each log in plastic wrap. Refrigerate 2 to 3 hours or overnight.

Preheat oven to 350°F. Grease cookie sheets. Cut logs into ¼-inch-thick slices; decorate with candies or colored sugar, if desired. (Or leave plain and decorate with icing later.) Place at least 2 inches apart on cookie sheets.

Bake 11 to 13 minutes or until edges are light brown. Transfer to wire racks to cool.

Makes about 4 dozen cookies

Molded Scotch Shortbread

Ultimate Sugar Cookies

1¼ cups granulated sugar
  1 Butter Flavor* CRISCO® Stick or
    1 cup Butter Flavor* CRISCO®
    all-vegetable shortening
  2 eggs
  ¼ cup light corn syrup or regular
    pancake syrup
  1 tablespoon vanilla
  3 cups all-purpose flour plus
    4 tablespoons, divided
  ¾ teaspoon baking powder
  ½ teaspoon baking soda
  ½ teaspoon salt
    Decorations of your choice:
    granulated sugar, colored sugar
    crystals, frosting, decors, candies,
    chips, nuts, raisins, decorating gel

Butter Flavor Crisco is artificially flavored.

1. Combine sugar and shortening in large bowl. Beat at medium speed of electric mixer until well blended. Add eggs, syrup and vanilla. Beat until well blended and fluffy.

2. Combine 3 cups flour, baking powder, baking soda and salt. Add gradually to creamed mixture at low speed. Mix until well blended. Divide dough into 4 quarters.

3. Heat oven to 375°F. Place sheets of foil on countertop for cooling cookies.

4. Spread 1 tablespoon flour on large sheet of waxed paper. Place one fourth of dough on floured paper. Flatten slightly with hands. Turn dough over and cover with another large sheet of waxed paper. Roll dough to ¼-inch thickness. Remove top sheet of waxed paper.

5. Cut out cookies with floured cutter. Transfer to ungreased baking sheet with large pancake turner. Place 2 inches apart. Sprinkle with granulated sugar, colored sugar crystals, decors or leave plain to frost or decorate when cooled. Roll out remaining dough.

6. Bake one baking sheet at a time at 375°F for 5 to 9 minutes, depending on size of cookies. (Bake smaller, thinner cookies closer to 5 minutes; larger cookies closer to 9 minutes.) *Do not overbake.* Cool 2 minutes on baking sheet. Remove cookies to foil to cool completely, then decorate if desired.

Makes about 3 to 4 dozen cookies

Tip: For well-defined cookie edges, or if dough is too sticky or too soft to roll, wrap each quarter of dough with plastic wrap. Refrigerate 1 hour. Keep dough balls refrigerated until ready to roll.

Ultimate Sugar Cookies

Gingerbread People

2¼ cups all-purpose flour
2 teaspoons ground ginger
2 teaspoons ground cinnamon
1 teaspoon baking powder
½ teaspoon salt
¼ teaspoon ground cloves
¼ teaspoon ground nutmeg
¾ cup butter, softened
½ cup packed light brown sugar
½ cup dark molasses
1 egg
    Tube frosting (optional)
    Candies and other decorations
      (optional)

Combine flour, ginger, cinnamon, baking powder, salt, cloves and nutmeg in large bowl.

Beat butter and brown sugar in large bowl with electric mixer at medium speed until light and fluffy. Beat in molasses and egg. Gradually add flour mixture; beat at low speed until well blended. Shape dough into 3 disks. Wrap in plastic wrap; refrigerate 1 hour or until firm.

Preheat oven to 350°F. Working with one disk at a time, place on lightly floured surface. Roll out dough with lightly floured rolling pin to ¼-inch thickness. Cut out gingerbread people with floured 5-inch cookie cutters; place on ungreased cookie sheets. Press dough trimmings together gently; reroll and cut out more cookies.

Bake 12 minutes or until edges are golden. Let cookies stand on cookie sheets 1 minute; transfer to wire racks to cool completely.

Decorate cooled cookies with piped icing; garnish with candies, if desired. Let stand at room temperature 20 minutes or until set. Store tightly covered at room temperature or freeze up to 3 months.

Makes about 16 large cookies

Holiday Sugar Cookies

1 cup butter, softened
¾ cup sugar
1 egg
2 cups all-purpose flour
1 teaspoon baking powder
¼ teaspoon salt
¼ teaspoon ground cinnamon
    Colored sprinkles or sugar, for
      decorating (optional)

Beat butter and sugar in large bowl with electric mixer until creamy. Add egg; beat until fluffy.

Stir in flour, baking powder, salt and cinnamon until well blended. Form dough into a ball; wrap in plastic wrap and flatten. Refrigerate about 2 hours or until firm.

Preheat oven to 350°F. Roll out dough, a small portion at a time, to ¼-inch thickness on lightly floured surface with lightly floured rolling pin. (Keep remaining dough wrapped in refrigerator.)

Cut out cookies with 3-inch cookie cutters. Sprinkle with colored sprinkles or sugar, if desired. Transfer to ungreased cookie sheets.

Bake 7 to 9 minutes until edges are lightly browned. Cool on cookie sheets 1 minute; transfer to wire racks.

Makes 3 dozen cookies

Gingerbread People

Old-Fashioned Oatmeal Cookies

¾ Butter Flavor* CRISCO® Stick or
⅓ cup Butter Flavor* CRISCO®
all-vegetable shortening
1¼ cups firmly packed brown sugar
1 egg
⅓ cup milk
1½ teaspoons vanilla
3 cups quick oats, uncooked
1 cup all-purpose flour
½ teaspoon baking soda
½ teaspoon salt
¼ teaspoon ground cinnamon
1 cup raisins
1 cup coarsely chopped walnuts

Butter Flavor Crisco is artificially flavored.

1. Heat oven to 375°F. Grease baking sheets with shortening. Place sheets of foil on countertop for cooling cookies.

2. Combine shortening, brown sugar, egg, milk and vanilla in large bowl. Beat at medium speed of electric mixer until well blended.

3. Combine oats, flour, baking soda, salt and cinnamon. Mix into shortening mixture at low speed just until blended. Stir in raisins and walnuts.

4. Drop by rounded measuring tablespoonfuls of dough 2 inches apart onto prepared baking sheets.

5. Bake one baking sheet at a time at 375°F for 10 to 12 minutes or until lightly browned. *Do not overbake.* Cool 2 minutes on baking sheets. Remove cookies to foil to cool.
Makes about 2½ dozen cookies

Pfeffernüesse

3½ cups all-purpose flour
2 teaspoons baking powder
1½ teaspoons ground cinnamon
1 teaspoon ground ginger
½ teaspoon baking soda
½ teaspoon salt
½ teaspoon ground cloves
½ teaspoon ground cardamom
¼ teaspoon ground black pepper
1 cup butter, softened
1 cup granulated sugar
¼ cup dark molasses
1 egg
Powdered sugar

Combine flour, baking powder, cinnamon, ginger, baking soda, salt, cloves, cardamom and pepper in large bowl.

Beat butter and sugar in large bowl with electric mixer at medium speed until light and fluffy. Beat in molasses and egg. Gradually add flour mixture. Beat at low speed until dough forms. Shape dough into disk; wrap in plastic wrap and refrigerate until firm, 30 minutes or up to 3 days.

Preheat oven to 350°F. Grease cookie sheets. Roll dough into 1-inch balls. Place 2 inches apart on prepared cookie sheets.

Bake 12 to 14 minutes or until golden brown. Transfer cookies to wire racks; dust with sifted powdered sugar. Cool completely.
Makes 5 dozen cookies

Pfeffernüesse

Yuletide Linzer Bars

1⅓ cups butter, softened
¾ cup sugar
1 egg
1 teaspoon grated lemon peel
2½ cups all-purpose flour
1½ cups whole almonds, ground
1 teaspoon ground cinnamon
¾ cup raspberry preserves
Powdered sugar

Preheat oven to 350°F. Grease 13×9-inch baking pan.

Beat butter and sugar in large bowl with electric mixer until creamy. Beat in egg and lemon peel until blended. Mix in flour, almonds and cinnamon until well blended.

Press 2 cups dough into bottom of prepared pan. Spread preserves over crust. Press remaining dough, a small amount at a time, evenly over preserves.

Bake 35 to 40 minutes until golden brown. Cool in pan on wire rack. Sprinkle with powdered sugar; cut into bars.

Makes 3 dozen bars

Pecan Pie Bars

¾ cup butter, softened
½ cup powdered sugar
1½ cups all-purpose flour
3 eggs
2 cups coarsely chopped pecans
1 cup granulated sugar
1 cup light corn syrup
2 tablespoons butter, melted
1 teaspoon vanilla

Preheat oven to 350°F. For crust, beat butter in large bowl with electric mixer at medium speed until smooth. Add powdered sugar; beat at medium speed until well blended.

Add flour gradually, beating at low speed after each addition. (Mixture will be crumbly but presses together easily.)

Press dough evenly into ungreased 13×9-inch baking pan. Press mixture slightly up sides of pan (less than ¼ inch) to form lip to hold filling. Bake 20 to 25 minutes.

Meanwhile, for filling, beat eggs lightly in medium bowl with fork. Add pecans, granulated sugar, corn syrup, melted butter and vanilla; mix well.

Pour filling over partially baked crust. Return to oven; bake 35 to 40 minutes or until filling is set.

Loosen edges with knife. Let cool completely on wire rack before cutting into squares. Cover and refrigerate until 10 to 15 minutes before serving time. (Do not freeze.)

Makes 4 dozen bars

Yuletide Linzer Bars

Pecan Toffee Filled Ravioli Cookies

1 cup packed brown sugar
¼ cup butter, melted
½ cup chopped pecans
2 tablespoons all-purpose flour
2 recipes Butter Cookie Dough
    (recipe follows)

1. Stir brown sugar into butter in large bowl until well blended. Add pecans and flour; mix well.

2. Transfer brown sugar filling to waxed paper; shape into 7-inch square. Cut filling into 36 (1¼-inch) pieces. Refrigerate 1 hour or overnight.

3. Prepare Butter Cookie Dough. Cover; refrigerate about 4 hours or until firm. Roll half of dough on well-floured sheet of waxed paper to 12-inch square.

4. Repeat with second half of dough. If dough becomes soft, refrigerate 1 hour.

5. Preheat oven to 350°F. Lightly score 1 layer of dough at 2 inch intervals to form 36 squares.

6. Place 1 square of brown sugar filling in center of each dough square. Carefully place second layer of dough over brown sugar mixture. Press gently between rows. Cut with knife, ravioli wheel or pastry cutter.

7. Transfer filled ravioli to ungreased cookie sheets. Bake 14 to 16 minutes or until lightly browned. Cool on cookie sheets 5 minutes. Remove to wire racks; cool completely.

Makes 3 dozen cookies

Butter Cookie Dough

¾ cup butter, softened
¼ cup granulated sugar
¼ cup packed light brown sugar
1 egg yolk
1¾ cups all-purpose flour
¾ teaspoon baking powder
⅛ teaspoon salt

Combine butter, granulated sugar, brown sugar and egg yolk in medium bowl. Add flour, baking powder and salt; mix well.

No-Fuss Bar Cookies

2 cups graham cracker crumbs
1 cup semisweet chocolate chips
1 cup flaked coconut
¾ cup coarsely chopped walnuts
1 can (14 ounces) sweetened
    condensed milk

Preheat oven to 350°F. Grease 13×9-inch baking pan; set aside.

Combine crumbs, chips, coconut and walnuts in medium bowl; stir to blend. Add milk; stir until blended. Spread batter evenly in prepared pan.

Bake 15 to 18 minutes or until edges are golden brown. Let pan stand on wire rack until completely cool. Cut into bars.

Makes 20 bars

No-Fuss Bar Cookies

Currant Cheesecake Bars

½ cup butter, softened
1 cup all-purpose flour
½ cup packed light brown sugar
½ cup finely chopped pecans
1 package (8 ounces) cream cheese, softened
¼ cup granulated sugar
1 egg
1 tablespoon milk
2 teaspoons grated lemon peel
⅓ cup currant jelly or seedless raspberry jam

Preheat oven to 350°F. Grease 9-inch square baking pan. Beat butter in medium bowl with electric mixer at medium speed until smooth. Add flour, brown sugar and pecans; beat at low speed until well blended. Press mixture into bottom and partially up sides of prepared pan.

Bake about 15 minutes or until light brown. If sides of crust have shrunk down, press back up and reshape with spoon. Let cool 5 minutes on wire rack.

Meanwhile, beat cream cheese in large bowl with electric mixer at medium speed until smooth. Add granulated sugar, egg, milk and lemon peel; beat until well blended.

Heat jelly in small saucepan over low heat 2 to 3 minutes or until smooth, stirring occasionally.

Pour cream cheese mixture over crust. Drizzle jam in 7 to 8 horizontal strips across filling with spoon. Swirl jam through filling with knife to create marbleized effect.

Return pan to oven; bake 20 to 25 minutes or until filling is set. Let cool completely on wire rack before cutting into bars.

Makes about 32 bars

Luscious Lemon Bars

2 cups all-purpose flour
1 cup butter
½ cup powdered sugar
4 teaspoons grated lemon peel, divided
¼ teaspoon salt
1 cup granulated sugar
3 eggs
⅓ cup fresh lemon juice
Sifted powdered sugar

Preheat oven to 350°F. Grease 13×9-inch baking pan.

Combine flour, butter, powdered sugar, 1 teaspoon lemon peel and salt in food processor. Process until crumbly. Press mixture evenly into prepared pan. Bake 18 to 20 minutes or until golden.

Meanwhile, beat remaining 3 teaspoons lemon peel, granulated sugar, eggs and lemon juice in medium bowl with electric mixer at medium speed until well blended.

Pour mixture evenly over warm crust. Return pan to oven; bake 18 to 20 minutes or until center is set and edges are golden brown. Remove pan to wire rack to cool completely.

Dust with sifted powdered sugar; cut into bars. Store tightly covered at room temperature. (Do not freeze.)

Makes 3 dozen bars

Currant Cheesecake Bars

FESTIVE CAKES & CHEESECAKES

Pecan Spice Cake

MAZOLA NO STICK® Cooking Spray
1 package (18.25 ounces) spice cake mix plus ingredients as label directs

½ cup finely chopped pecans
Coconut-Pecan Filling (page 320)
Luscious Chocolate Frosting (page 320)

Preheat oven to 350°F. Spray 2 (9-inch) round cake pans with cooking spray. Prepare cake mix as label directs; stir in pecans. Pour batter into pans. Bake as directed. Cool on wire racks 10 minutes. Remove from pans; cool completely. When cool, split layers horizontally in half. Place one cake layer on serving plate. Spread with one-third of Coconut-Pecan Filling. Top with second cake layer; spread with about ⅔ cup Luscious Chocolate Frosting. Top with third cake layer; spread with one-third of filling. Top with fourth cake layer. Frost side of cake with remaining frosting. Spread top of cake with remaining filling. Refrigerate 2 hours or until set. *Makes 12 to 16 servings*

(continued on page 320)

Pecan Spice Cake

(**Pecan Spice Cake,** *continued from page 318*)

Coconut-Pecan Filling

½ cup **KARO® Light Corn Syrup**
½ cup **evaporated milk**
¾ cup **sugar**
½ cup **(1 stick) MAZOLA® Margarine or butter**
3 **egg yolks, slightly beaten**
1 **teaspoon vanilla**
1⅓ cups **flaked coconut**
1 cup **finely chopped pecans**

In medium saucepan combine corn syrup, evaporated milk, sugar, margarine, egg yolks and vanilla. Stirring frequently, cook over medium heat until thickened, 10 to 12 minutes. Remove from heat. Stir in coconut and pecans. Cool until thick enough to spread, stirring occasionally.

Makes about 2¼ cups filling

Luscious Chocolate Frosting

1 **package (3 ounces) cream cheese**
¼ cup **KARO® Light Corn Syrup**
2 **tablespoons MAZOLA® Margarine or butter**
2 cups **confectioners' sugar**
⅓ cup **unsweetened cocoa**
½ teaspoon **vanilla**

In small bowl beat cream cheese, corn syrup and margarine until creamy. Beat in confectioners' sugar, cocoa and vanilla until frosting is of spreading consistency.

Makes 1⅓ cups frosting

Apple-Gingerbread Mini Cakes

1 large **Cortland or Jonathan apple, cored and cut into quarters**
1 package **(14½ ounces) gingerbread cake and cookie mix**
1 cup **water**
1 large **egg**
Powdered sugar

1. Lightly grease 10 (6- to 7-ounce) custard cups; set aside. Grate apple in food processor or with hand-held grater. Combine grated apple, cake mix, water and egg in medium bowl; stir until well blended. Spoon about ⅓ cup mix into each custard cup, filling cups half full.

2. Arrange 5 custard cups in microwave. Microwave at HIGH (100% power) 2 minutes. Rotate cups ½ turn. Microwave 1 minute more or until cakes are springy when touched lightly and slightly moist on top. Cool on wire rack. Repeat with remaining cakes.

3. To unmold cakes, run a small knife around edge of custard cups to loosen cakes while still warm. Invert onto cutting board and tap lightly until cake drops out. Place on plates. Dust with powdered sugar. Serve warm or at room temperature.   *Makes 10 servings*

Prep and cook time: 20 minutes

Serving Suggestion: Serve with whipped cream, vanilla ice cream or crème anglaise.

Apple-Gingerbread Mini Cakes

Spicy Butterscotch Snack Cake

1 cup (2 sticks) butter or margarine, softened
1 cup granulated sugar
2 eggs
½ teaspoon vanilla extract
½ cup applesauce
2½ cups all-purpose flour
1½ to 2 teaspoons ground cinnamon
1 teaspoon baking soda
½ teaspoon salt
1⅔ cups (10-ounce package) HERSHEY'S Butterscotch Chips
1 cup chopped pecans (optional)
   Powdered sugar or frozen non-dairy whipped topping, thawed (optional)

Heat oven to 350°F. Lightly grease 13×9-inch baking pan. In large bowl, beat butter and sugar until light and fluffy. Add eggs and vanilla; beat well. Mix in applesauce. Stir together flour, cinnamon, baking soda and salt; gradually add to butter mixture, beating until well blended. Stir in butterscotch chips and pecans, if desired. Spread into prepared pan. Bake 35 minutes or until wooden pick inserted in center comes out clean. Cool completely in pan. Dust with powdered sugar or serve with whipped topping, if desired. *Makes 12 servings*

Scrumptious Apple Cake

3 egg whites
1½ cups sugar
1 cup unsweetened applesauce
1 teaspoon vanilla
2 cups all-purpose flour
2 teaspoons ground cinnamon
1 teaspoon baking soda
¼ teaspoon salt
4 cups cored peeled tart apple slices (McIntosh or Crispin)
   Yogurt Glaze (recipe follows)

Preheat oven to 350°F. Beat egg whites until slightly foamy; add sugar, applesauce and vanilla. Combine flour, cinnamon, baking soda and salt in separate bowl; add to applesauce mixture. Spread apples in 13×9-inch pan or 9-inch round springform pan sprayed with nonstick cooking spray. Spread batter over apples. Bake 35 to 40 minutes or until wooden toothpick inserted in center comes out clean; cool on wire rack. Prepare Yogurt Glaze; spread over cooled cake.
Makes 15 to 20 servings

Yogurt Glaze
Combine 1½ cups plain or vanilla nonfat yogurt, 3 tablespoons brown sugar (or to taste) and 1 teaspoon vanilla or 1 teaspoon lemon juice. Stir together until smooth.

Nutrients per Serving:

Calories:	170	Cholesterol:	1 mg
Total Fat:	<1 g	Sodium:	130 mg

Favorite recipe from **New York Apple Association**

Scrumptious Apple Cake

Lemon Poppy Seed Cake

6 tablespoons margarine, softened
½ cup firmly packed light brown
    sugar
½ cup plain low-fat yogurt
1 whole egg
2 egg whites
3 teaspoons fresh lemon juice
1¾ cups all-purpose flour
1 teaspoon baking powder
½ teaspoon baking soda
¼ teaspoon salt
⅓ cup fat-free (skim) milk
2 tablespoons poppy seeds
1 tablespoon grated lemon peel

LEMON GLAZE
1 cup powdered sugar
2 tablespoons plus 1½ teaspoons
    lemon juice
½ teaspoon poppy seeds

Preheat oven to 350°F. Grease and flour 6-cup Bundt® pan. Beat margarine in large bowl with electric mixer until fluffy. Beat in brown sugar, yogurt, whole egg, egg whites and 3 teaspoons lemon juice. Set aside. Combine flour, baking powder, baking soda and salt in medium bowl. Add flour mixture to margarine mixture alternately with milk, beginning and ending with flour mixture. Mix in 2 tablespoons poppy seeds and lemon peel. Pour batter into prepared pan.

Bake about 40 minutes or until cake is golden brown and toothpick inserted in center comes out clean. Cool in pan on wire rack 10 minutes. Remove from pan to wire rack; cool completely.

For glaze, mix powdered sugar with 2 tablespoons plus 1½ teaspoons lemon juice until of desired consistency. Spoon glaze over cake and sprinkle with ½ teaspoon poppy seeds. *Makes 12 servings*

Angel Food Cake with Pineapple Sauce

1 can (20 ounces) DOLE® Crushed
    Pineapple
2 tablespoons sugar
1 tablespoon cornstarch
1 tablespoon orange marmalade,
    peach or apricot fruit spread
1 prepared angel food cake

• Combine undrained pineapple, sugar, cornstarch and orange marmalade in small saucepan. Bring to a boil. Reduce heat to low; cook 2 minutes, stirring constantly, or until sauce thickens. Cool slightly. Sauce can be served warm or chilled.

• Cut angel food cake into 12 slices. To serve, spoon sauce over each slice.

Makes 12 servings

Prep time: 10 minutes
Cook time: 5 minutes

Nutrients per Serving:

Calories:	116	Cholesterol:	0 mg
Total Fat:	0 g	Sodium:	213 mg

Lemon Poppy Seed Cake

Mom's Favorite White Cake

2¼ cups cake flour
1 tablespoon baking powder
½ teaspoon salt
½ cup margarine or butter, softened
1½ cups sugar
4 egg whites
2 teaspoons vanilla
1 cup milk
Strawberry Frosting
(recipe follows)
Fruit Filling (recipe follows)
Fresh strawberries (optional)

Preheat oven to 350°F. Line bottoms of two 9-inch round cake pans with waxed paper; lightly grease paper. Combine flour, baking powder and salt in medium bowl; set aside.

Beat margarine and sugar in large bowl with electric mixer at medium speed until light and fluffy. Add egg whites, two at a time, beating well after each addition. Add vanilla; beat until blended. With electric mixer at low speed, add flour mixture alternately with milk, beating well after each addition. Pour batter evenly into prepared pans.

Bake 25 minutes or until wooden pick inserted into centers comes out clean. Cool layers in pans on wire rack 10 minutes. Loosen edges and invert layers onto rack to cool completely.

Prepare Strawberry Frosting and Fruit Filling. To fill and frost cake, place one layer on cake plate; spread top with Fruit Filling. Place second layer over filling. Frost top and sides with Strawberry Frosting. Place strawberries on top of cake, if desired. Refrigerate; allow cake to stand at room temperature 15 minutes before serving.

Makes 12 servings

Strawberry Frosting

2 envelopes (1.3 ounces *each*)
whipped topping mix
⅔ cup milk
1 cup (6 ounces) white chocolate
chips, melted
¼ cup strawberry jam

Beat whipped topping mix and milk in medium bowl with electric mixer on low speed until blended. Beat on high speed 4 minutes until topping thickens and forms peaks. With mixer at low speed, beat melted chocolate into topping. Add jam; beat until blended. Chill 15 minutes or until of spreading consistency.

Fruit Filling

1 cup Strawberry Frosting
(recipe above)
1 can (8 ounces) crushed pineapple,
drained
1 cup sliced strawberries

Combine Strawberry Frosting, pineapple and strawberries in medium bowl; mix well.

Mom's Favorite White Cake

Pineapple Upside-Down Cake

1 (8-ounce) can crushed pineapple in juice, undrained
2 tablespoons margarine, melted, divided
½ cup firmly packed light brown sugar
6 whole maraschino cherries
1½ cups all-purpose flour
2 tablespoons baking powder
¼ teaspoon salt
1 cup granulated sugar
½ cup MOTT'S® Natural Apple Sauce
1 whole egg
3 egg whites, beaten until stiff

1. Preheat oven to 375°F. Drain pineapple; reserve juice. Spray sides of 8-inch square baking pan with nonstick cooking spray.

2. Spread 1 tablespoon melted margarine evenly in bottom of prepared pan. Sprinkle with brown sugar; top with pineapple. Slice cherries in half. Arrange cherries, cut side up, so that when cake is cut, each piece will have cherry half in center.

3. In small bowl, combine flour, baking powder and salt.

4. In large bowl, combine granulated sugar, apple sauce, whole egg, remaining 1 tablespoon melted margarine and reserved pineapple juice.

5. Add flour mixture to apple sauce mixture; stir until well blended. Fold in egg whites. Gently pour batter over fruit, spreading evenly.

6. Bake 35 to 40 minutes or until lightly browned. Cool on wire rack 10 minutes. Invert cake onto serving plate. Serve warm or cool completely. Cut into 12 pieces.

Makes 12 servings

Nutrients per Serving:

Calories:	200	Cholesterol:	20 mg
Total Fat:	3 g	Sodium:	240 mg

Pinwheel Cake and Cream

2 cups cold milk
1 package (4-serving size) JELL-O® Vanilla or French Vanilla Flavor Instant Pudding & Pie Filling
1 cup thawed COOL WHIP® Whipped Topping
1 small peach or nectarine, chopped
1 teaspoon grated orange peel
1 package (12 ounces) pound cake, cut into slices
2 cups summer fruits, such as sliced peaches, nectarines or plums; seedless grapes; strawberries, raspberries, or blueberries

POUR milk into large bowl. Add pudding mix. Beat with wire whisk 1 minute. Gently stir in whipped topping, chopped peach and grated peel.

ARRANGE pound cake slices on serving plate. Spoon pudding mixture evenly over cake. Top with fruits. Serve immediately or cover and refrigerate until ready to serve.

Makes 10 servings

Polenta Apricot Pudding Cake

¼ cup chopped dried apricots
2 cups orange juice
1 cup part-skim ricotta cheese
3 tablespoons honey
¾ cup sugar
½ cup cornmeal
½ cup all-purpose flour
¼ teaspoon grated nutmeg
¼ cup slivered almonds

1. Preheat oven to 300°F. Soak apricots in ¼ cup water in small bowl 15 minutes. Drain and discard water. Pat apricots dry with paper towels; set aside.

2. Combine orange juice, ricotta cheese and honey in medium bowl. Beat on medium speed of electric mixer 5 minutes or until smooth. Combine sugar, cornmeal, flour and nutmeg in small bowl. Gradually add sugar mixture to orange juice mixture; blend well. Slowly stir in apricots.

3. Spray 10-inch nonstick springform pan with nonstick cooking spray. Pour batter into prepared pan. Sprinkle with almonds. Bake 60 to 70 minutes or until center is firm and cake is golden brown. Garnish with powdered sugar, if desired. Serve warm.

Makes 8 servings

Polenta Apricot Pudding Cake

Easy Carrot Cake

½ cup **Prune Purée (page 331)**
2 cups **all-purpose flour**
2 teaspoons **ground cinnamon**
1½ teaspoons **baking soda**
½ teaspoon **salt**
4 cups **shredded DOLE® Carrots**
2 cups **sugar**
½ cup **DOLE® Pineapple Juice**
2 **eggs**
2 teaspoons **vanilla extract**
Vegetable cooking spray

• Prepare Prune Purée; set aside.

• Combine flour, cinnamon, baking soda and salt in medium bowl; set aside.

• Beat together Prune Purée, carrots, sugar, juice, eggs and vanilla in large bowl until blended. Add flour mixture; stir until well blended.

• Spread batter into 13×9-inch baking dish sprayed with vegetable cooking spray.

• Bake at 375°F 30 to 35 minutes or until toothpick inserted in center comes out clean. Cool completely in dish on wire rack. Dust with powdered sugar and garnish with carrot curls, if desired.   *Makes 12 servings*

Prep time: 15 minutes
Bake time: 35 minutes

Easy Carrot Cake

Prune Purée

Combine 1⅓ cups DOLE® Pitted Prunes, halved, and ½ cup hot water in food processor or blender container. Process until prunes are finely chopped, stopping to scrape down sides occasionally. (Purée can be refrigerated in airtight container for up to 1 week.)

Nutrients per Serving:

Calories:	240	Cholesterol:	32 mg
Total Fat:	1 g	Sodium:	244 mg

Apple-Streusel Pound Cake

3 cups all-purpose flour
⅓ cup cornmeal
1½ teaspoons baking soda
1½ teaspoons baking powder
½ teaspoon salt
1 cup granulated sugar
1 cup skim milk
1 cup nonfat sour cream
½ cup MOTT'S® Natural Apple Sauce
1 whole egg
2 tablespoons vegetable oil
2 teaspoons vanilla extract
3 egg whites, beaten until stiff
¾ cup firmly packed light brown
 sugar
¾ cup peeled, chopped apple
½ cup uncooked rolled oats
2 teaspoons ground cinnamon

1. Preheat oven to 350°F. Spray 10-inch (12-cup) Bundt® pan with nonstick cooking spray; flour lightly.

2. In medium bowl, combine 3 cups flour, cornmeal, baking soda, baking powder and salt.

3. In large bowl, combine granulated sugar, milk, sour cream, apple sauce, whole egg, oil and vanilla.

4. Add flour mixture to apple sauce mixture; stir until well blended. Gently fold in beaten egg whites.

5. In small bowl, combine brown sugar, apple, oats and cinnamon.

6. Spread half of batter into prepared pan; sprinkle with oat mixture. Spread remaining batter over oat mixture.

7. Bake 60 to 70 minutes or until toothpick inserted in center comes out clean. Cool on wire rack 15 minutes before removing from pan. Place cake, fluted side up, on serving plate. Serve warm or cool completely. Cut into 24 slices.   *Makes 24 servings*

Nutrients per Serving:

Calories:	160	Cholesterol:	10 mg
Total Fat:	2 g	Sodium:	140 mg

Flourless Chocolate Cake with Raspberry Sauce

CAKE
   7 ounces semisweet baking chocolate, broken into pieces
   12 tablespoons unsalted butter
   5 eggs, separated
   1 teaspoon vanilla
   1/3 cup sugar
   2 tablespoons unsweetened cocoa powder
   1/8 teaspoon salt
      Additional unsweetened cocoa powder

RASPBERRY SAUCE
   1 package (12 ounces) frozen unsweetened raspberries, thawed
   1/3 to 1/2 cup sugar

1. For cake, preheat oven to 350°F. Grease 9-inch springform pan. Heat chocolate and butter in medium saucepan over low heat until melted, stirring frequently. Remove from heat; whisk in egg yolks and vanilla. Blend in sugar, cocoa and salt.

2. Beat egg whites to soft peaks in large bowl. Stir about one-fourth of egg whites into chocolate mixture. Fold chocolate mixture into remaining egg whites.

3. Spread batter evenly in prepared pan. Bake about 30 minutes or until toothpick inserted in center comes out clean and edge of cake begins to pull away from side of pan. Cool cake in pan on wire rack 2 to 3 minutes; carefully loosen edge of cake with sharp knife and remove side of pan. Cool cake completely. Cover and refrigerate overnight.

4. Blend raspberries in blender or food processor until smooth. Strain sauce and discard seeds; stir in sugar to taste. Cut cake into wedges. Sift additional cocoa over cake; serve with sauce.   *Makes 8 to 10 servings*

Cherry-Topped Icebox Cake

   20 whole graham crackers, divided
   1 package (6-serving size) JELL-O® Vanilla or Chocolate Flavor Instant Pudding & Pie Filling
   2 cups cold milk
   1¾ cups thawed COOL WHIP® Whipped Topping
   2 cans (21 ounces each) cherry pie filling

Line 13×9-inch pan with one third of the graham crackers, breaking crackers, if necessary.

Prepare pudding mix with cold milk as directed on package. Let stand 5 minutes. Gently stir in whipped topping. Spread half the pudding mixture over crackers. Add second layer of crackers; top with remaining pudding mixture. Add third layer of crackers. Top with cherry pie filling. Refrigerate 3 hours.   *Makes 12 servings*

Chocolate-Frosted Icebox Cake: Prepare Cherry-Topped Icebox Cake as directed, substituting ¾ cup ready-to-spread chocolate fudge frosting for the cherry pie filling. Carefully spread frosting over top layer of graham crackers.

Flourless Chocolate Cake with Raspberry Sauce

Cappuccino Cake

½ cup (3 ounces) semisweet chocolate chips

½ cup chopped hazelnuts, walnuts or pecans

1 (18.25-ounce) package yellow cake mix

¼ cup instant espresso coffee powder

2 teaspoons ground cinnamon

1¼ cups water

3 large eggs

⅓ cup FILIPPO BERIO® Pure or Extra Light Tasting Olive Oil

Powdered sugar

1 (15-ounce) container ricotta cheese

2 teaspoons granulated sugar

Additional ground cinnamon

Preheat oven to 325°F. Grease 10-inch (12-cup) Bundt® pan or 10-inch tube pan with olive oil. Sprinkle lightly with flour.

In small bowl, combine chocolate chips and hazelnuts. Spoon evenly into bottom of prepared pan.

In large bowl, combine cake mix, coffee powder and 2 teaspoons cinnamon. Add water, eggs and olive oil. Beat with electric mixer at low speed until dry ingredients are moistened. Beat at medium speed 2 minutes. Pour batter over topping in pan.

Cappuccino Cake

Bake 60 minutes or until toothpick inserted in center comes out clean. Cool on wire rack 15 minutes. Remove from pan. Place cake, fluted side up, on serving plate. Cool completely. Sprinkle with powdered sugar.

In medium bowl, combine ricotta cheese and granulated sugar. Sprinkle with cinnamon. Serve alongside slices of cake. Serve cake with cappuccino, espresso or your favorite coffee, if desired.

Makes 12 to 16 servings

Hershey's Special Chocolate Cake

1¼ **cups all-purpose flour**
⅓ **cup HERSHEY'S Cocoa**
1 **teaspoon baking soda**
6 **tablespoons extra light corn oil spread**
1 **cup sugar**
1 **cup skim milk**
1 **tablespoon white vinegar**
½ **teaspoon vanilla extract**
Special Cocoa Frosting or Almond Frosting (recipes follow)

Heat oven to 350°F. Spray two 8-inch round baking pans with vegetable cooking spray. In small bowl, stir together flour, cocoa and baking soda. In medium saucepan over low heat, melt corn oil spread; stir in sugar. Remove from heat. Add milk, vinegar and vanilla to mixture in saucepan; stir. Add flour mixture; stir with whisk until well blended. Pour batter into prepared pans.

Bake 20 minutes or until wooden pick inserted in centers comes out clean. Cool 10 minutes; remove from pans to wire racks. Cool completely. To assemble, place one cake layer on serving plate; spread half of frosting over top. Set second cake layer on top; spread remaining frosting over top. Refrigerate 2 to 3 hours or until chilled before serving. Garnish as desired. Cover; refrigerate leftover cake.

Makes 12 servings

Special Cocoa Frosting

In small bowl, stir together 1 envelope (1.3 ounces) dry whipped topping mix, ½ cup cold skim milk, 1 tablespoon HERSHEY'S Cocoa and ½ teaspoon vanilla extract. Beat on high speed of electric mixer until soft peaks form.

Almond Frosting

Omit ½ teaspoon vanilla extract. Add ¼ teaspoon almond extract. Continue as directed above.

Four Way Fudgey Chocolate Cake

1¼ cups all-purpose flour
1 cup sugar
1 cup skim milk
⅓ cup HERSHEY'S Cocoa or
   HERSHEY'S Dutch Processed
   Cocoa
⅓ cup unsweetened applesauce
1 tablespoon white vinegar
1 teaspoon baking soda
½ teaspoon vanilla extract
   Toppings (optional): Frozen light
   non-dairy whipped topping,
   thawed, REESE'S® Peanut Butter
   Chips, sliced strawberries,
   chopped almonds, raspberries

Heat oven to 350°F. Spray 9-inch square baking pan or 11×7×2-inch baking pan with vegetable cooking spray. In large mixer bowl, stir together flour, sugar, milk, cocoa, applesauce, vinegar, baking soda and vanilla; beat on low speed of electric mixer until blended. Pour batter into prepared pan. Bake 30 to 35 minutes or until wooden pick inserted in center comes out clean. Cool completely in pan on wire rack. Spoon whipped topping into pastry bag fitted with star tip; pipe stars in two lines to divide cake into four squares or rectangles. Using plain tip, pipe lattice design into one square; place peanut butter chips onto lattice. Place strawberries into another square. Sprinkle almonds into third square. Place raspberries into remaining square. Serve immediately. Store ungarnished cake, covered, at room temperature.   *Makes 12 servings*

Chocolate Espresso Cake

2 cups cake flour
1½ teaspoons baking soda
½ teaspoon salt
½ cup margarine or butter, softened
1 cup granulated sugar
1 cup packed light brown sugar
3 eggs
4 squares (1 ounce *each*)
   unsweetened chocolate, melted
¾ cup sour cream
1 teaspoon vanilla
1 cup brewed espresso*
   Creamy Chocolate Frosting
   (page 337)
   White chocolate curls (optional)

*Use fresh brewed espresso, instant espresso powder prepared according to directions on jar or 1 tablespoon instant coffee powder dissolved in 1 cup hot water.

Preheat oven to 350°F. Line bottoms of two 9-inch round cake pans with waxed paper; lightly grease paper. Combine flour, baking soda and salt in medium bowl; set aside.

Beat margarine and sugars in large bowl with electric mixer at medium speed until light and fluffy. Add eggs, one at a time, beating well after each addition. Add melted chocolate, sour cream and vanilla; beat until blended. Add flour mixture alternately with espresso, beating well after each addition. Pour batter evenly into prepared pans.

Bake 35 minutes or until wooden pick inserted into centers comes out clean. Cool layers in pans on wire rack 10 minutes. Loosen edges and invert layers onto rack to cool completely.

Prepare Creamy Chocolate Frosting. To fill and frost cake, place one layer on cake plate; frost top with Creamy Chocolate Frosting. Place second layer over frosting. Frost top and sides with frosting; smooth frosting. Place White Chocolate Curls on cake, if desired. *Makes 12 servings*

Creamy Chocolate Frosting

½ **cup margarine or butter, softened**
4 **cups powdered sugar**
5 **to 6 tablespoons brewed espresso, divided**
½ **cup (3 ounces) semisweet chocolate chips, melted**
1 **teaspoon vanilla**
 Dash salt

Beat margarine in large bowl with electric mixer at medium speed until creamy. Gradually add powdered sugar and 4 tablespoons espresso; beat until smooth. Beat in melted chocolate, vanilla and salt. Add remaining espresso, 1 tablespoon at a time, until frosting is desired spreading consistency.

Chocolate Espresso Cake

White Chocolate Cheesecake

CRUST
½ cup (1 stick) butter
¼ cup sugar
½ teaspoon vanilla
1 cup all-purpose flour

FILLING
4 (8-ounce) packages PHILADELPHIA BRAND® Cream Cheese, softened
½ cup sugar
1 teaspoon vanilla
4 eggs
12 ounces white chocolate, melted, slightly cooled

• Heat oven to 325°F.

CRUST
• Cream butter, sugar and vanilla in small bowl at medium speed with electric mixer until light and fluffy. Gradually add flour, mixing at low speed until blended. Press onto bottom of 9-inch springform pan; prick with fork.

• Bake 25 minutes or until edges are light golden brown.

FILLING
• Beat cream cheese, sugar and vanilla at medium speed with electric mixer until well blended. Add eggs, 1 at a time, mixing at low speed after each addition, just until blended.

• Blend in melted chocolate; pour over crust.

• Bake 55 to 60 minutes or until center is almost set. Run knife or metal spatula around rim of pan to loosen cake; cool before removing rim of pan. Refrigerate 4 hours or overnight. Garnish with chocolate curls and powdered sugar, if desired.

Makes 12 servings

Prep time: 35 minutes
Cook time: 1 hour

Macadamia Nut Cheesecake: Stir 1 (3½-ounce) jar macadamia nuts, chopped (about ¾ cup) into batter.

White Chocolate Cheesecake

Creamy Banana Cheesecake

20 vanilla sandwich cream cookies
¼ cup margarine or butter, melted
3 packages (8 ounces *each*) cream cheese, softened
⅔ cup sugar
2 tablespoons cornstarch
3 eggs
¾ cup mashed bananas
½ cup whipping cream
2 teaspoons vanilla
¼ fresh peeled pineapple, cut in chunks or 1 can (20 ounces) pineapple chunks, drained
1 pint strawberries, cut into halves
2 tablespoons hot fudge ice cream topping
Mint leaves (optional)

Preheat oven to 350°F. Place cookies in food processor or blender; process until finely crushed. Add margarine; process until blended. Press crumb mixture onto bottom of 10-inch springform pan; refrigerate.

Beat cream cheese in large bowl with electric mixer at medium speed until creamy. Add sugar and cornstarch; beat well. Add eggs, one at a time, beating well after each addition. Beat in bananas, whipping cream and vanilla.

Pour cream cheese mixture into prepared crust. Place pan on cookie sheet and bake 15 minutes. *Reduce oven temperature to 200°F.* Continue baking 1 hour 15 minutes or until center is almost set. Loosen edge of cheesecake; cool completely on wire rack before removing rim of pan.

Creamy Banana Cheesecake

Refrigerate cheesecake, uncovered, 6 hours or overnight. Place pineapple and strawberries over top of cake. Allow cheesecake to stand at room temperature 15 minutes before serving. For fudge drizzle, place topping in small resealable plastic freezer bag; seal bag. Microwave at HIGH 20 seconds. Cut off tiny corner of bag; drizzle over fruit. Garnish with mint leaves, if desired.   *Makes 8 servings*

Chocolate Swirled Cheesecake

Yogurt Cheese (recipe follows)
**2 tablespoons graham cracker
    crumbs**
**1 package (8 ounces) Neufchâtel
    cheese (⅓ less fat cream cheese
    cream cheese), softened**
1½ teaspoons vanilla extract
¾ cup sugar
1 tablespoon cornstarch
**1 container (8 ounces) liquid egg
    substitute**
¼ cup HERSHEY's Cocoa
¼ teaspoon almond extract

Prepare Yogurt Cheese. Heat oven to 325°F. Spray bottom of 8- or 9-inch springform pan with vegetable cooking spray. Sprinkle graham cracker crumbs on bottom of pan. In large mixer bowl, beat Yogurt Cheese, Neufchâtel cheese and vanilla on medium speed of electric mixer until smooth. Add sugar and cornstarch; beat just until well blended. Gradually add egg substitute, beating on low speed until blended. Transfer 1½ cups batter to medium bowl; add cocoa. Beat until well blended. Stir almond extract

into vanilla batter. Alternately spoon vanilla and chocolate batters into prepared pan. With knife or metal spatula, cut through batters for marble effect.

Bake 35 minutes for 8-inch pan, 40 minutes for 9-inch pan or until edge is set. With knife, loosen cheesecake from side of pan. Cool completely in pan on wire rack. Cover; refrigerate at least 6 hours before serving. Just before serving, remove side of pan. Garnish as desired. Cover; refrigerate leftover cheesecake.   *Makes 16 servings*

Yogurt Cheese
Use one 16-ounce container plain lowfat yogurt, no gelatin added. Line non-rusting colander or sieve with large piece of double thickness cheesecloth or large coffee filter; place colander over deep bowl. Spoon yogurt into prepared colander; cover with plastic wrap. Refrigerate until liquid no longer drains from yogurt, about 24 hours. Remove yogurt from cheesecloth and place in separate bowl; discard liquid.

Nutrients per Serving:

Calories:	110	Cholesterol:	15 mg
Total Fat:	4 g	Sodium:	100 mg

Lemon Cheesecake

CRUST
35 vanilla wafers
¾ cup slivered almonds, toasted
⅓ cup sugar
¼ cup butter, melted

FILLING
3 packages (8 ounces *each*) cream
  cheese, softened
¾ cup sugar
4 eggs
⅓ cup whipping cream
¼ cup lemon juice
1 tablespoon grated lemon peel
1 teaspoon vanilla

TOPPING
1 pint strawberries, sliced
2 tablespoons sugar

1. Preheat oven to 375°F. For crust, combine wafers, almonds and ⅓ cup sugar in food processor; process until fine crumbs are formed. Combine sugar mixture with melted butter in medium bowl. Press mixture evenly on bottom and 1 inch up side of 9-inch springform pan. Set aside.

2. For filling, beat cream cheese and ¾ cup sugar in large bowl on high speed of electric mixer until fluffy. Add eggs one at a time, beating after each addition. Add whipping cream, lemon juice, lemon peel and vanilla; beat just until blended. Pour into prepared crust. Place springform pan on baking sheet. Bake 45 to 55 minutes or until set. Loosen cake from rim of pan with knife. Cool completely. Cover and refrigerate overnight.

3. For topping, combine strawberries and sugar. Let stand 15 minutes; serve.

Makes 16 servings

Philly 3-Step™ Cheesecake

2 (8-ounce) packages PHILADELPHIA
  BRAND® Cream Cheese or
  PHILADELPHIA BRAND®
  Neufchâtel Cheese, ⅓ Less Fat
  Than Cream Cheese, softened
½ cup sugar
½ teaspoon vanilla
2 eggs
1 ready-to-use graham cracker crumb
  crust (6 ounces or 9 inches)

1. MIX cream cheese, sugar and vanilla with electric mixer on medium speed until well blended. Add eggs; mix until blended.

2. POUR into crust.

3. BAKE at 350°F 40 minutes or until center is almost set. Cool. Refrigerate 3 hours or overnight.   *Makes 8 servings*

Prep time: 10 minutes
Cook time: 40 minutes

Fruit Topped Cheesecake: Top with 2 cups assorted cut-up fruit or 1 (21-ounce) can cherry pie filling.

Lemon Cheesecake: Stir 1 tablespoon fresh lemon juice and ½ teaspoon grated lemon peel into batter.

Chocolate Chip Cheesecake: Stir ½ cup miniature semi-sweet chocolate chips into batter. Sprinkle with additional ¼ cup chips before baking.

Lemon Cheesecake

Chocolate Turtle Cheesecake

24 chocolate sandwich cookies,
  ground (about 2¾ cups)
2 tablespoons butter, melted
2 packages (8 ounces *each*) cream
  cheese, softened
⅓ cup sugar
¼ cup sour cream
2 eggs
1 teaspoon vanilla
½ cup prepared caramel sauce
½ cup prepared fudge sauce
½ cup pecan halves

1. Preheat oven to 350°F. Combine ground cookies and butter in medium bowl; pat evenly on bottom and 1 inch up side of 9-inch springform pan. Place in freezer while preparing filling.

2. Beat cream cheese in large bowl with electric mixer until fluffy. Beat in sugar, sour cream, eggs and vanilla until smooth. Pour mixture into prepared crust.

3. Bake cheesecake 30 to 35 minutes or until almost set in center. Cool on wire rack. Refrigerate, loosely covered, 8 hours or overnight.

4. Remove side of springform pan from cheesecake; place on serving plate. Drizzle caramel and fudge sauces over cake; cut cake into wedges. Top each serving with 2 to 3 pecan halves.   *Makes 12 servings*

Philly 3-Step™ Toffee Crunch Cheesecake

2 (8-ounce) packages PHILADELPHIA
  BRAND® Cream Cheese, softened
½ cup sugar
½ teaspoon vanilla
2 eggs
1 ready-to-use graham cracker pie
  crust (6 ounces or 9 inches)
4 (1.4-ounce) bars chocolate covered
  English toffee, chopped (1 cup)

1. MIX cream cheese, sugar and vanilla at medium speed with electric mixer until well blended. Add eggs; mix until blended.

2. POUR into crust. Sprinkle with toffee.

3. BAKE at 350°F 40 minutes or until center is almost set. Cool. Refrigerate overnight.
                              Makes 8 servings

Prep time: 10 minutes
Cook time: 40 minutes

Peanut Butter Caramel Nut Cheesecake:
Omit toffee. Beat ⅓ cup peanut butter in with cream cheese. Sprinkle with 1 cup chopped milk chocolate with nuts and caramel candy bars (three 2.07 ounce bars) before baking.

Chocolate Turtle Cheesecake

Luscious Chocolate Cheesecake

2 cups (1 pound) nonfat cottage cheese
¾ cup liquid egg substitute
⅔ cup sugar
4 ounces (½ of 8-ounce package) Neufchâtel cheese, softened
⅓ cup HERSHEY'S Cocoa or HERSHEY'S European Style Cocoa
½ teaspoon vanilla extract
Yogurt Topping (page 347)
Sliced strawberries or mandarin orange segments (optional)

Heat oven to 300°F. Spray 9-inch springform pan with vegetable cooking spray. In food processor, place cottage cheese, egg substitute, sugar, Neufchâtel cheese, cocoa and vanilla; process until smooth. Pour into prepared pan. Bake 35 minutes or until edges are set. Meanwhile, prepare Yogurt Topping. Carefully spread topping over cheesecake. Continue baking 5 minutes. Remove from oven to wire rack. With knife, loosen cheesecake from side of pan. Cool completely. Cover; refrigerate until chilled. Remove side of pan. Serve with strawberries or mandarin orange segments, if desired. Refrigerate leftover cheesecake.

Makes 12 servings

Luscious Chocolate Cheesecake

Yogurt Topping

⅔ cup plain nonfat yogurt
2 tablespoons sugar

In small bowl, stir together yogurt and sugar until well blended.

Nutrients per Serving *(no garnishes):*

Calories:	120	Cholesterol:	10 mg
Fat:	3 g	Sodium:	210 mg

Chilled Raspberry Cheesecake

1½ cups vanilla wafer crumbs (about 45 wafers, crushed)
⅓ cup powdered sugar
⅓ cup HERSHEY'S Cocoa
⅓ cup butter or margarine, melted
1 package (10 ounces) frozen raspberries, thawed
1 envelope unflavored gelatin
½ cup cold water
½ cup boiling water
2 packages (8 ounces each) cream cheese, softened
½ cup granulated sugar
1 teaspoon vanilla extract
3 tablespoons seedless red raspberry preserves
Chocolate Whipped Cream (recipe follows)

Heat oven to 350°F. In medium bowl, stir together crumbs, powdered sugar and cocoa; stir in melted butter. Press mixture onto bottom and 1½ inches up side of 9-inch springform pan. Bake 10 minutes; cool completely. Purée and strain raspberries; set aside. In small bowl, sprinkle gelatin over cold water; let stand several minutes to soften. Add boiling water; stir until gelatin dissolves completely and mixture is clear. In large bowl, beat cream cheese, granulated sugar and vanilla until smooth. Gradually add raspberry purée and gelatin, mixing thoroughly; pour into prepared crust. Refrigerate several hours or overnight. With knife, loosen cake from side of pan; remove side of pan. Spread raspberry preserves over top. Garnish with Chocolate Whipped Cream. Cover; refrigerate leftovers.

Makes 10 to 12 servings

Chocolate Whipped Cream

In medium bowl, stir together ½ cup powdered sugar and ¼ cup HERSHEY'S Cocoa. Add 1 cup chilled whipping cream and 1 teaspoon vanilla extract; beat until stiff.

DIVINE

DESSERTS

Rum and Spumoni Layered Torte

1 package (18 to 19 ounces)
   moist butter recipe yellow
   cake mix
3 eggs
½ cup butter, softened
⅓ cup plus 2 teaspoons rum,
   divided
⅓ cup water

1 quart spumoni ice cream,
   softened
1 cup whipping cream
1 tablespoon powdered sugar
   Mixed candied fruit
   Red and green sugars for
   decorating (optional)

Preheat oven to 375°F. Grease and flour 15½×10½×1-inch jelly-roll pan. Combine cake mix, eggs, butter, ⅓ cup rum and water in large bowl. Beat with electric mixer at low speed until moistened. Beat at high speed 4 minutes. Pour evenly into prepared pan.

(continued on page 350)

Rum and Spumoni Layered Torte

(Rum and Spumoni Layered Torte,
*continued from page 348***)**

Bake 20 to 25 minutes or until toothpick inserted in center comes out clean. Cool in pan 10 minutes. Cool completely on wire rack.

Cut cake into three 10×5-inch pieces. Place one cake layer on serving plate. Spread with half the ice cream. Cover with second cake layer. Spread with remaining ice cream. Place remaining cake layer on top. Wrap cake in plastic wrap and freeze at least 4 hours.

Just before serving, combine cream, powdered sugar and remaining 2 teaspoons rum in small chilled bowl. Beat at high speed with chilled beaters until stiff peaks form. Remove cake from freezer. Spread thin layer of whipped cream mixture over top of cake.

Place star tip in pastry bag; fill with remaining whipped cream mixture. Pipe rosettes around outer top edges of cake. Place candied fruit in narrow strip down center of cake. Sprinkle colored sugars over rosettes, if desired. Serve immediately.

Makes 8 to 10 servings

Chocolate Cream Torte

1 package DUNCAN HINES® Moist Deluxe Devil's Food Cake Mix
1 package (8 ounces) cream cheese, softened
½ cup sugar
1 teaspoon vanilla extract
1 cup finely chopped pecans
1 cup whipping cream, chilled Strawberry halves for garnish Mint leaves for garnish

1. Preheat oven to 350°F. Grease and flour two 8- or 9-inch round cake pans.

2. Prepare, bake and cool cake following package directions for basic recipe. Chill layers for ease in splitting.

3. Place cream cheese, sugar and vanilla extract in small bowl. Beat at low speed with electric mixer until smooth. Add pecans; stir until blended. Set aside. Beat whipping cream in small bowl until stiff peaks form. Fold whipped cream into cream cheese mixture.

4. To assemble, split each cake layer in half horizontally (see Tip). Place one cake layer on serving plate. Spread layer with one-fourth of filling. Repeat with remaining layers and filling. Garnish with strawberry halves and mint leaves, if desired. Refrigerate.

Makes 12 to 16 servings

Tip: To split layers evenly, measure cake with ruler. Divide into 2 equal layers. Mark with toothpicks. Cut through layers with serrated knife, using toothpicks as guide.

Pineapple Mousse Torte

Chocolate Crumb Crust
  (recipe follows)
1 package (8 ounces) cream cheese,
  softened
1¼ cups sugar
 ½ teaspoon grated lemon peel
1 can (15¼ ounces) DEL MONTE®
  FreshCut™ Brand Crushed
  Pineapple In Its Own Juice,
  undrained
1 can (8 ounces) DEL MONTE®
  FreshCut™ Pineapple Tidbits In
  Its Own Juice, undrained
2 envelopes unflavored gelatin
2¼ cups whipping cream, whipped

1. Prepare crumb crust; set aside.

2. Blend cream cheese with sugar and lemon peel.

3. Drain juice from crushed pineapple and tidbits into small saucepan. Sprinkle gelatin over juice. Place over low heat and stir until gelatin is completely dissolved.

4. Add crushed pineapple to cream cheese mixture; stir in gelatin mixture until blended. Thoroughly fold in whipped cream.

5. Pour filling into crust. Chill at least 5 hours or overnight. Remove sides of pan. Top with pineapple tidbits and garnish, if desired.
Makes 10 to 12 servings

Prep time: 20 minutes
Chill time: 5 hours

Chocolate Crumb Crust

2¼ cups chocolate wafer crumbs
 ½ cup butter or margarine, melted

Mix ingredients; press firmly onto bottom of 9-inch springform pan.

Pineapple Mousse Torte

Chocolate Truffle Mousse

1 cup whipping cream, divided
1 egg yolk
2 tablespoons corn syrup
2 tablespoons margarine or butter
4 squares (1 ounce *each*) semisweet
    chocolate, coarsely chopped
4 squares (1 ounce *each*) milk
    chocolate, coarsely chopped
5 teaspoons powdered sugar
½ teaspoon vanilla
    Sweetened whipped cream, fresh
    raspberries and mint leaves
    (optional)

Whisk ½ cup cream, egg yolk, corn syrup and margarine in medium heavy saucepan over medium heat until mixture simmers. Continue whisking while mixture simmers 2 minutes. Remove from heat; add chocolates, stirring until smooth. Cool to room temperature.

Beat remaining ½ cup cream in medium bowl with electric mixer at high speed until soft peaks form. Add powdered sugar and vanilla; beat until stiff peaks form.

Stir whipped cream into cooled chocolate mixture. Pour into medium serving bowl. Chill 4 hours or overnight. Garnish with sweetened whipped cream, fresh raspberries and mint leaves, if desired.
Makes 6 servings

Apple Sauce Bread Pudding

1 (16-ounce) loaf light white bread,
    sliced
1 cup raisins
2 teaspoons ground cinnamon
2 cups skim milk
8 egg whites
1 cup MOTT'S® Natural Apple Sauce
½ cup firmly packed light brown
    sugar
1½ teaspoons vanilla extract

1. Preheat oven to 350°F. Spray 9-inch square baking pan with nonstick cooking spray.

2. Cut bread into ½-inch cubes. In large bowl, toss bread with raisins and cinnamon.

3. In medium bowl, stir together milk, egg whites, apple sauce, brown sugar and vanilla. Pour over bread cube mixture; mix well. Let stand 25 minutes. Pour mixture into prepared pan.

4. Bake 35 to 40 minutes or until knife inserted in center comes out clean. Cool 15 to 20 minutes before serving. Refrigerate leftovers. *Makes 10 servings*

Nutrients per Serving:

Calories:	210	Cholesterol:	0 mg
Total Fat:	1 g	Sodium:	75 mg

Chocolate Truffle Mousse

Bavarian Rice Cloud with Bittersweet Chocolate Sauce

1 envelope unflavored gelatin
1½ cups skim milk
3 tablespoons sugar
2 cups cooked rice
2 cups frozen light whipped topping, thawed
1 tablespoon almond-flavored liqueur
½ teaspoon vanilla extract
Bittersweet Chocolate Sauce (recipe follows)
2 tablespoons sliced almonds, toasted

Sprinkle gelatin over milk in small saucepan; let stand 1 minute or until gelatin is softened. Cook over low heat, stirring constantly, until gelatin dissolves. Add sugar and stir until dissolved. Add rice; stir well. Cover; chill until the consistency of unbeaten egg whites. Fold in whipped topping, liqueur, and vanilla. Spoon into 4-cup mold coated with nonstick cooking spray. Cover; chill until firm. Unmold; spoon sauce over dessert. Sprinkle with almonds.   *Makes 10 servings*

Bittersweet Chocolate Sauce
Combine 3 tablespoons sugar and 3 tablespoons cocoa powder in small saucepan. Add ½ cup low-fat buttermilk, mixing well. Place over medium heat; cook until sugar dissolves. Stir in 1 tablespoon almond-flavored liqueur; remove from heat.

Favorite recipe from **USA Rice Federation**

Bavarian Rice Cloud with Bittersweet Chocolate Sauce

Rice Pudding

1¼ cups water, divided
½ cup uncooked long-grain rice
2 cups evaporated skim milk
½ cup granulated sugar
½ cup raisins
½ cup MOTT'S® Natural Apple Sauce
3 tablespoons cornstarch
1 teaspoon vanilla extract
   Brown sugar or nutmeg (optional)
   Fresh raspberries (optional)
   Orange peel strips (optional)

1. In medium saucepan, bring 1 cup water to a boil. Add rice. Reduce heat to low and simmer, covered, 20 minutes or until rice is tender and water is absorbed.

2. Add milk, granulated sugar, raisins and apple sauce. Bring to a boil. Reduce heat to low and simmer for 3 minutes, stirring occasionally.

3. Combine cornstarch and remaining ¼ cup water in small bowl. Stir into rice mixture. Simmer about 20 minutes or until mixture thickens, stirring occasionally. Remove from heat; stir in vanilla. Cool 15 to 20 minutes before serving. Sprinkle each serving with brown sugar or nutmeg and garnish with raspberries and orange peel, if desired. Refrigerate leftovers. *Makes 8 servings*

Nutrients per Serving:

Calories:	190	Cholesterol:	2 mg
Total Fat:	1 g	Sodium:	75 mg

Rich Chocolate Pudding

⅔ cup sugar
¼ cup unsweetened cocoa powder
3 tablespoons cornstarch
2 cups reduced-fat (2%) milk
1 egg
½ teaspoon vanilla
1 tablespoon butter

1. Combine sugar, cocoa and cornstarch in medium saucepan; whisk in milk. Cook over medium-high heat, stirring frequently, until mixture boils. Continue boiling 1 minute, stirring constantly.

2. Beat egg in small bowl. Whisk about ½ cup hot milk mixture into egg; whisk egg mixture back into saucepan. Cook over medium heat 2 minutes, stirring constantly.

3. Remove pudding from heat; stir in vanilla and butter. Pour into serving dishes. Serve warm or cover and refrigerate until ready to serve. *Makes 4 servings*

Rich Mocha Pudding: Add 1 to 1½ teaspoons instant coffee crystals to sugar mixture in step 1.

Luscious Cold Chocolate Soufflés

1 envelope unflavored gelatin
¼ cup cold water
2 tablespoons reduced-calorie tub
    margarine
1½ cups cold skim milk, divided
½ cup sugar
⅓ cup HERSHEY'S Cocoa or
    HERSHEY'S European Style Cocoa
2½ teaspoons vanilla extract, divided
1 envelope (1.3 ounces) dry whipped
    topping mix

Measure lengths of foil to fit around 6 small soufflé dishes (about 4 ounces each); fold in thirds lengthwise. Tape securely to outsides of dishes to form collars, allowing collars to extend 1 inch above rims of dishes. Lightly oil insides of foil.

In small microwave-safe bowl, sprinkle gelatin over water; let stand 2 minutes to soften. Microwave at HIGH (100%) 40 seconds; stir thoroughly. Stir in margarine until melted; let stand 2 minutes or until gelatin is completely dissolved. In small mixer bowl, stir together 1 cup milk, sugar, cocoa and 2 teaspoons vanilla. Beat on low speed of electric mixer while gradually pouring in gelatin mixture. Beat until well blended. Prepare topping mix as directed on package, using remaining ½ cup milk and remaining ½ teaspoon vanilla; carefully fold into chocolate mixture until well blended.

Spoon into prepared soufflé dishes, filling ½ inch from tops of collars. Cover; refrigerate until firm, about 3 hours. Carefully remove foil. Garnish as desired. *Makes 6 servings*

Note: Six (6-ounce) custard cups may be used in place of soufflé dishes; omit foil collars.

Nutrients per Serving:

Calories:	150	Cholesterol:	0 mg
Total Fat:	3 g	Sodium:	55 mg

Chocolate Fruit Dip

1 container (8 ounces) vanilla lowfat
    yogurt
⅓ cup packed light brown sugar
1 tablespoon HERSHEY'S Cocoa
½ teaspoon vanilla extract
    Dash ground cinnamon
    Assorted fresh fruit, cut up
    (optional)

In small bowl, combine all ingredients except fruit. Stir with whisk until smooth. Cover; refrigerate until well chilled. Serve with assorted fresh fruit, if desired. Cover and refrigerate leftover dip.

Makes 10 servings

Nutrients per Serving *(2 tablespoons):*

Calories:	50	Cholesterol:	0 mg
Total Fat:	0 g	Sodium:	20 mg

Luscious Cold Chocolate Soufflés

Fantasy in Berries

1 bag (12 ounces) frozen
    unsweetened raspberries, thawed
¼ cup plus 2 tablespoons sugar,
    divided
1 tablespoon fresh lemon juice
2 cups sliced fresh strawberries
1 cup fresh raspberries
1 cup fresh blueberries
1 cup low-fat ricotta cheese
1 teaspoon vanilla extract
¼ teaspoon almond extract

1. To prepare raspberry sauce, place thawed frozen raspberries, ¼ cup sugar and lemon juice in blender or food processor; blend until smooth. Pour through strainer to remove seeds. Spoon 3 tablespoons raspberry sauce on each of 8 plates. Tilt each plate, rotating to spread raspberry sauce over bottom of plate.

2. Arrange ¼ cup sliced strawberries, 2 tablespoons fresh raspberries and 2 tablespoons fresh blueberries on top of sauce in desired pattern on each plate.

3. Place cheese, remaining 2 tablespoons sugar and vanilla and almond extracts in clean blender or food processor; blend until smooth and satiny. Spoon cheese mixture into pastry bag and pipe onto berries, using about 2 tablespoons per serving. (Use star tip to make rosettes or various sizes of writing tips to drizzle mixture over berries.) Before serving, garnish with mint sprigs and edible flowers, such as pansies, violets or nasturtiums, if desired. *Makes 8 servings*

Swedish Apple Nut Strip

1½ cups all-purpose flour
3 tablespoons sugar, divided
½ teaspoon salt
½ cup margarine
1 egg, slightly beaten
1 cup MOTT'S® Cinnamon Apple
    Sauce
¼ cup finely chopped walnuts
1 teaspoon ground cinnamon

Preheat oven to 375°F. In bowl, mix flour, 2 tablespoons sugar and salt; cut in margarine until mixture is crumbly. Stir in egg; shape dough into ball. Cover; refrigerate 15 minutes. Divide dough in half. On lightly greased baking sheet, shape each half into 10×2-inch rectangle. Make a 1-inch-wide indentation down center length of each rectangle; fill each with ½ cup apple sauce. Mix remaining 1 tablespoon sugar, walnuts and cinnamon; sprinkle on dough along sides of apple sauce filling. Bake 20 minutes. Cool slightly on wire rack. Cut into 1-inch diagonal slices. Cool completely. Store in airtight container. *Makes 20 bars*

Berry Delicious Trifles

1 package (4-serving size) instant
vanilla pudding and pie filling
mix
2¼ cups milk
1 cup sliced strawberries
1 cup raspberries
1 cup blueberries
1 frozen pound cake (10¾ ounces),
thawed
2 tablespoons orange-flavored liqueur
or orange juice
¼ cup orange marmalade
Sweetened whipped cream and
mint leaves (optional)

Beat pudding mix and milk in medium bowl
with electric mixer on low speed 2 minutes;
set aside. Combine strawberries, raspberries
and blueberries in medium bowl; set aside.

Slice cake into 12 slices, each about ½-inch
wide. Brush one side of each piece with
liqueur; spread marmalade over liqueur.

Cut cake slices in half lengthwise. Place
4 pieces of cake each against side of 6 martini
or parfait glasses with marmalade side toward
center of glass.

Place ¼ cup berries in bottom of each glass;
top each with heaping ⅓ cup pudding mix
and then ¼ cup berries. Refrigerate 30
minutes. Garnish with sweetened whipped
cream and mint leaves, if desired.

Makes 6 servings

Berry Delicious Trifle

Baked Apple Crisp

8 cups unpeeled, thinly sliced apples
  (about 8 medium)
2 tablespoons granulated sugar
4½ teaspoons lemon juice
4 teaspoons ground cinnamon,
  divided
1½ cups MOTT'S® Natural Apple Sauce
1 cup uncooked rolled oats
½ cup firmly packed light brown
  sugar
⅓ cup all-purpose flour
⅓ cup evaporated skimmed milk
¼ cup nonfat dry milk powder
1 cup vanilla nonfat yogurt

1. Preheat oven to 350°F. Spray 2-quart casserole dish with nonstick cooking spray.

2. In large bowl, toss apple slices with granulated sugar, lemon juice and 2 teaspoons cinnamon. Spoon into prepared dish. Spread apple sauce evenly over apple mixture.

3. In medium bowl, combine oats, brown sugar, flour, evaporated milk, dry milk powder and remaining 2 teaspoons cinnamon. Spread over apple sauce.

4. Bake 35 to 40 minutes or until lightly browned and bubbly. Cool slightly; serve warm. Top each serving with dollop of yogurt. *Makes 12 servings*

Nutrients per Serving:

Calories:	185	Cholesterol:	0 mg
Total Fat:	2 g	Sodium:	35 mg

Fresh Berry Pizza

Ginger Cookie Crust
  (recipe follows)
1½ cups fat-free ricotta cheese
3 tablespoons sugar
1 tablespoon lemon juice
2 teaspoons grated lemon peel
1 pint fresh raspberries
½ pint fresh blueberries

1. Prepare Ginger Cookie Crust; cool. Gently slide onto flat serving platter or board.

2. Combine ricotta, sugar, lemon juice and lemon peel in medium bowl. Stir until smooth. Spread evenly over crust leaving ½- to 1-inch border. Arrange raspberries and blueberries on top. Serve, or cover with plastic wrap and refrigerate up to 6 hours. Cut into 8 wedges. Garnish as desired.
Makes 8 servings

Ginger Cookie Crust

35 vanilla wafers
20 gingersnaps
1 egg white, slightly beaten

1. Preheat oven to 375°F. Combine vanilla wafers and gingersnaps in food processor or blender; process until coarse crumbs form. Transfer to medium bowl. Stir egg white into crumbs until evenly mixed.

2. Spray 12- to 14-inch pizza pan with nonstick cooking spray. Press crumb mixture evenly into pan. Bake on center rack in oven 8 to 10 minutes or until firm and lightly browned. Cool in pan. *Makes 1 crust*

Baked Apple Crisp

Smucker's® Double Apple Turnovers

½ cup SMUCKER'S® Apple Butter
½ cup apple cider or juice
½ teaspoon ground cinnamon
    Grated peel of 1 orange
¼ cup golden raisins
4 large firm apples, peeled, cored and
    chopped
1 package frozen phyllo dough
    Nonstick cooking spray
    Powdered sugar for garnish

Preheat oven to 375°F. Place Smucker's® Apple Butter, cider, cinnamon and orange peel in medium saucepan; simmer 5 minutes. Add raisins; heat 2 minutes. Add apples; cook over medium heat about 10 minutes or until apples begin to soften and most of liquid evaporates. Cool in refrigerator.

Unwrap phyllo dough. Remove one sheet of dough, keeping remaining sheets covered with damp cloth. Coat dough with cooking spray, then cover with second sheet of dough. Spray top sheet with cooking spray.

Spoon about ⅓ cup of apple filling on lower right corner of dough. Fold dough over filling to form large rectangle. Then fold turnover as if it were a flag, making triangular packet with each turn. Continue process with remaining dough and filling until 6 turnovers are made. Place finished turnovers on baking sheet. Bake 25 minutes or until golden. Sprinkle with powdered sugar before serving.

Makes 6 turnovers

Prep time: 30 minutes
Cook time: 40 minutes

Nutrients per Serving:

Calories:	214	Cholesterol:	0 mg
Total Fat:	1 g	Sodium:	2 mg

Summertime Fruit Medley

2 large ripe peaches, peeled and
    sliced
2 large ripe nectarines, sliced
1 large mango, peeled and cut into
    1-inch chunks
1 cup blueberries
2 cups orange juice
¼ cup amaretto *or* ½ teaspoon
    almond extract
2 tablespoons sugar
    Mint leaves for garnish

1. Combine peaches, nectarines, mango and blueberries in large bowl.

2. Whisk orange juice, amaretto and sugar in small bowl until sugar is dissolved. Pour over fruit mixture; toss. Marinate 1 hour at room temperature, gently stirring occasionally. Garnish with mint leaves, if desired.

Makes 8 servings

Smucker's® Double Apple Turnover

Double Dipped Apples

MAZOLA NO STICK® Cooking Spray
5 medium apples
5 wooden sticks
1 package (14 ounces) caramel
    candies, unwrapped
¼ cup KARO® Light or Dark Corn
    Syrup
¾ cup chopped walnuts
1 cup (6 ounces) semisweet chocolate
    chips
1 teaspoon MAZOLA® Corn Oil

1. Spray small cookie sheet with cooking spray; set aside. Wash and dry apples; insert stick into stem end.

2. In small, deep microwavable bowl, microwave caramels and corn syrup at HIGH 3 to 4 minutes or until caramels are melted and smooth, stirring after each minute.

3. Dip apples in hot caramel mixture, turning to coat well. Allow caramel to drip from apples for a few seconds, then scrape excess from bottom of apples. Roll bottom half in walnuts. Place on prepared cookie sheet. Refrigerate at least 15 minutes.

4. In small microwavable bowl, microwave chocolate and corn oil at HIGH 1 to 2 minutes; stir until melted.

5. Drizzle apples with chocolate. Refrigerate 10 minutes or until chocolate is firm. Wrap apples individually; store in refrigerator.

Makes 5 apples

Prep time: 20 minutes, plus cooling

Fresh Nectarine-Pineapple Cobbler

1 DOLE® Fresh Pineapple
3 cups sliced ripe DOLE® Fresh
    Nectarines or Peaches
½ cup sugar
2 tablespoons all-purpose flour
½ teaspoon ground cinnamon
1 cup buttermilk baking mix
½ cup low fat milk

• Twist crown off pineapple. Cut pineapple in half. Refrigerate one half for another use. Cut remaining pineapple half in half. Remove fruit from shell; core fruit. Cut fruit into cubes.

• Combine pineapple, nectarines, sugar, flour and cinnamon in 8×8-inch glass baking dish; spread fruit evenly in dish.

• Stir together baking mix and milk in small bowl until just combined. Pour over fruit.

• Bake at 400°F 40 to 45 minutes or until fruit is tender and crust is browned.

Makes 8 servings

Prep time: 20 minutes
Bake time: 45 minutes

Nutrients per Serving:

Calories:	212	Cholesterol:	1 mg
Total Fat:	3 g	Sodium:	200 mg

Double Dipped Apples

Spiced Apple & Cranberry Compote

2½ cups cranberry juice cocktail
1 package (6 ounces) dried apples
½ cup (2 ounces) dried cranberries
½ cup Rhine wine or apple juice
½ cup honey
2 cinnamon sticks, broken in half
 Frozen yogurt or ice cream
  (optional)
 Additional cinnamon sticks
  (optional)

Mix juice, apples, cranberries, wine, honey and cinnamon stick halves in slow cooker. Cover and cook on low 4 to 5 hours or until liquid is absorbed and fruit is tender. Remove and discard cinnamon stick halves. Ladle compote into bowls. Serve warm, at room temperature or chilled with scoop of frozen yogurt or ice cream and garnish with additional cinnamon sticks, if desired.

Makes 6 servings

Cranberry-Walnut Pear Wedges

3 firm ripe pears
¼ cup triple sec*
2 tablespoons orange juice
½ cup prepared cranberry fruit relish
¼ cup finely chopped walnuts
¼ cup (1 ounce) crumbled blue cheese

*Omit liqueur, if desired. Increase orange juice to
¼ cup. Add 2 tablespoons honey and 2 tablespoons
balsamic vinegar to marinade.*

1. Cut each pear lengthwise into quarters; remove cores.

2. Place pears in resealable plastic food storage bag. Pour liqueur and orange juice over pears; seal bag. Turn bag over several times to coat pears evenly. Refrigerate at least 1 hour, turning bag occasionally.

3. Drain pears; discard marinade. Place pears on serving platter. Spoon cranberry relish evenly into pear cavities; sprinkle with walnuts and cheese. Garnish, if desired.

Makes 12 servings

Black Forest Parfaits

1 package (8 ounces) PHILADELPHIA
  BRAND® Cream Cheese, softened
2 cups cold milk
1 package (4-serving size) JELL-O®
  Chocolate Flavor Instant Pudding
  & Pie Filling
1 can (21 ounces) cherry pie filling
1 tablespoon cherry liqueur
½ cup chocolate wafer cookie crumbs

BEAT cream cheese with ½ cup milk at low speed until smooth. Add pudding mix and remaining milk. Beat until smooth, 1 to 2 minutes.

MIX cherry pie filling and liqueur. Reserve a few cherries for garnish, if desired. Spoon ½ of pudding mixture evenly into individual dessert dishes; sprinkle with cookie crumbs. Top with pie filling, then with remaining pudding mixture. Refrigerate until ready to serve. Garnish with reserved cherries and additional cookie crumbs, if desired.

Makes 4 to 6 servings

Frozen Chocolate-Covered Bananas

2 ripe medium bananas
4 wooden sticks
½ cup low-fat granola cereal without raisins
⅓ cup hot fudge sauce, at room temperature

1. Cover baking sheet or 15×10-inch jelly-roll pan with waxed paper; set aside.

2. Peel bananas; cut each in half crosswise. Insert wooden stick into center of cut end of each banana about 1½ inches into banana half. Place on prepared baking sheet; freeze until firm, at least 2 hours.

3. Place granola in large plastic food storage bag; crush slightly using rolling pin or meat mallet. Transfer granola to shallow plate. Place fudge sauce in shallow dish.

4. Working with 1 banana at a time, place frozen banana in fudge sauce; turn banana and spread fudge sauce evenly on banana with small rubber scraper. Immediately place banana on plate with granola; turn to coat lightly. Return to baking sheet in freezer. Repeat with remaining bananas.

5. Freeze until fudge sauce is very firm, at least 2 hours. Place on small plates; let stand 5 minutes before serving.

Makes 4 servings

Frozen Chocolate-Covered Bananas

Fudge Brownie Sundaes

1 cup all-purpose flour
¾ cup granulated sugar
½ cup unsweetened cocoa powder, divided
2 teaspoons baking powder
½ teaspoon salt
½ cup skim milk
¼ cup MOTT'S® Natural Apple Sauce
1 teaspoon vanilla extract
1½ cups hot water
¾ cup firmly packed light brown sugar
½ gallon frozen nonfat vanilla yogurt
Maraschino cherries (optional)

1. Preheat oven to 350°F. Spray 8-inch square baking pan with nonstick cooking spray.

2. In large bowl, combine flour, granulated sugar, ¼ cup cocoa, baking powder and salt. Add milk, apple sauce and vanilla; stir until well blended. Pour batter into prepared pan.

3. In medium bowl, combine hot water, brown sugar and remaining ¼ cup cocoa. Pour over batter. Do not stir.

4. Bake 40 minutes or until center is almost set. Cool completely on wire rack. Cut into 12 bars. Top each bar with ½-cup scoop of frozen yogurt; spoon sauce from bottom of pan over yogurt. Garnish with cherry, if desired. *Makes 12 servings*

Nutrients per Serving:

Calories:	300	Cholesterol:	5 mg
Total Fat:	3 g	Sodium:	200 mg

Mocha Parfaits

1½ tablespoons margarine
⅓ cup unsweetened cocoa powder
1 cup boiling water
½ cup sugar
1 tablespoon instant coffee granules
1 teaspoon vanilla
1 pint coffee-flavored nonfat frozen yogurt
12 whole coffee beans (optional)

Melt margarine in heavy saucepan over low heat. Add cocoa; cook and stir 3 minutes. Add boiling water, sugar and coffee; cook and stir until thickened. Remove from heat; stir in vanilla. Cool.

Place 2 tablespoons frozen yogurt in bottom of each of 4 parfait glasses. Top each with 1 tablespoon sauce. Top sauce with another 2 tablespoons frozen yogurt; top frozen yogurt with 2 tablespoons sauce. Repeat layering twice more ending with sauce. Top each parfait with 3 coffee beans, if desired.
Makes 4 servings

Mocha Parfaits

Color-Bright Ice Cream Sandwiches

¾ cup (1½ sticks) butter or margarine, softened
¾ cup creamy peanut butter
1¼ cups firmly packed light brown sugar
1 large egg
1 teaspoon vanilla extract
1½ cups all-purpose flour
1 teaspoon baking soda
¼ teaspoon salt
1¾ cups "M&M's"® Chocolate Mini Baking Bits, divided
2 quarts vanilla or chocolate ice cream, slightly softened

Preheat oven to 350°F. In large bowl cream butter, peanut butter and sugar until light and fluffy; beat in egg and vanilla. In medium bowl combine flour, baking soda and salt; blend into creamed mixture. Stir in 1⅓ cups "M&M's"® Chocolate Mini Baking Bits. Shape dough into 1¼-inch balls. Place about 2 inches apart on ungreased cookie sheets. Gently flatten to about ½-inch thickness with fingertips. Place 7 or 8 of the remaining "M&M's"® Chocolate Mini Baking Bits on each cookie; press in lightly. Bake 10 to 12 minutes or until edges are light brown. Do not overbake. Cool about 1 minute on cookie sheets; cool completely on wire racks. Assemble cookies in pairs with about ⅓ cup ice cream; press cookies together lightly. Wrap each sandwich in plastic wrap; freeze until firm.

Makes about 24 ice cream sandwiches

Color-Bright Ice Cream Sandwiches

Citrus Sorbet

1 can (12 ounces) DOLE® Orange
    Peach Mango or Tropical Fruit
    Frozen Juice Concentrate
1 can (8 ounces) DOLE® Crushed
    Pineapple or Pineapple Tidbits,
    drained
½ cup plain nonfat or low fat yogurt
2½ cups cold water

• Combine frozen juice concentrate,
pineapple and yogurt in blender or food
processor container; blend until smooth. Stir
in water.

• Pour mixture into container of ice cream
maker.* Freeze according to manufacturer's
directions.

• Serve sorbet in dessert dishes.

Makes 10 servings

*Or, pour sorbet mixture into 8-inch square metal
pan; cover. Freeze 1½ to 2 hours or until slightly firm.
Place in large bowl; beat with electric mixer on
medium speed 1 minute or until slushy. Return
mixture to metal pan; repeat freezing and beating
steps. Freeze until firm, about 6 hours or overnight.*

Prep time: 20 minutes
Freeze time: 20 minutes

Passion-Banana Sorbet: Substitute DOLE®
Pine-Orange-Banana Frozen Juice Concentrate
for frozen juice concentrate. Prepare sorbet
as directed above except reduce water to
2 cups and omit canned pineapple.

Nutrients per Serving:

Calories:	99	Cholesterol:	0 mg
Total Fat:	0 g	Sodium:	26 mg

Frozen Orange Cream

1 package (4-serving size) JELL-O®
    Brand Orange Flavor Sugar Free
    Gelatin
¾ cup boiling water
2 cups skim milk
1 can (6 ounces) frozen apple juice
    concentrate, thawed
1 cup thawed COOL WHIP® LITE®
    Whipped Topping
1 can (11 ounces) mandarin orange
    segments, well drained

Completely dissolve gelatin in boiling water.
Stir in milk and apple juice concentrate.
(Mixture will appear curdled but will be
smooth when frozen.) Pour into 13×9-inch
metal pan. Freeze until about 1 inch of icy
crystals forms around edges, about 1 hour.
Spoon mixture into chilled bowl; beat with
electric mixer until smooth. Gently stir in
whipped topping. Spoon a scant ⅔ cup
mixture into each of 8 custard cups. Freeze
about 6 hours or overnight.

To serve, reserve 8 orange segments for
garnish. Process remaining oranges in
blender until smooth. Remove custard cups
from freezer; let stand 15 minutes. Run knife
around edges of cups; invert onto dessert
plates and unmold. Garnish each dessert
with about 1 tablespoon puréed oranges,
1 reserved orange segment and a mint leaf, if
desired. Store leftover desserts in freezer.

Makes 8 servings

Nutrients per Serving:

Calories:	100	Cholesterol:	0 mg
Total Fat:	1 g	Sodium:	75 mg

Tiramisu

3 cups water
3 tablespoons honey
1 cup instant nonfat dry milk
2 tablespoons cornstarch
¼ teaspoon ground cinnamon
⅛ teaspoon salt
⅛ teaspoon ground cloves
½ cup cholesterol-free egg substitute
½ cup espresso coffee
2 tablespoons orange extract
12 ladyfingers, cut in half lengthwise
¼ cup grated semisweet chocolate
    Powdered sugar for garnish

1. Bring water and honey to a boil in medium saucepan over high heat. Reduce heat; simmer, uncovered, 20 minutes. Remove from heat.

2. Combine dry milk, cornstarch, cinnamon, salt and cloves in medium bowl. Add milk mixture to honey mixture, stirring until smooth. Bring to a boil, stirring constantly, over medium heat. Remove from heat.

3. Pour egg substitute into small bowl. Add ½ cup hot milk mixture to egg substitute; blend well. Stir egg mixture back into remaining milk mixture in saucepan. Cook over low heat 2 minutes or until thickened. Cool 15 minutes. Combine coffee with orange extract in another small bowl. Set aside.

4. Arrange 6 ladyfingers in 1-quart serving bowl. Drizzle half the coffee mixture over ladyfingers. Spread half the custard over ladyfingers. Sprinkle with half the grated chocolate. Repeat layers; cover and refrigerate 2 hours. Spoon into individual bowls. Garnish with powdered sugar, if desired.   *Makes 6 servings*

Crème Caramel

½ cup sugar, divided
1 tablespoon hot water
2 cups fat-free (skim) milk
⅛ teaspoon salt
½ cup cholesterol-free egg substitute
½ teaspoon vanilla
⅛ teaspoon maple extract

Heat ¼ cup sugar in heavy saucepan over low heat, stirring constantly until melted and straw colored. Remove from heat; stir in water. Return to heat; stir 5 minutes or until mixture is dark caramel color. Divide melted sugar evenly among 6 custard cups. Set aside.

Preheat oven to 350°F. Combine milk, remaining ¼ cup sugar and salt in medium bowl. Add egg substitute, vanilla and maple extract; mix well. Pour ½ cup mixture into each custard cup. Place cups in heavy baking pan and pour 1 to 2 inches hot water into pan.

Bake 40 to 45 minutes or until knife inserted near edge of each cup comes out clean. Cool on wire rack. Refrigerate 4 hours or overnight. Before serving, run knife around edge of custard cup. Invert custard onto serving plate; remove cup.

Makes 6 servings

The publishers would like to thank the companies and organizations listed below for the use of their recipes and photographs in this publication.

A.1.® Steak Sauce
Alpine Lace Brands, Inc.
American Italian Pasta Company
BC-USA, Inc.
BelGioioso® Cheese, Inc.
Best Foods
Birds Eye®
Bob Evans®
California Olive Industry
Chef Paul Prudhomme's Magic
    Seasoning Blends®
Cherry Marketing Institute, Inc.
Chilean Fresh Fruit Association
Christopher Ranch Garlic
COLLEGE INN® Broth
Del Monte Corporation
Delmarva Poultry Industry, Inc.
Dole Food Company, Inc.
Egg Beaters® Healthy Real Egg
    Substitute
Filippo Berio Olive Oil
Florida Department of Agriculture and
    Consumer Services, Bureau of
    Seafood and Aquaculture
Golden Grain®
Grey Poupon® Mustard
Guiltless Gourmet®
Healthy Choice®
Hershey Foods Corporation
Hormel Foods Corporation
The HV Company
The J.M. Smucker Company
Kellogg Company
Kikkoman International Inc.
The Kingsford Products Company
Kraft Foods, Inc.

Lawry's® Foods, Inc.
Lipton®
M & M/MARS
McIlhenny Company (Tabasco®
    Pepper Sauce)
Michigan Apple Committee
MOTT'S® Inc., a division of Cadbury
    Beverages Inc.
National Broiler Council
National Cattlemen's Beef Association
National Fisheries Institute
National Foods
National Pork Producers Council
National Turkey Federation
Nestlé USA, Inc.
New York Apple Association, Inc.
North Dakota Beef Commission
Pacific Coast Canned Pear Service
Perdue Farms Incorporated
The Procter & Gamble Company
The Quaker® Kitchens
Reckitt & Colman Inc.
RED STAR® Yeast & Products, a
    Division of Universal Foods
    Corporation
Riviana Foods Inc.
Sargento® Foods Inc.
Sonoma® Dried Tomatoes
StarKist® Seafood Company
The Sugar Association, Inc.
USA Dry Pea & Lentil Council
USA Rice Federation
Veg-All®
Walnut Marketing Board
Washington Apple Commission
Wisconsin Milk Marketing Board

METRIC CONVERSION CHART

VOLUME MEASUREMENTS (dry)

⅛ teaspoon = 0.5 mL
¼ teaspoon = 1 mL
½ teaspoon = 2 mL
¾ teaspoon = 4 mL
1 teaspoon = 5 mL
1 tablespoon = 15 mL
2 tablespoons = 30 mL
¼ cup = 60 mL
⅓ cup = 75 mL
½ cup = 125 mL
⅔ cup = 150 mL
¾ cup = 175 mL
1 cup = 250 mL
2 cups = 1 pint = 500 mL
3 cups = 750 mL
4 cups = 1 quart = 1 L

VOLUME MEASUREMENTS (fluid)

1 fluid ounce (2 tablespoons) = 30 mL
4 fluid ounces (½ cup) = 125 mL
8 fluid ounces (1 cup) = 250 mL
12 fluid ounces (1½ cups) = 375 mL
16 fluid ounces (2 cups) = 500 mL

WEIGHTS (mass)

½ ounce = 15 g
1 ounce = 30 g
3 ounces = 90 g
4 ounces = 120 g
8 ounces = 225 g
10 ounces = 285 g
12 ounces = 360 g
16 ounces = 1 pound = 450 g

DIMENSIONS

1/16 inch = 2 mm
⅛ inch = 3 mm
¼ inch = 6 mm
½ inch = 1.5 cm
¾ inch = 2 cm
1 inch = 2.5 cm

OVEN TEMPERATURES

250°F = 120°C
275°F = 140°C
300°F = 150°C
325°F = 160°C
350°F = 180°C
375°F = 190°C
400°F = 200°C
425°F = 220°C
450°F = 230°C

BAKING PAN SIZES

Utensil	Size in Inches/Quarts	Metric Volume	Size in Centimeters
Baking or Cake Pan (square or rectangular)	8×8×2	2 L	20×20×5
	9×9×2	2.5 L	23×23×5
	12×8×2	3 L	30×20×5
	13×9×2	3.5 L	33×23×5
Loaf Pan	8×4×3	1.5 L	20×10×7
	9×5×3	2 L	23×13×7
Round Layer Cake Pan	8×1½	1.2 L	20×4
	9×1½	1.5 L	23×4
Pie Plate	8×1¼	750 mL	20×3
	9×1¼	1 L	23×3
Baking Dish or Casserole	1 quart	1 L	—
	1½ quart	1.5 L	—
	2 quart	2 L	—